# HOW TO BUILD
# BRICK CARS

## DETAILED LEGO® DESIGNS FOR
## SPORTS CARS, RACE CARS, AND MUSCLE CARS

PETER BLACKERT

motorbooks

Inspiring | Educating | Creating | Entertaining

Brimming with creative inspiration, how-to projects, and useful information to enrich your everyday life, Quarto Knows is a favourite destination for those pursuing their interests and passions. Visit our site and dig deeper with our books into your area of interest: Quarto Creates, Quarto Cooks, Quarto Homes, Quarto Lives, Quarto Drives, Quarto Explores, Quarto Gifts, or Quarto Kids.

First Published in 2017 by Motorbooks, an imprint of The Quarto Group, 100 Cummings Center, Suite 265-D, Beverly, MA 01915, USA.
T (978) 282-9590 F (978) 283-2742 QuartoKnows.com

Motorbooks titles are also available at discount for retail, wholesale, promotional, and bulk purchase. For details, contact the Special Sales Manager by email at specialsales@quarto.com or by mail at The Quarto Group, Attn: Special Sales Manager, 100 Cummings Center, Suite 265-D, Beverly, MA 01915, USA.

10 9 8 7 6 5 4 3

ISBN: 978-0-7603-5265-6

Library of Congress Cataloging-in-Publication Data

Names: Blackert, Peter, 1972- author.
Title: How to build brick cars : detailed LEGO designs for sports cars, race cars, and muscle cars / Peter Blackert.
Description: Minneapolis, MN : Motorbooks, an imprint of The Quarto Group, 2017.
Identifiers: LCCN 2017015625 | ISBN 9780760352656 (hc)
Subjects: LCSH: Automobiles--Models. | Vehicles--Models. | LEGO toys. | Models and modelmaking.
Classification: LCC TL237 .B53 2017 | DDC 629.22/12--dc23
LC record available at https://lccn.loc.gov/2017015625


Acquiring Editor: Jordan Wiklund
Project Managers: Alyssa Lochner / Madeleine Vasaly
Art Director: James Kegley
Layout: Rebecca Pagel


On the front cover: BMW i8 Hybrid Coupe
On the back cover: 1971 Plymouth HEMI 'Cuda


Printed in China

# ACKNOWLEDGMENTS

Thanks to the editorial team at Motorbooks for giving me the opportunity to share my passion for cars and LEGO® vehicle building. Thanks to my publisher, Zack Miller—I have subsequently discovered how much you like that particular Porsche 911. My editor, Jordan Wiklund, thanks for your enthusiasm—I hope you get a kick out of building the cars in the book. And thank you to the skilled team who helped put together all those pages to help my work look its best.

Thanks to the Ford Motor Company and my fellow engineering teams for allowing me to work in the field that I love—the creation of the automobile.

Thanks to my loving family: my wife, J, and children É, L, and M. Thank you for bearing with me through the creation of the material for this book, whilst I was so very busy and being an intolerable bore.

Thanks to Miles for not smashing up the cars before I managed to get the instructions and photos completed.

Peter Blackert (lego911)

# CONTENTS

# PREFACE

What is it that drives a fascination toward cars? Far more than just a mechanical horse, the car has been the transformative technology of the twentieth century. The car wraps up two centuries of advances in science and technology in a product polished by stylists and marketing departments for your personal freedom.

The automobile is the driver of so many technological changes in our lives—we are more likely to have first had a computer in our car than in our house. And unless you have flown to the moon, your car was probably the first product you've been in that was designed on computer too.

Whole societies have been transformed by the automobile, which fueled the growth of cities, highways, shopping malls, and suburbs. From its origins in late-nineteenth-century Europe during the Industrial Revolution, the car has also come to represent our hopes and dreams. Postwar American optimism was reflected in gleaming two-tone paint, rocket pods, towering fins, and chrome.

It is sports cars, muscle cars, and race cars, though, that feed high-octane excitement into our bloodstreams. Power, noise, speed, and fast, fast styling are mechanical interpretations of our fears of and appreciation for the animals that lurk, linger, and growl. Dangerous animals with claws, teeth, and talons. Animals we're warned about and that haunt our dreams. Automotive history is filled with cars named after these animals—Pantera (panther), Bronco, Cobra, Stingray, and Viper. (Section 3 of this book includes the Plymouth Hemi 'Cuda—the wildest of the wild muscle cars from the early 1970s.)

The industry that creates these cars has drawn in passionate artists, stylists, engineers, marketers, and visionary dreamers. Men and women pour their sweat and tears in pursuit of a hero vehicle—cars that set our imaginations alight. These hero vehicles can be found on posters on teenagers' bedroom walls, on the screensavers of coworkers, and polished to perfection in the garages of car enthusiasts the world over.

In *How to Build Brick Cars*, I hope to bring these cars to life in 3-D brick form: cars made from LEGO® bricks. In creating the cars for this book, I have drawn on a small portion of the thousands of brick vehicles I have built over the years, married to more than a decade of automotive design engineering at the Ford Motor Company.

LEGO has been instrumental in developing the skills now termed STEM or STEAM—creative skills in science, technology, engineering, art, and mathematics—of people in diverse, exciting careers, including those who design and develop cars.

LEGO has been part of my own experience in developing these skills and applying them to my own specialist field of advanced vehicle architecture.

These are some of the most significant sports cars, muscle cars, and race cars over the past one hundred years. I hope you enjoy building them as much as I have designing them.

Best Regards,
Peter Blackert

# WHY BUILD BRICK CARS?

People often ask me what I do for a living—a normal question when you meet someone for the first time. I respond in any number of ways: "I work for Ford," or "I am a car design engineer," or something similar. If I give them my real job title, they just stare at me blankly, sometimes even when the question is asked by one of the engineers who works in the same building.

When it comes to discussing what I do for fun, the idea that an adult designs cars made from LEGO® bricks is perhaps a bit more unusual. Kids, of course, think this is a fantastic hobby.

The next question is, "Why?"

Again, there is always more than one answer.

I build cars from LEGO because it is a relaxing and enjoyable creative pastime.

But I also build cars from LEGO because it allows me to quickly solve problems that I encounter when I design real vehicles, in a way that's much less expensive and time-consuming. It allows me to demonstrate the solutions in a 3-D interactive form that people can see and hold. LEGO is not a static object either. The suspension systems used in this book in the Intermediate and Advanced sections rely on the engineering properties of LEGO that are poorly understood and seldom exploited, properties that exist in all materials and that we rely on every day without appreciating their significance.

For further reading, I suggest researching "torsion bars"—the spring method used in this book—along with "elastic properties of materials." These subjects are usually first encountered at a college or university, but the opportunity to experience them in a LEGO-built model can provide invaluable insight.

It may come as a surprise, but the chief practice of engineering is to solve problems. If there are no problems to solve, I don't have a job to do. Thankfully (I guess?) there seems to be an overabundance of problems to solve, even if we are challenged to make "minor" changes to a vehicle that we designed a couple of years earlier. Real vehicle engineering is like this—the various stakeholders (corporate, government, customer, and manufacturing) all move the goal posts forward in pursuit of a better car, whether it's in regards to safety, environmental pollution, comfort, cost, convenience, or features. Cars are pretty complex, and understanding how everything works together is challenging—we create models in one form or another all the time to try to simplify the concepts and appreciate their interactions.

When you can build your world in LEGO, you can create models of your problems as well as models of your solutions.

This is also true of fields outside automotive engineering. LEGO has always had an architectural focus, and LEGO robotics sets have added problem-solving with software code, sensors, motors, and gears to the LEGO-based STEM toolkit. My involvement with Ford Motor Company includes mentoring programs with local schools using these tools.

And lastly, I build cars from LEGO because I love cars and I love LEGO.

# HOW TO USE THIS BOOK

Designing LEGO® cars is a skill set that has taken me a great many pleasurable years of building to master. In writing this book, and through the detailed instructions, I have endeavored to provide inspirational material to aid builders, new and experienced alike, with design techniques and solutions that they can use to create their own model vehicles.

The selection of cars spans the 1930s to today and represents the evolution of a number of engineering technologies, including V engines, all-wheel drive, independent suspension, mid-engine layouts, and other real-life features, scaled down to model size.

On first reading, a new builder may find some of the advanced designs beyond their LEGO parts collection, building experience, or comfort zone. I hope that a slow progression through the Beginner and Intermediate designs, and experimentation with some of the techniques introduced into your own builds, will give you the confidence to move to the more advanced designs when you are ready for those challenges.

For the advanced builder, I hope that the less-complex models are nonetheless a rewarding building exercise at a smaller scale and that the more-complex models reveal an advanced world of model building, one that more closely reflects the challenges and rewards of designing and engineering real cars for the real world.

| Build Introduction | Symbol/Nomenclature/ Technique | What does it mean? What should I do? |
|---|---|---|
| '32 Ford |  | The instructions for the 1932 Ford V-8 allow the builder to create either a coupe or a roadster version of the car. The instructions for both are common for most of the construction, with unique instructions to build one or the other detailed at the end of the build. This technique is used again for the Ferrari 488 and the Jaguar E-Type. |
| '32 Ford | **1** **29** | The large bold numbers for the instructions start at 1 and number progressively. This helps keep track of the stage that the build is in overall and provides some guidance to the next instruction step when alternative designs can be chosen. |
| '32 Ford | **1** **4** | The small bold numbers included in the colored box fields show the step level when creating an assembly. An assembly is a collection of parts that create a cohesive structure prior to being joined to the main model. |
| '32 Ford | **2** × | A number followed by × indicates that the builder should assemble that number of common assemblies. This is usually the case for wheels, seats, and engine parts. |
| '32 Ford |  ↻ | This symbol indicates that the assembly or model should be rotated to aid the next step or to see what it looks like from the reverse side. |
| '32 Ford | 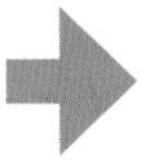 ➡ | This symbol indicates that alternative assemblies can be chosen and points to the beginning of the first step of building the assembly shown to the left of the arrow. |
| '32 Ford |  ➜ | This symbol indicates the construction sequence to attach an assembly to the main structure of the model. |
| Ferrari GTB & Spider | **5**  ◿ **LHS** | This symbol indicates that the following assembly steps show how to build the left-hand side (LHS) of the model. It also indicates that this assembly stage should be built in a reflected right-hand side assembly as well. |

The building instructions introduce various symbols and nomenclature progressively through the chapters, allowing for the instruction set to be condensed while still maintaining instruction clarity. The following symbols and typography are there to aid the builder in selecting the correct parts at each building stage, preparing intermediate assemblies, and connecting them to the base model architecture.

A note on part numbers: You will see each part required for the model in the form of xxxx-yy. The xxxx refers to the LEGO Part ID. This part type number is used in LDD and other software. It is also the part number that you need to use to order parts from LEGO or a third-party seller. The yy refers to the part color. LEGO uses these numbers to identify specific colors. For example, red is color 21.

One of the most fun things about LEGO is the vibrancy and range of colors you can use. Colors for the models in this book have been selected satisfy a generally available palette. In each chapter, a color guide will indicate which colors should be used, but beauty is in the eye of the beholder—let your imagination run wild!

| Chapter Introduction | Symbol/Nomenclature/ Technique | What does it mean? What should I do? |
|---|---|---|
| Ferrari GTB & Spider | | Arrows (red, black, or orange) indicate the position for smaller assemblies to be placed on the main model, where this might be difficult to see clearly. |
| Ferrari GTB & Spider | | This symbol, which is also used in the parts list, indicates the length (in standard bricks) of the LEGO Technic axle to be used at this assembly stage. |
| Citroën | | Many of the car models have brick-built windows. The instructions to build these can be quite confusing. To aid the process, the parts to be added at each instruction stage are colored pale yellow. |
| Jaguar E-Type | **A** | The use of [A] and [B] symbols indicates that a choice of designs can be considered. The [A] or [B] logo will sit in the corner of the finished assembly and guide the following assembly instructions. |
| Ford F-150 | 29 | Similar to the red arrow symbol, the arrow followed by a number, e.g. [29], indicates that the main instruction stage 29 is the assembly that should be attached at the position indicated by the arrow. |
| Ford F-150 | Tile 1 × 3 | Where there is no easy indication as to which part exactly is required, a word description is used to make this clear. |
| Ford F-150 | LHS + RHS | To aid the correct orientation of small assemblies, they are pictured in the same orientation as the main vehicle. LHS and RHS text indicates which part goes where. |

# FOUNDATION

T he models in Section 1 are some of the most recognizable vehicles in the history of the automobile. We recognize these cars from their designs—distinct silhouettes arriving at historically significant moments in time.

These models are not generic LEGO® cars for kids. They are detailed models at a smaller scale (1:28), take less time to build, and do not require many specialist pieces. These models can seat LEGO minifigures.

The builds become more detailed and complex as you work through the section. The 1932 Ford V-8, Ferrari 488, and Jaguar E-Type also provide instructions to build these cars in both convertible and coupe forms, along with some other modeling differences, such as wheels.

## 1932 FORD
# V-8 COUPE & ROADSTER

The Ford Model 18 (as it was officially named) marked the beginning of an era of affordable power for the common man. The Model 18 was Ford's V-8—a configuration otherwise confined to high-price luxury cars. Priced from $490 for coupes ($495 for roadsters), the V-8 was significantly less expensive than any car offering 8 cylinders. The concurrent 4-cylinder "B" Model (priced at just $10 less) would have been a failure but for Ford's inability to produce greater numbers of V-8 engines and cars.

A V-8 had many advantages. Chiefly, it offered smooth running and high power density for its overall length. The engine was barely heavier than an inline-four and lighter than an inline-six. This made for a fantastic recipe: small car + big engine = maximum mayhem. All getaway drivers knew this. Bonnie and Clyde, while on the run, famously penned a thank-you note to Henry Ford:

*Dear Sir*
*While I still have got breath in my lungs I will tell you what a dandy car you make. I have drove Fords exclusivly when I could get away with one. For sustained speed and freedom from trouble the Ford has got every other car skinned and even if my business hasn't been strickly legal it don't hurt anything to tell you what a fine car you got in the V-8.*
*Yours truly,*
*Clyde Champion Barrow [April 10th, 1934]*

After World War II, returned servicemen sought the adrenaline a modified Ford V-8 could offer. The Ford V-8 was the original hot rod. The culture of hot rodding came to life chiefly thanks to cheaply available prewar Ford V-8s. Roadsters and coupes were the favored styles, and very few cars from this period are left in original condition.

The Ford V-8 was updated in 1933 to the Model 40 and in 1934 to the 40B, offering a styling change to a more shovel-like radiator and hood line.

| | |
|---|---|
| **COUNTRY OF ORIGIN:** | USA |
| **PRODUCTION:** | 1932 |
| **NUMBER MADE:** | 298,647 |
| **LAYOUT / DRIVE:** | Front engine / Rear-wheel drive |
| **ENGINE:** | V, 8 cylinders, 221 cid (3.6L) |
| **CAPACITY:** | 65 hp (48 kW) |
| **CONSTRUCTION:** | Separate frame, steel body/ 2-door coupe and roadster |

This model can also be built in the folowing colors: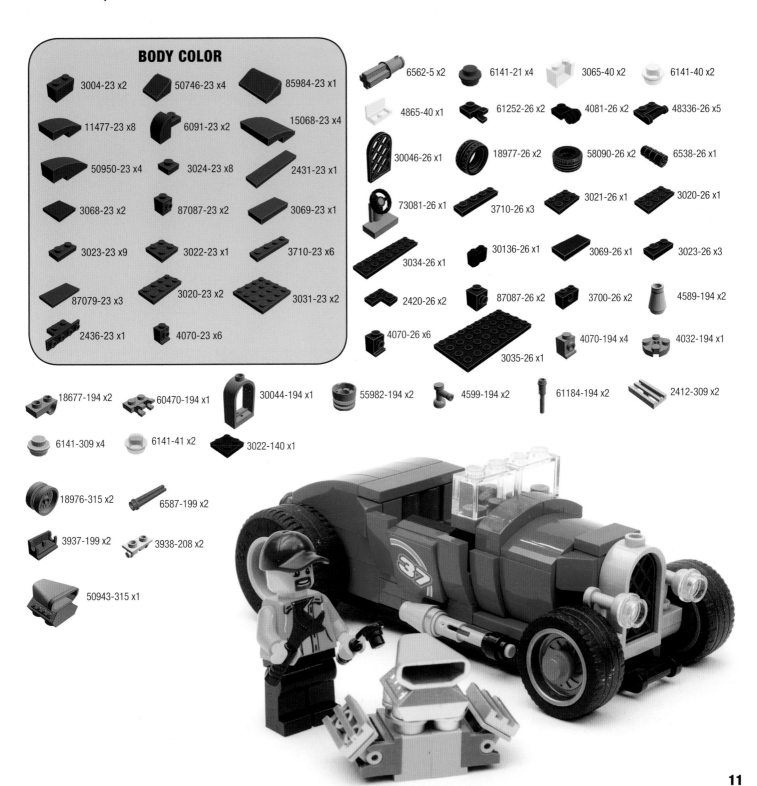

Number of parts: 155

**BODY COLOR**

3004-23 x2
50746-23 x4
85984-23 x1

11477-23 x8
6091-23 x2
15068-23 x4

50950-23 x4
3024-23 x8
2431-23 x1

3068-23 x2
87087-23 x2
3069-23 x1

3023-23 x9
3022-23 x1
3710-23 x6

87079-23 x3
3020-23 x2
3031-23 x2

2436-23 x1
4070-23 x6

6562-5 x2
6141-21 x4
3065-40 x2
6141-40 x2

4865-40 x1
61252-26 x2
4081-26 x2
48336-26 x5

30046-26 x1
18977-26 x2
58090-26 x2
6538-26 x1

73081-26 x1
3710-26 x3
3021-26 x1
3020-26 x1

3034-26 x1
30136-26 x1
3069-26 x1
3023-26 x3

2420-26 x2
87087-26 x2
3700-26 x2
4589-194 x2

4070-26 x6
3035-26 x1
4070-194 x4
4032-194 x1

18677-194 x2
60470-194 x1
30044-194 x1
55982-194 x2
4599-194 x2
61184-194 x2
2412-309 x2

6141-309 x4
6141-41 x2
3022-140 x1

18976-315 x2
6587-199 x2

3937-199 x2
3938-208 x2

50943-315 x1

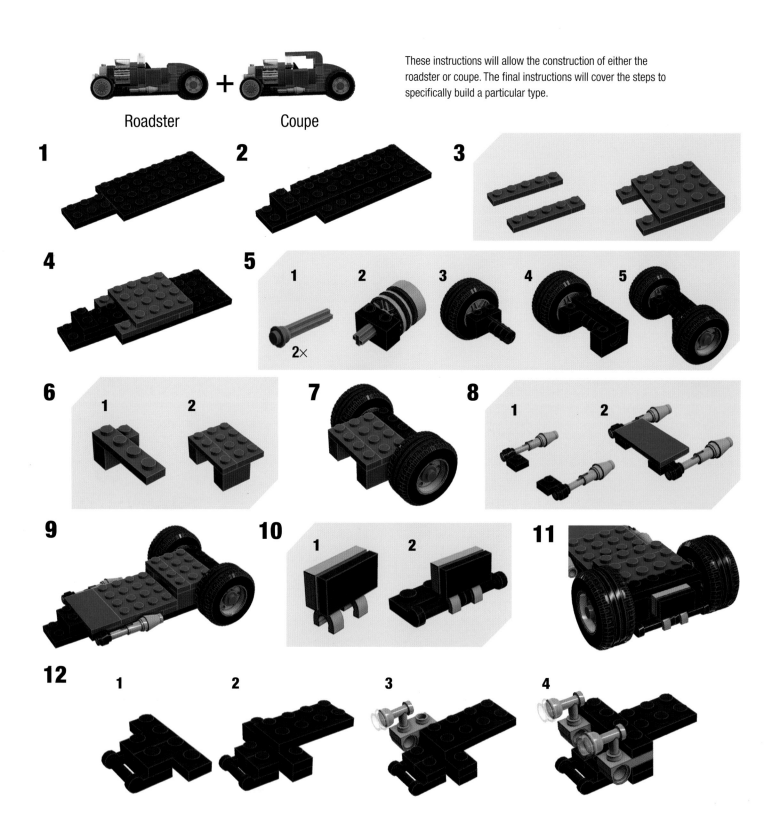

Roadster + Coupe

These instructions will allow the construction of either the roadster or coupe. The final instructions will cover the steps to specifically build a particular type.

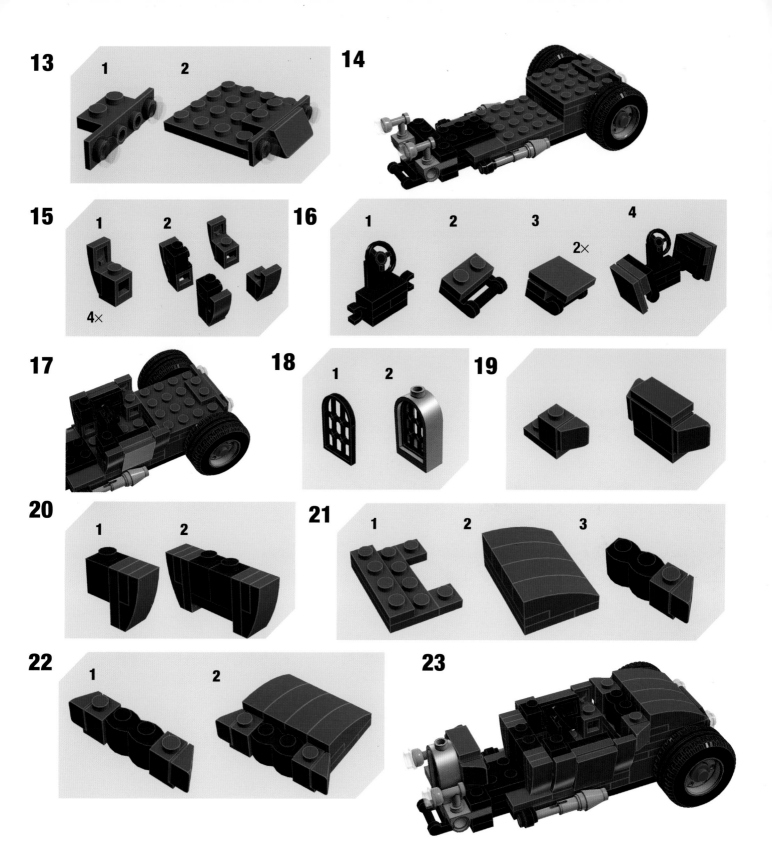

**13**

1  2

**14**

**15**

1  2

4×

**16**

1  2  3  4

2×

**17**

**18**

1  2

**19**

**20**

1  2

**21**

1  2  3

**22**

1  2

**23**

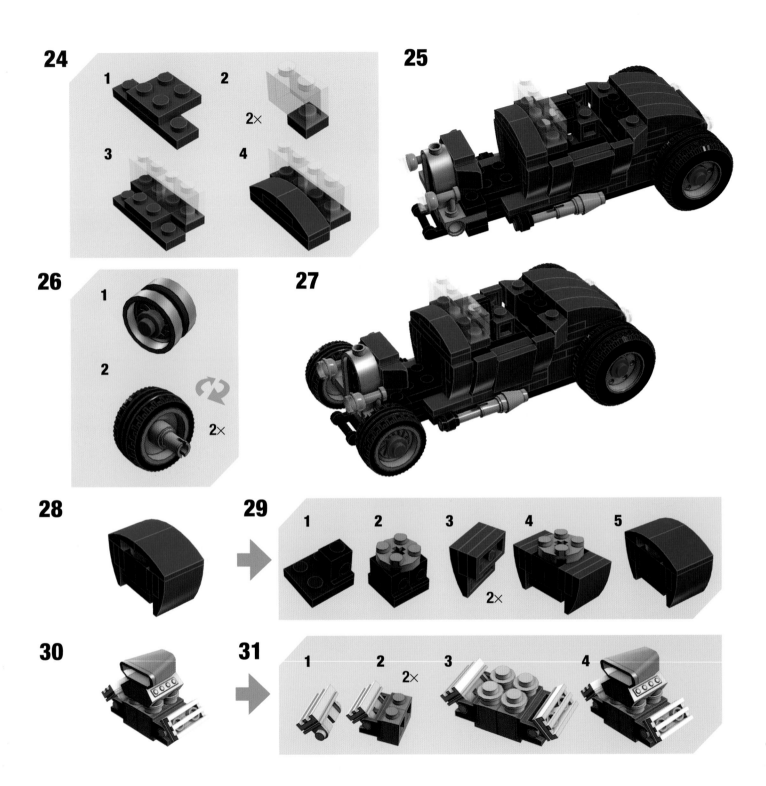

**32**

Roadster

**33**

Coupe

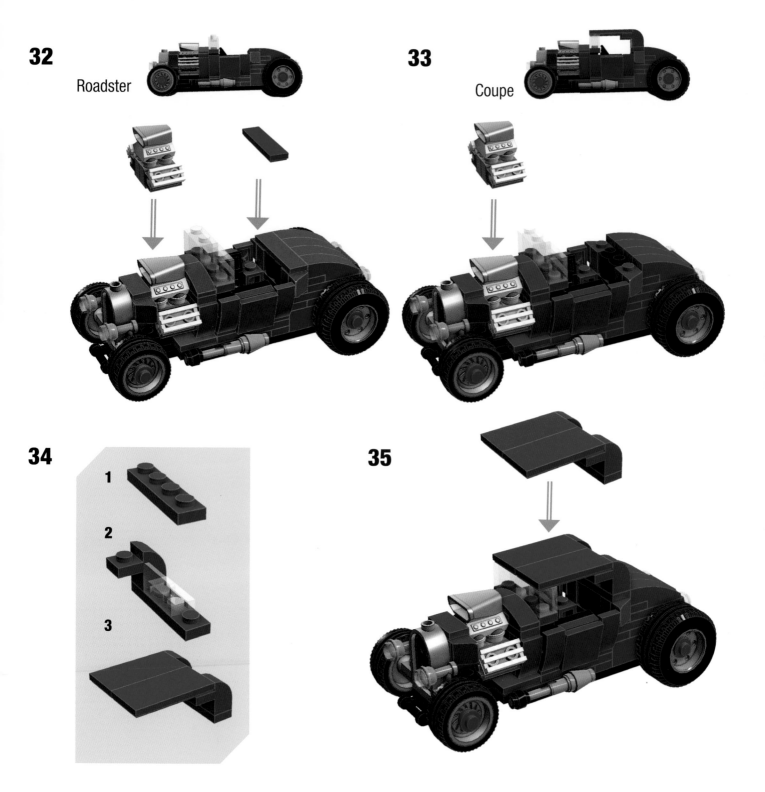

**34**

1

2

3

**35**

# 488 GTB & 488 SPIDER

Familiar and yet different. The Ferrari 488 GTB, launched in 2015, in many ways closely resembled the 458 Berlinetta model it replaced. The car looked very similar in overall form, size, and proportion.

The heart and soul of any Ferrari, though, is the engine. In the 488, the V-8 engine remains. Capacity was reduced from 4.5L to 3.9, but two turbochargers were added. The turbos add power and, more importantly, torque. For each measure, the 488 has the highest specific power and torque of any road Ferrari engine ever. This means that for every cubic centimeter of engine capacity, the 488 produces the most useable go. Power is transmitted to the rear wheels via a twin-clutch, 7-speed gearbox. This gearbox design uses two independent clutches. One clutch engages gears 1, 3, 5, and 7, while the second operates on 2, 4, 6, and reverse. The gears are preselected electromechanically for the next shift.

The 488 is available as both a Berlinetta (coupe) and Spider (convertible), the names commonly used for these body styles in Italy.

Ferrari was founded by Enzo Ferrari in 1948, after he had run the racing team for rival Alfa Romeo. Originally he had built very limited numbers of road cars for well-heeled and well-connected customers—primarily to fund his racing team, Scuderia Ferrari. Early road cars were almost exclusively V-12 and front-engined. Ferrari introduced a companion brand with assistance from FIAT and produced a V-6 mid-engine design in the mid-1960s. It was named "Dino" after his son Alfredino Ferrari, a name he also used for the V-6 engine that Alfredino helped design. In 1975, the V-6 Dino 246 was replaced by a new V-8 engine model—the 308, with a 3.0-liter engine. The V-8 line moved through the 1980s to the 2010s with progressively larger engines. Along with a few low-capacity tax specials, Ferrari added turbos to the V-8 engine, high-performance 288 GTO, and F40 models—the pinnacle Ferraris of their day.

| | |
|---|---|
| **COUNTRY OF ORIGIN:** | Italy |
| **PRODUCTION:** | 2015–present |
| **NUMBER MADE:** | Currently in production |
| **LAYOUT / DRIVE:** | Mid engine / Rear-wheel drive |
| **ENGINE:** | 3,902 cc, 8 cylinders, V, turbocharged |
| **POWER / TORQUE:** | 661hp (493kW) / 561 lb-ft (760 Nm) |
| **CONSTRUCTION / DOORS:** | Aluminum-alloy spaceframe / 2 doors |

This model can also be built in the folowing colors: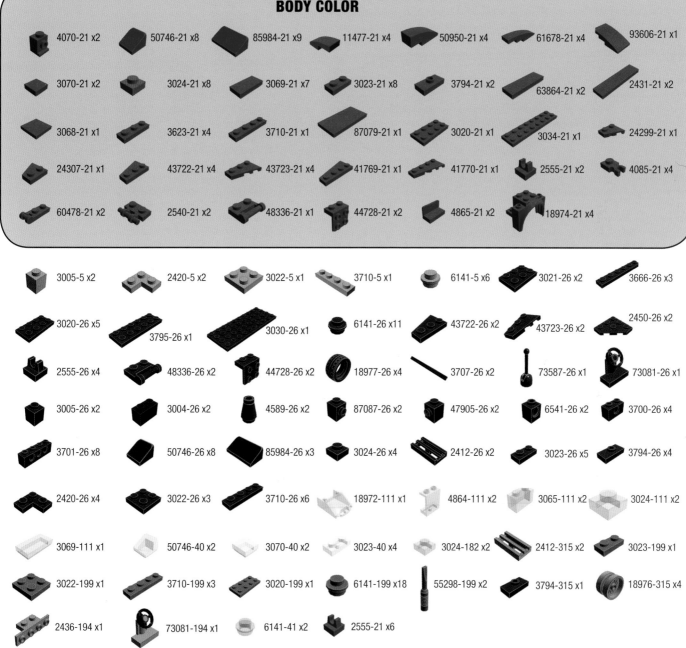

Number of parts: 284

## BODY COLOR

4070-21 x2    50746-21 x8    85984-21 x9    11477-21 x4    50950-21 x4    61678-21 x4    93606-21 x1

3070-21 x2    3024-21 x8    3069-21 x7    3023-21 x8    3794-21 x2    63864-21 x2    2431-21 x2

3068-21 x1    3623-21 x4    3710-21 x1    87079-21 x1    3020-21 x1    3034-21 x1    24299-21 x1

24307-21 x1    43722-21 x4    43723-21 x4    41769-21 x1    41770-21 x1    2555-21 x2    4085-21 x4

60478-21 x2    2540-21 x2    48336-21 x1    44728-21 x2    4865-21 x2    18974-21 x4

3005-5 x2    2420-5 x2    3022-5 x1    3710-5 x1    6141-5 x6    3021-26 x2    3666-26 x3

3020-26 x5    3795-26 x1    3030-26 x1    6141-26 x11    43722-26 x2    43723-26 x2    2450-26 x2

2555-26 x4    48336-26 x2    44728-26 x2    18977-26 x4    3707-26 x2    73587-26 x1    73081-26 x1

3005-26 x2    3004-26 x2    4589-26 x2    87087-26 x2    47905-26 x2    6541-26 x2    3700-26 x4

3701-26 x8    50746-26 x8    85984-26 x3    3024-26 x4    2412-26 x2    3023-26 x5    3794-26 x4

2420-26 x4    3022-26 x3    3710-26 x6    18972-111 x1    4864-111 x2    3065-111 x2    3024-111 x2

3069-111 x1    50746-40 x2    3070-40 x2    3023-40 x4    3024-182 x2    2412-315 x2    3023-199 x1

3022-199 x1    3710-199 x3    3020-199 x1    6141-199 x18    55298-199 x2    3794-315 x1    18976-315 x4

2436-194 x1    73081-194 x1    6141-41 x2    2555-21 x6

488 GTB Berlinetta

488 Spider

These instructions will allow the construction of either the Ferrari 488 GTB Berlinetta or the 488 Spider. The two body variations are common up to step 61. Beyond that, the 488 GTB will continue instructions in red. Jumping to step 77 will allow you to continue to build the 488 Spider. This section will be illustrated with a yellow car—though the parts list will give you the parts you need in red, or an alternative color of your choice.

**1**

**2**

**3**

**4**

1    2    3    4    5

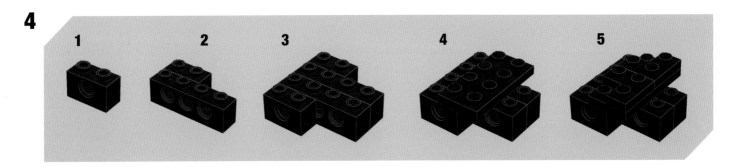

**5**

**6**

1    2    3

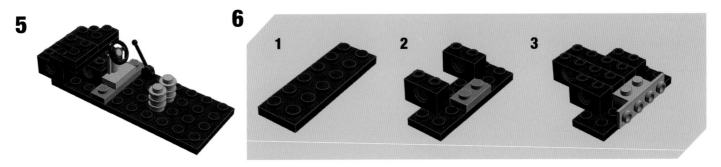

**7**

1    2    3

**8**

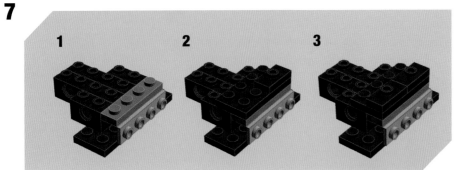

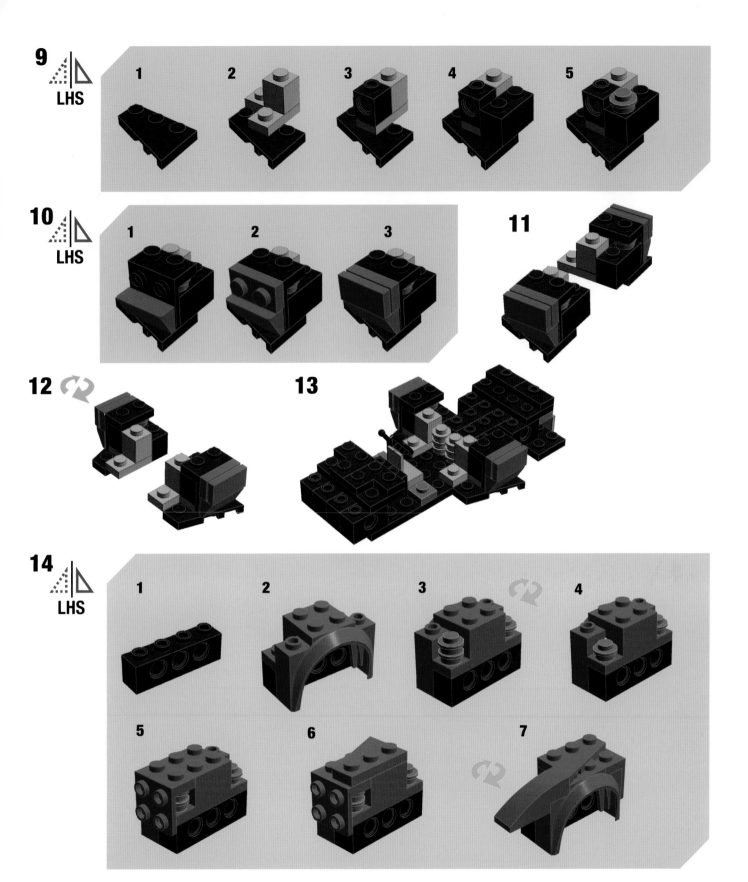

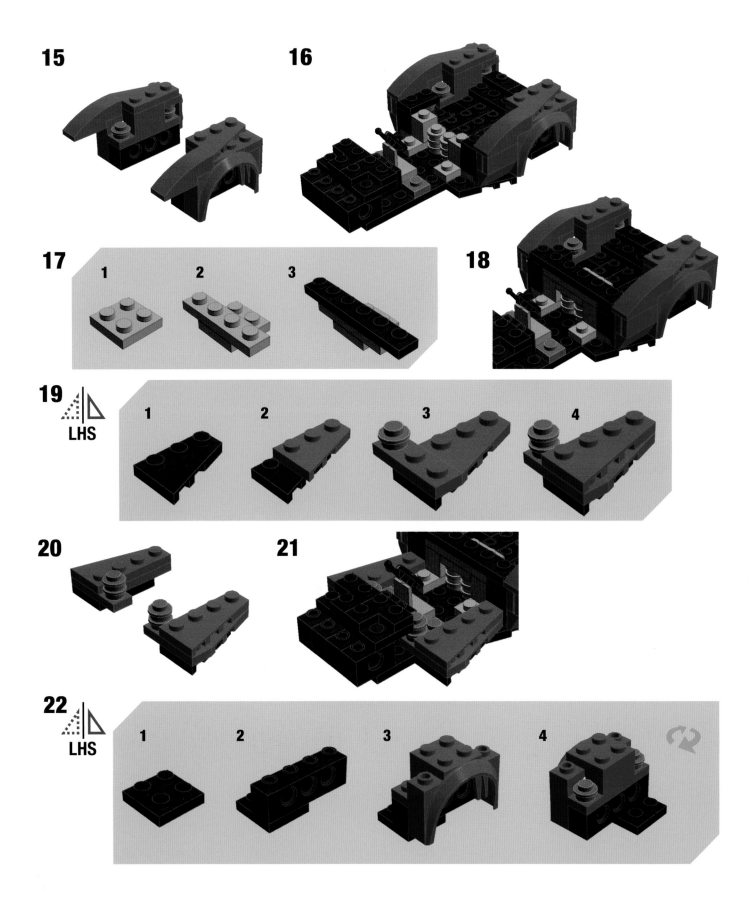

**15**

**16**

**17**

1

2

3

**18**

**19** LHS

1

2

3

4

**20**

**21**

**22** LHS

1

2

3

4

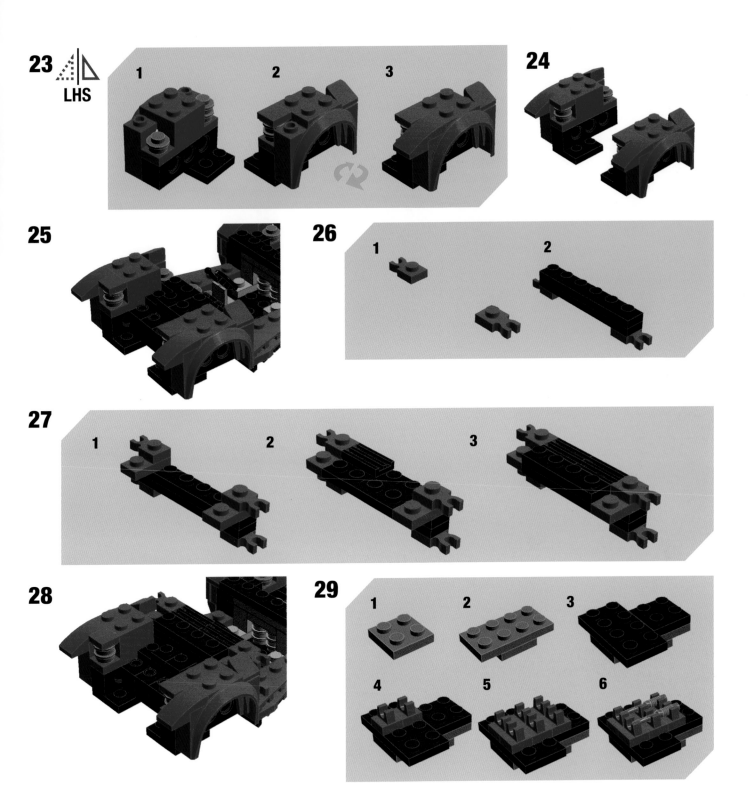

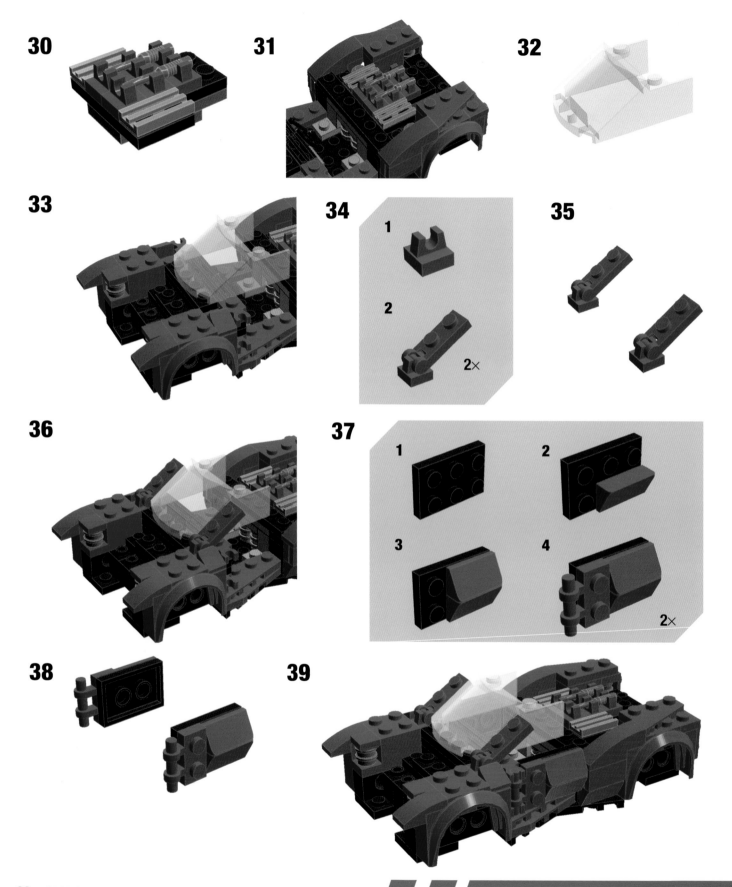

**30**

**31**

**32**

**33**

**34**
1
2
2×

**35**

**36**

**37**
1
2
3
4
2×

**38**

**39**

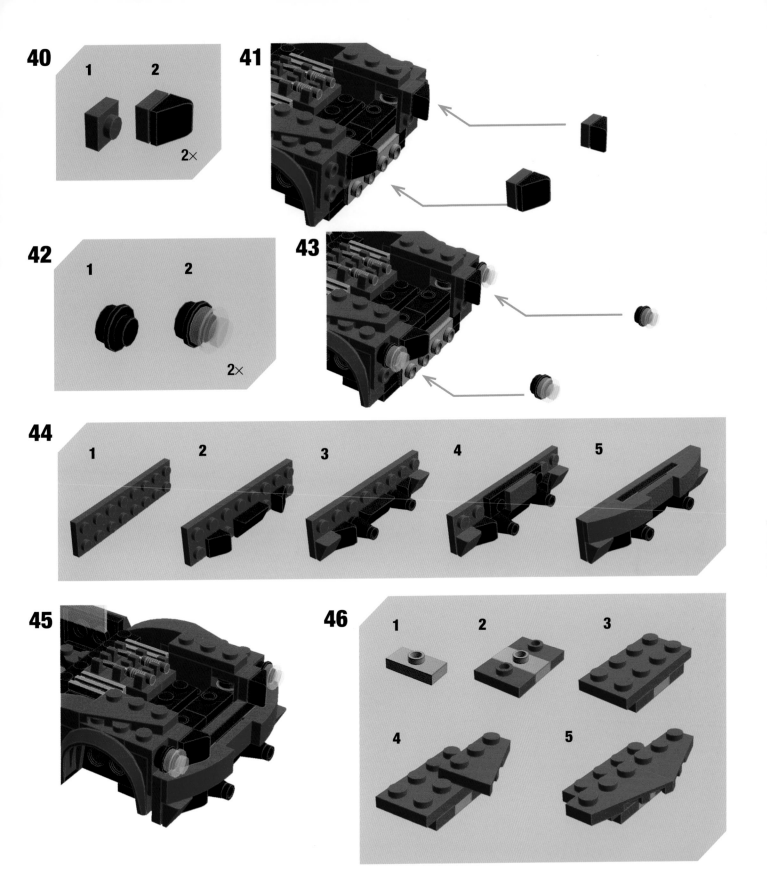

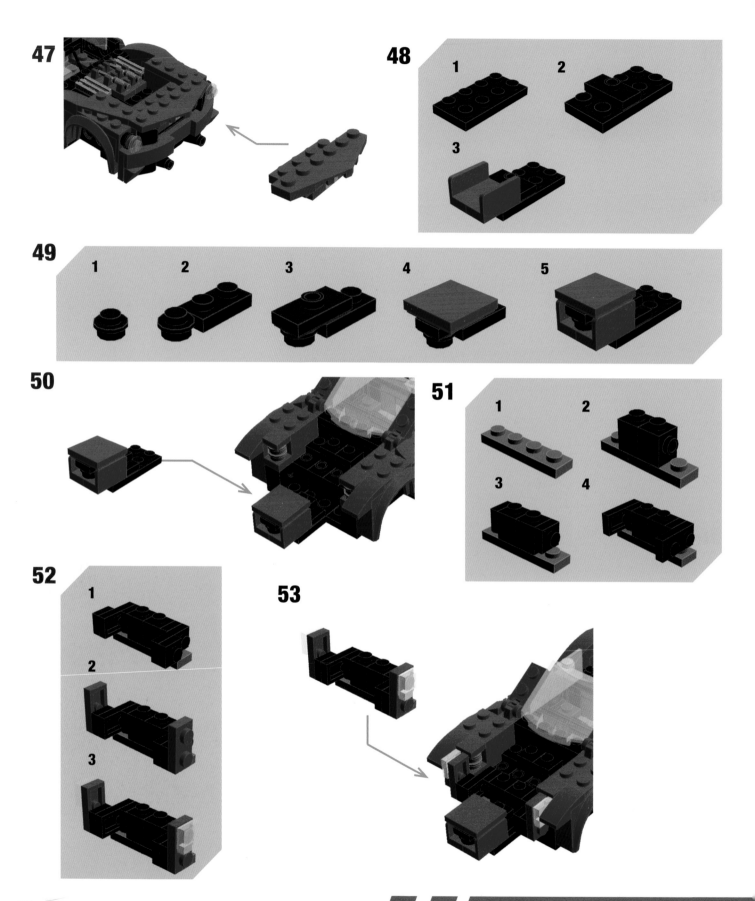

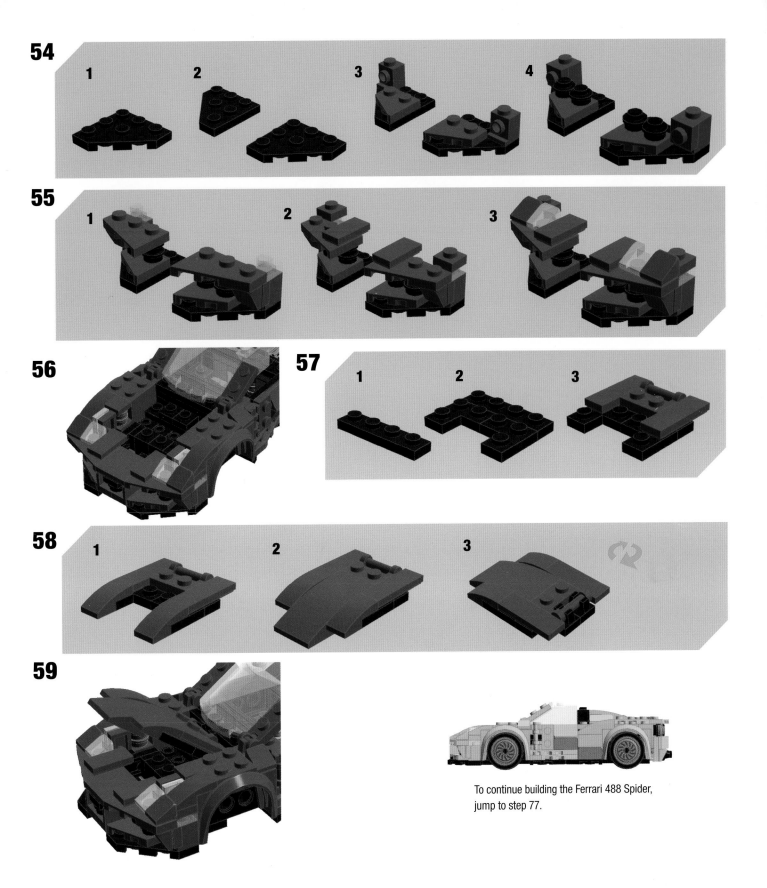

To continue building the Ferrari 488 Spider, jump to step 77.

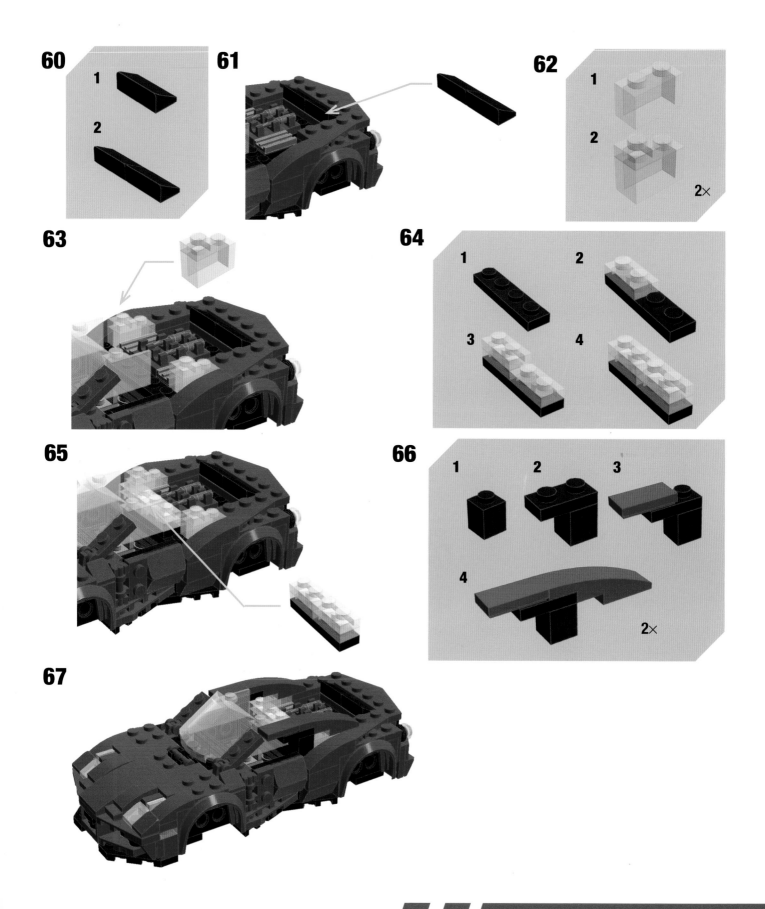

**60**

1

2

**61**

**62**

1

2

2×

**63**

**64**

1

2

3

4

**65**

**66**

1

2

3

4

2×

**67**

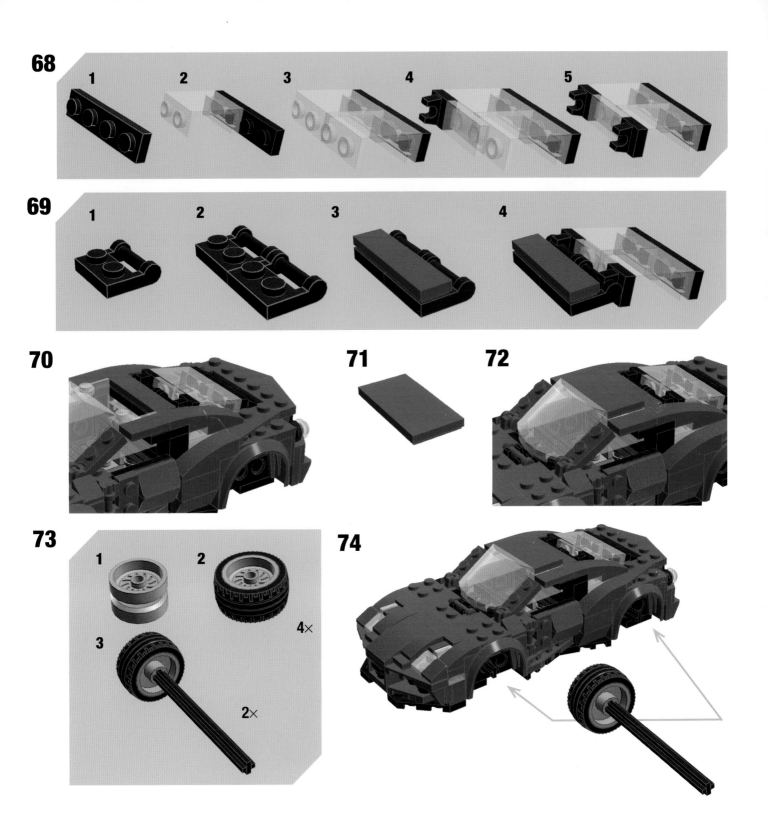

**75**

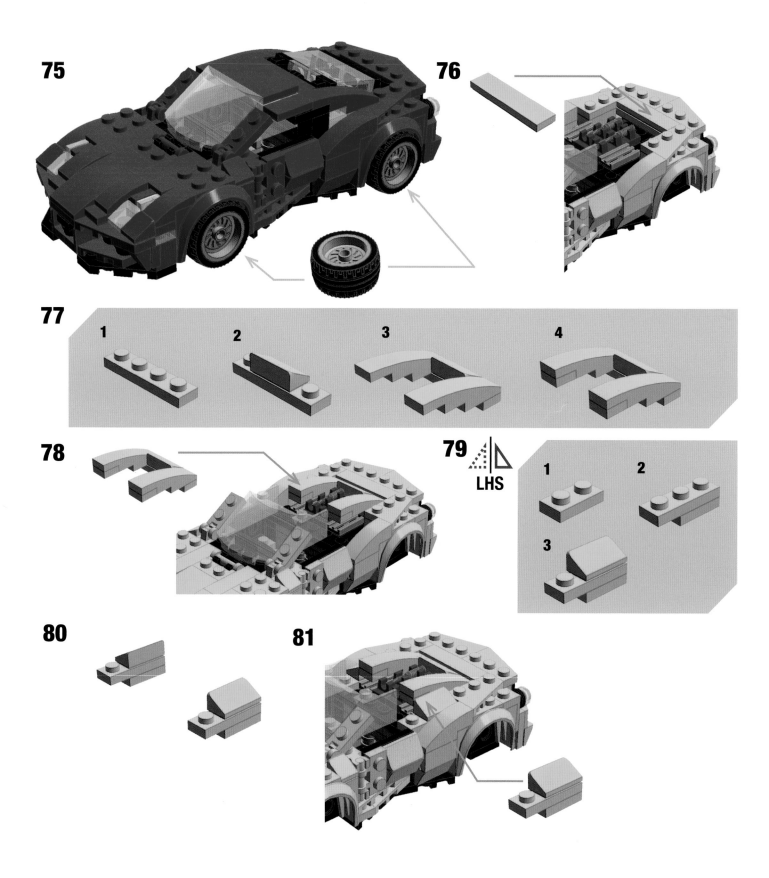

**76**

**77**
1   2   3   4

**78**

**79** LHS
1   2
3

**80**

**81**

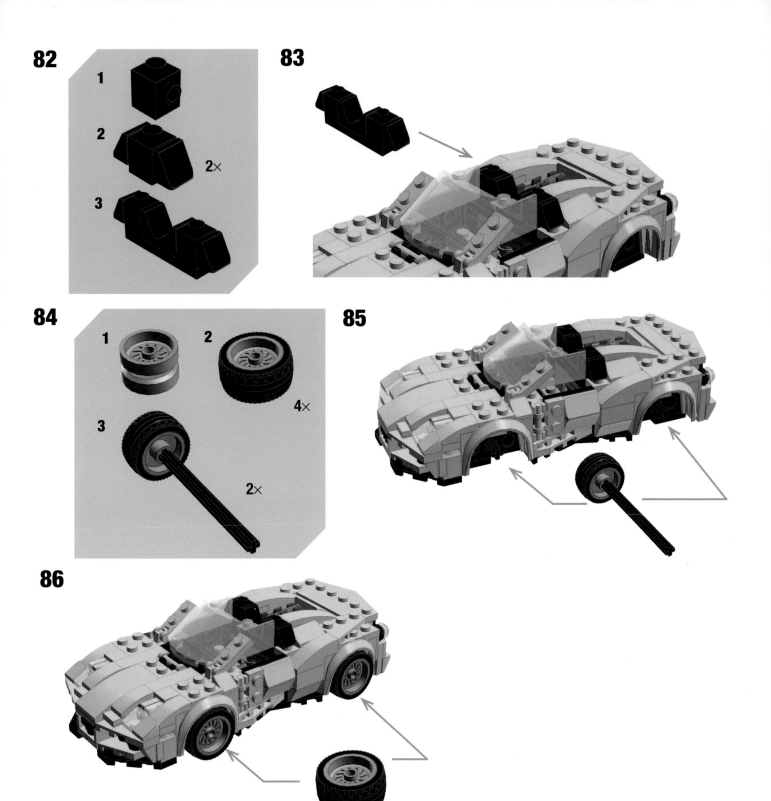

# 2CV CHARLESTON

The Citroën 2CV is a compact economy car developed in France leading up to World War II. The car began production in 1948 and quickly became a bestseller. Soft suspension settings made for dramatic lean during cornering but also made for a very smooth ride. The suspension interconnected the front and rear wheels, allowing the car to remain level but with long wheel travel. One of the original design requirements was to be able to carry eggs over a ploughed field without breaking any! The 2CV also formed the basis for small delivery vans and pickup trucks, ideal for compact European city streets.

The 2CV Charleston was introduced in 1980, originally as a special edition, and became a regular production model the following year. The Charleston introduced a limited number of colors combined with a black roof and fenders; it was one of many special editions released late in the 2CV's life to maintain interest in the model.

The Citroën 2CV had a remarkably long production period, finally ceasing in 1990. By that time, the car had become uncompetitive in areas such as safety, pollution control, and NVH (noise—vibration and harshness). At this point, the car was sold on quirky period design and charm. The 2CV was a very minimalist vehicle—the side windows hinged up from the middle because window winders were considered heavy and expensive!

By the time the 2CV Charleston was launched, the engine was a 602-cc, horizontally opposed 2-cylinder producing 29 hp. Earlier versions had smaller engines of 375 to 435 cc, with as little as 9 hp. (The 2CV was never considered to be anything but a slow car.) The early models could only achieve a top speed of 40 mph (64 km/h), but the Charleston could achieve 71 mph (115 km/h).

| | |
|---|---|
| **COUNTRY OF ORIGIN:** | France |
| **PRODUCTION:** | 1948–1990 |
| **NUMBER MADE:** | 3.8 million |
| **LAYOUT / DRIVE:** | Front engine / Front-wheel drive |
| **ENGINE:** | 602 cc, 2 cylinders, horizontally opposed |
| **POWER / TORQUE:** | 29 hp (22 kW) / 28.8 lb-ft (39 Nm) |
| **CONSTRUCTION / DOORS:** | Platform chassis / 4 doors |

This model can also be built in the folowing colors: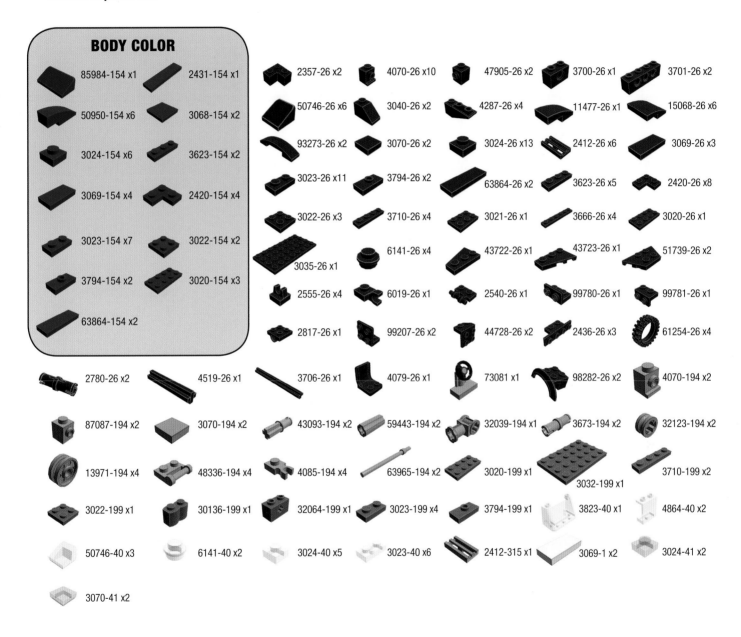

Number of parts: 249

**BODY COLOR**

85984-154 x1    2431-154 x1

50950-154 x6    3068-154 x2

3024-154 x6    3623-154 x2

3069-154 x4    2420-154 x4

3023-154 x7    3022-154 x2

3794-154 x2    3020-154 x3

63864-154 x2

2357-26 x2      4070-26 x10     47905-26 x2     3700-26 x1      3701-26 x2

50746-26 x6     3040-26 x2      4287-26 x4      11477-26 x1     15068-26 x6

93273-26 x2     3070-26 x2      3024-26 x13     2412-26 x6      3069-26 x3

3023-26 x11     3794-26 x2      63864-26 x2     3623-26 x5      2420-26 x8

3022-26 x3      3710-26 x4      3021-26 x1      3666-26 x4      3020-26 x1

3035-26 x1      6141-26 x4      43722-26 x1     43723-26 x1     51739-26 x2

2555-26 x4      6019-26 x1      2540-26 x1      99780-26 x1     99781-26 x1

2817-26 x1      99207-26 x2     44728-26 x2     2436-26 x3      61254-26 x4

2780-26 x2      4519-26 x1      3706-26 x1      4079-26 x1      73081 x1        98282-26 x2     4070-194 x2

87087-194 x2    3070-194 x2     43093-194 x2    59443-194 x2    32039-194 x1    3673-194 x2     32123-194 x2

13971-194 x4    48336-194 x4    4085-194 x4     63965-194 x2    3020-199 x1     3032-199 x1     3710-199 x2

3022-199 x1     30136-199 x1    32064-199 x1    3023-199 x4     3794-199 x1     3823-40 x1      4864-40 x2

50746-40 x3     6141-40 x2      3024-40 x5      3023-40 x6      2412-315 x1     3069-1 x2       3024-41 x2

3070-41 x2

31

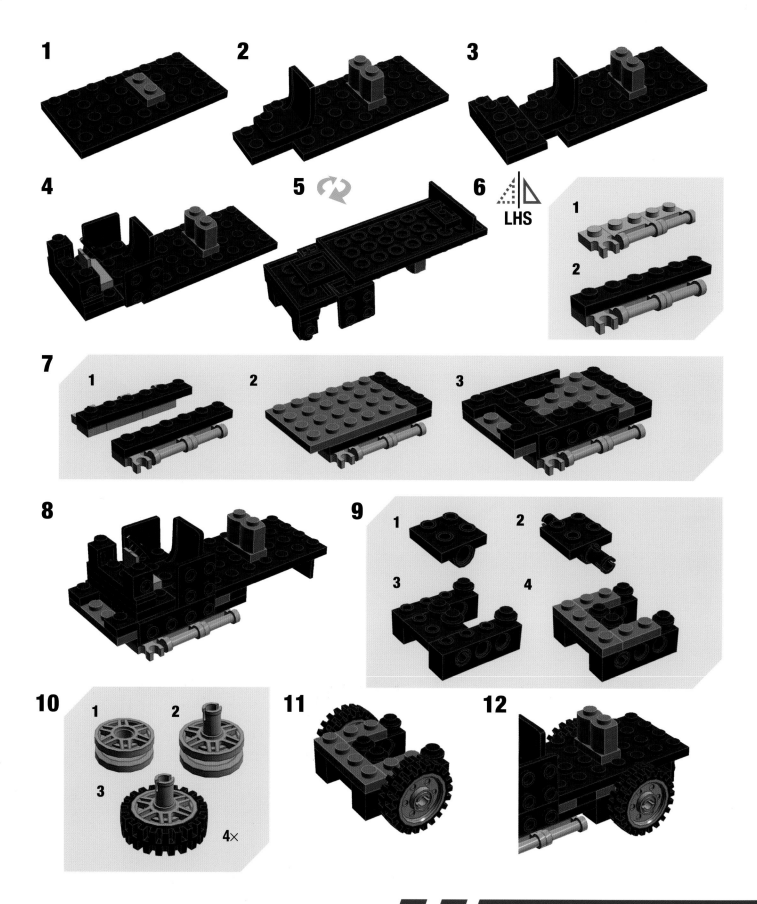

**1**

**2**

**3**

**4**

**5**

**6** LHS
1
2

**7**
1
2
3

**8**

**9**
1
2
3
4

**10**
1
2
3
4×

**11**

**12**

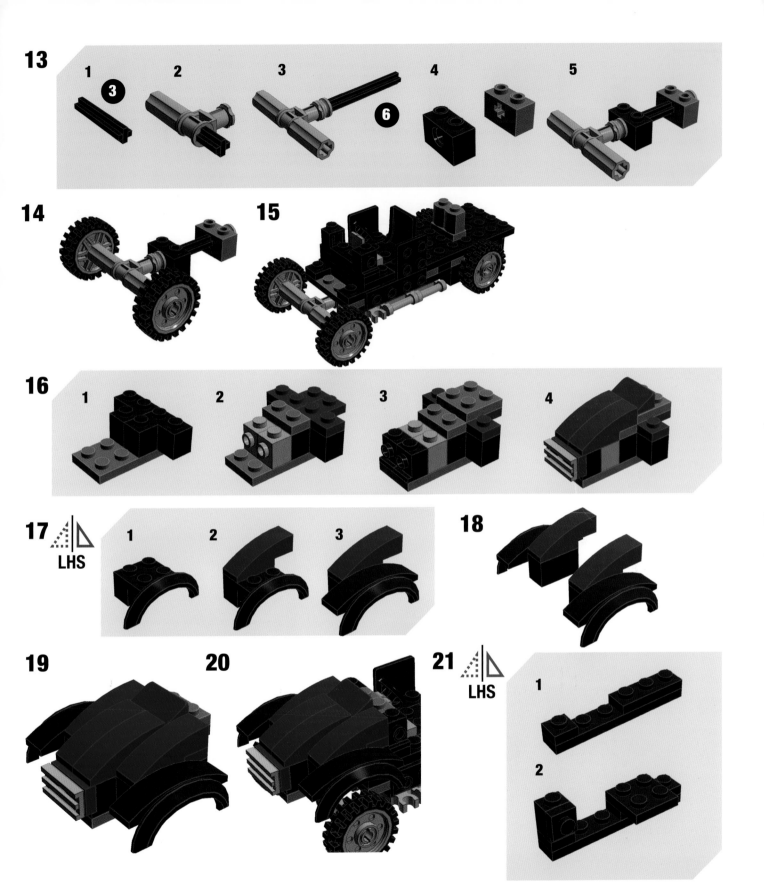

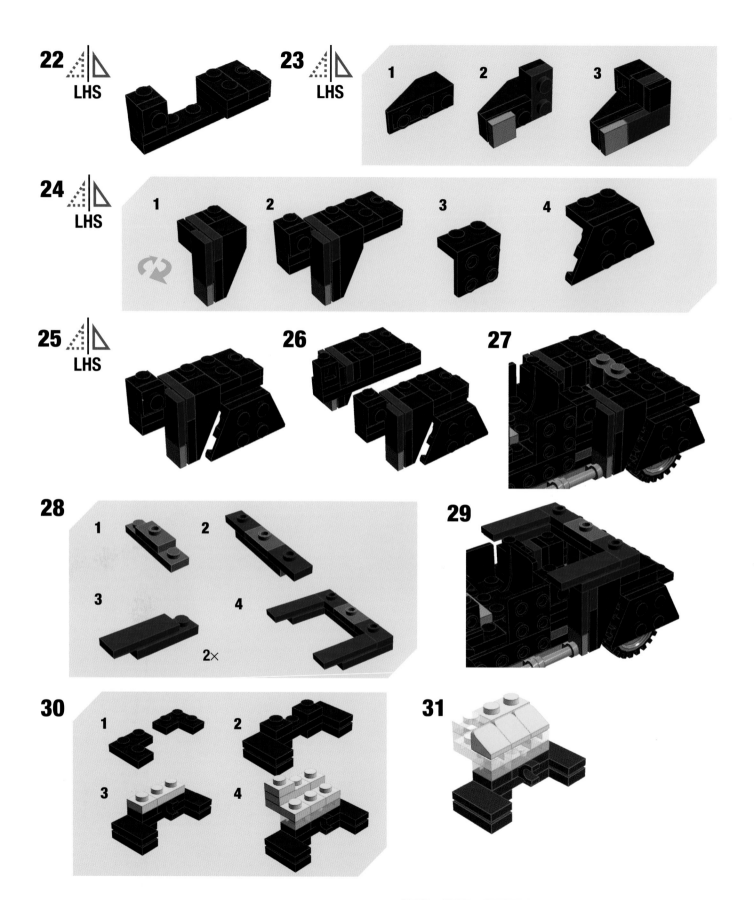

**22** LHS

**23** LHS

1 2 3

**24** LHS

1 2 3 4

**25** LHS

**26**

**27**

**28**

1 2

3 4

2×

**29**

**30**

1 2

3 4

**31**

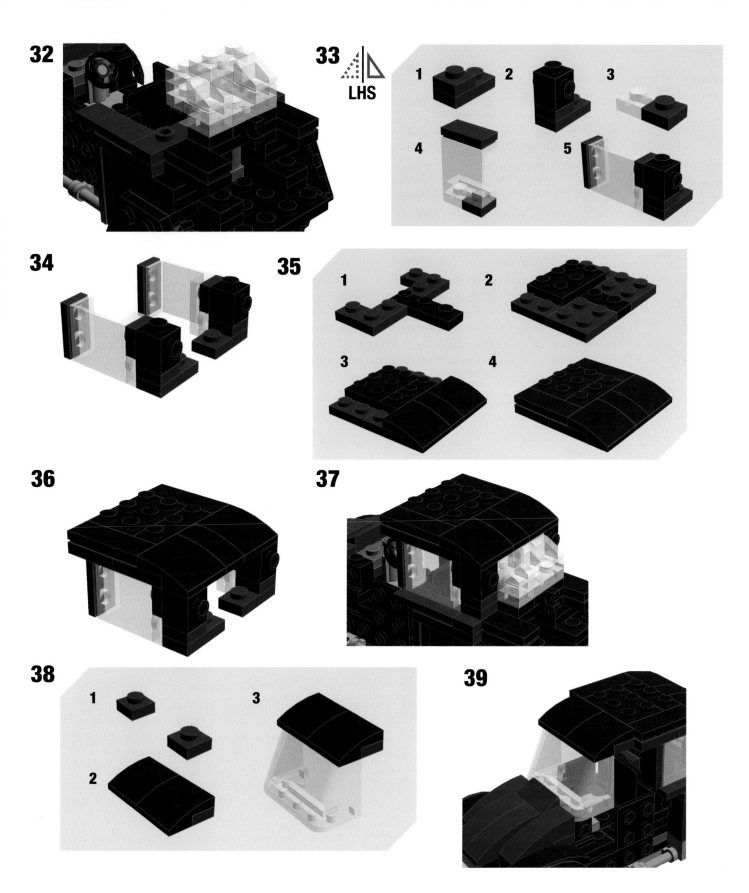

**32**

**33** LHS
1
2
3
4
5

**34**

**35**
1
2
3
4

**36**

**37**

**38**
1
2
3

**39**

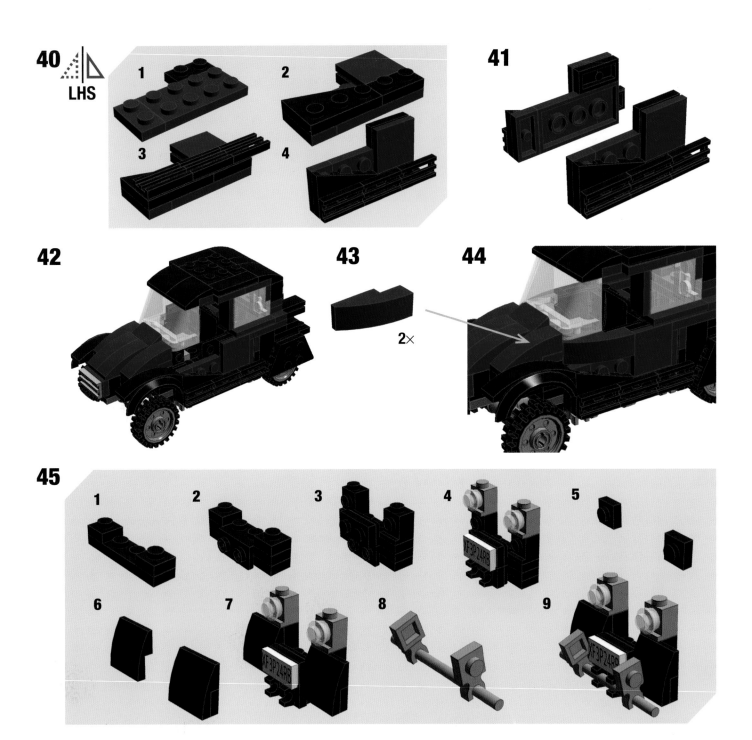

**40**

LHS

**41**

**42**

**43** 2×

**44**

**45**

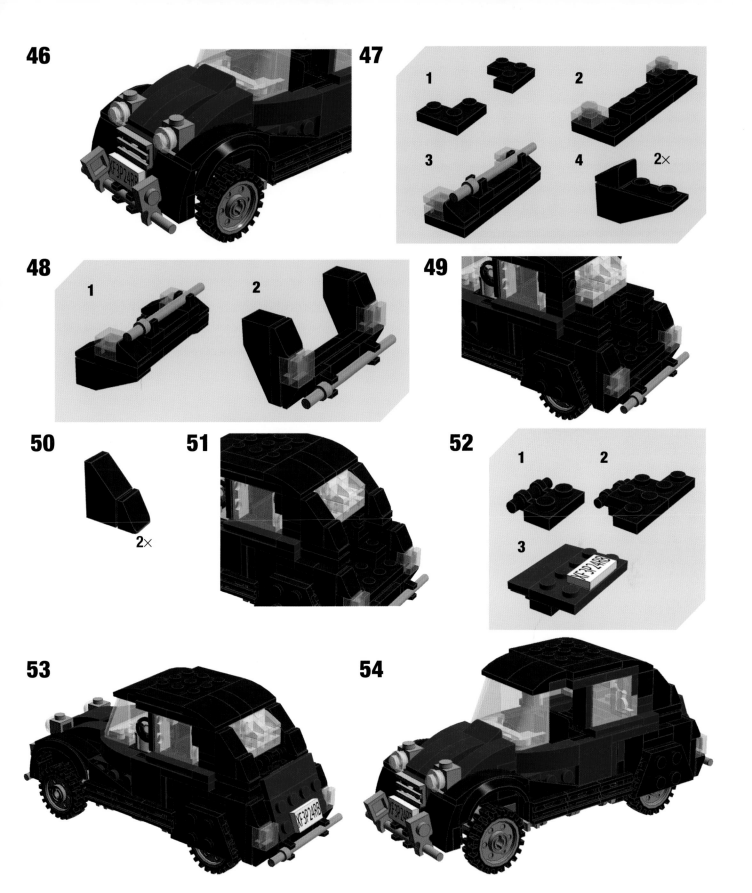

# E-TYPE COUPE & ROADSTER

A t its launch, Enzo Ferrari himself declared the E-Type "the most beautiful car ever made"—high praise indeed. Many polls conducted after 2000 declare it close to the top of the list of the most beautiful sports cars of the twentieth century. The E-Type is a template 1960s sports car. Long, long hood, slinky rounded lines, wire wheels, thin blade bumpers, and multiple exhaust pipes.

The car was not just all show—the Jaguar sports car had an evolved version of the XK 6-cylinder engine. Originally of 3.8L capacity and sporting twin overhead camshafts to produce 265 bhp (198 kW), in 1964 the engine was increased in capacity to 4.2L. The power remained the same at lower engine speeds with a 10 percent increase in maximum torque. In any guise, this made for a fast car: 0 to 60 mph (0 to 97 km/h) in 7.1 seconds and a maximum speed of 149.1 mph (240 km/h). Original press cars had been "optimized" with modification to the engines, tires, and other parts to achieve this performance—customer cars were a little slower.

At launch, two body styles were available, the fixed-head coupe (FHC) and the roadster. The cars shared basic dimensions and had seating for two. In 1966, a 2+2 coupe was added, with an additional 9 inches (225 mm) added to the body and the roofline changed to increase occupant space (but not attractiveness).

By the time of the Series 3 cars in 1971, the E-Type had begun to lose competitiveness as a sports car, despite the addition of a 5.3L V-12 engine. The car was now heavier and slower, and had lost handling prowess. The 12-cylinder, mid-engine exotics from Lamborghini and Ferrari had taken over the mantle of the ultimate supercar, though they lacked the beauty of the original E-Type Jag.

| | |
|---|---|
| **COUNTRY OF ORIGIN:** | England |
| **PRODUCTION:** | 1961–1975 |
| **NUMBER MADE:** | 75,515 (Series 1: 38,419) |
| **LAYOUT / DRIVE:** | Front engine / Rear-wheel drive |
| **ENGINE:** | 3.8L, 6 cylinders, inline |
| **POWER / TORQUE:** | 265 bhp (198 kW) / 240 lb-ft (325 Nm) |
| **CONSTRUCTION / DOORS:** | Steel monocoque with tubular steel subframe |

This model can also be built in the folowing colors:

Number of parts: 316

## BODY COLOR

| | | | |
|---|---|---|---|
| 3005-21 x2 | 3010-21 x1 | 4070-21 x4 | 50746-21 x6 |
| 85984-21 x11 | 3665-21 x6 | 4286-21 x2 | 3747-21 x2 |
| 11477-21 x2 | 50950-21 x2 | 61678-21 x8 | 3070-21 x5 |
| 3024-21 x3 | 2412-21 x4 | 3069-21 x5 | 3023-21 x15 |
| 3794-21 x10 | 63864-21 x2 | 2431-21 x3 | 3068-21 x3 |
| 3623-21 x3 | 2420-21 x13 | 3022-21 x2 | 3710-21 x2 |
| 87079-21 x2 | 3021-21 x4 | 3666-21 x4 | 3020-21 x2 |
| 3460-21 x2 | 2555-21 x2 | 48336-21 x6 | 52031-21 x1 |

| | | |
|---|---|---|
| 3005-194 x2 | 87087-194 x1 | 50746-194 x1 |
| 3665-194 x2 | 3070-194 x1 | 3024-194 x4 |
| 3069-194 x1 | 3023-194 x6 | 2420-194 x2 |
| 6141-194 x1 | 43722-194 x1 | 43723-194 x1 |
| 2450-194 x2 | 2555-194 x8 | 4081-194 x1 |
| 55982-194 x4 | 4274-194 x2 | 6589-194 x4 |
| 30374-194 x2 | 73587-194 x3 | 73081-194 x1 |
| 3065-40 x2 | 3024-40 x2 | 6141-40 x2 |

| | | | | | | |
|---|---|---|---|---|---|---|
| 4176-40 x1 | 4864-40 x2 | 48729-26 x2 | 73587-26 x3 | 73081-26 x1 | 3010-26 x1 | 3701-26 x1 |
| 3703-26 x2 | 50746-26 x2 | 85984-26 x3 | 3024-26 x2 | 2412-26 x1 | 3069-26 x2 | 3023-26 x10 |
| 3794-26 x1 | 2431-26 x1 | 3623-26 x4 | 2420-26 x4 | 3022-26 x2 | 3710-26 x4 | 6636-26 x1 |
| 87079-26 x1 | 3021-26 x4 | 3666-26 x2 | 3020-26 x1 | 3460-26 x4 | 3795-26 x1 | 3034-26 x1 |
| 3032-26 x2 | 6141-26 x6 | 12825-26 x2 | 4085-26 x4 | 63868-26 x2 | 2540-26 x2 | 48336-26 x2 |
| 60470-26 x2 | 99780-26 x1 | 99781-26 x1 | 10201-26 x4 | 4865-26 x2 | 89201-26 x4 | 3062B-199 x2 |
| 6188-199 x2 | 3023-199 x1 | 3710-199 x1 | 3021-199 x1 | 3020-199 x2 | 2654-199 x1 | 4032-199 x1 |
| 6587-199 x4 | 3024-41 x2 | 6141-182 x4 | 3069-1 x1 | 6141-315 x1 | | |

**E-Type Coupe**

**E-Type Roadster**

These instructions will allow the construction of either the Jaguar E-Type Coupe or the E-Type Roadster. The two body variations are common up to step 52. Beyond that the E-Type Coupe will continue instructions in red. Jumping to step 60 will allow you to continue to build the E-Type Roadster. This section will be illustrated with a green car—though the parts list will give you the parts you need in red, or an alternative color of your choice.

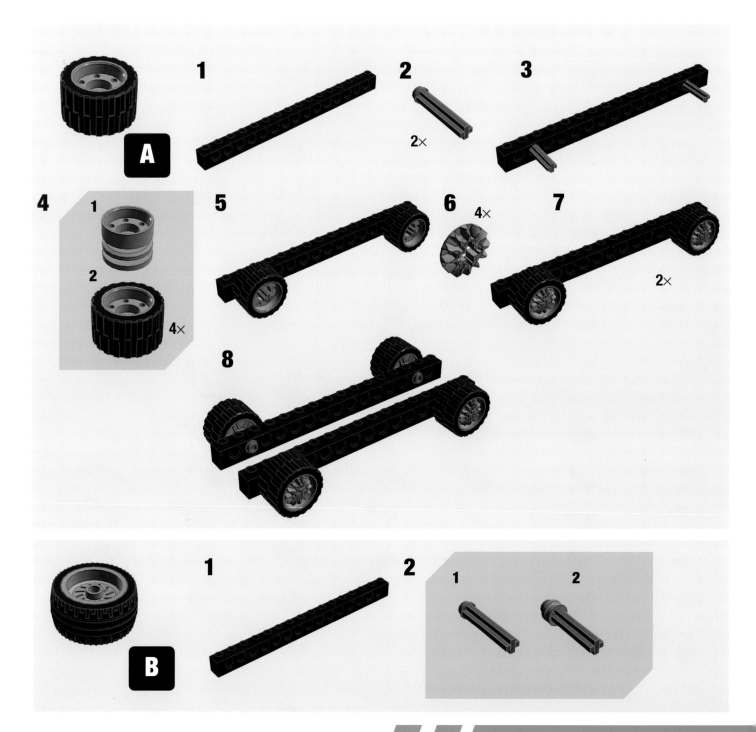

**A**

1

2   2×

3

4
  1
  2   4×

5

6   4×

7   2×

8

**B**

1

2
  1    2

**5**

1     2

4×

**Alternative Tires:**

332123-194 x8     18977-26 x4     18976-315 x4

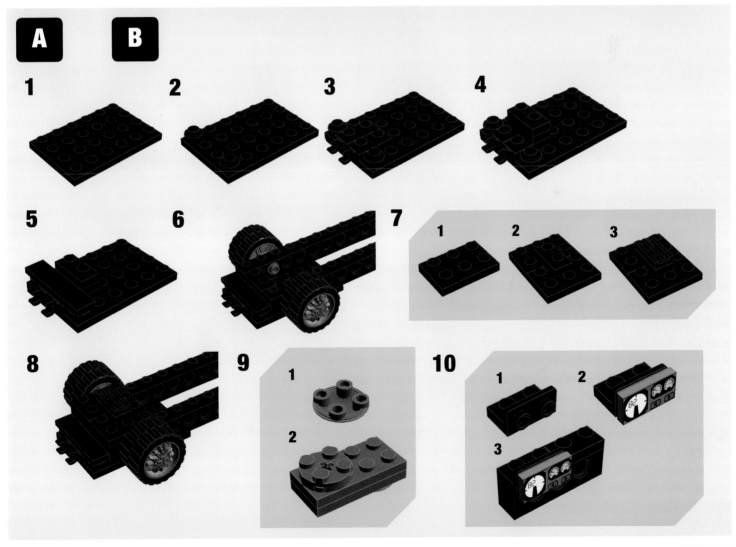

**A**   **B**

**JAGUAR E-TYPE COUPE & ROADSTER**   **41**

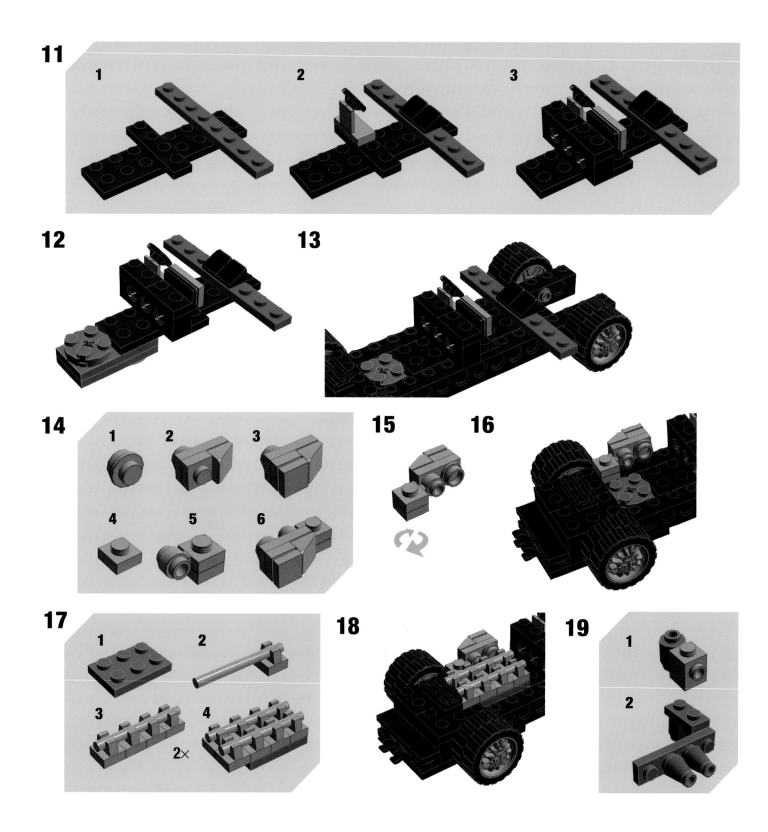

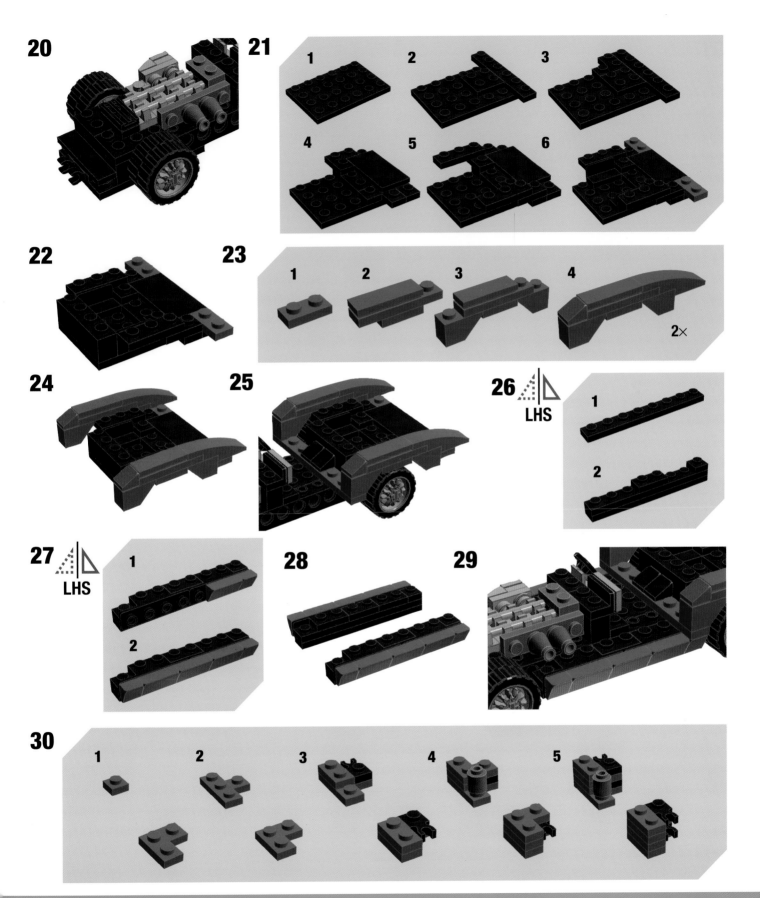

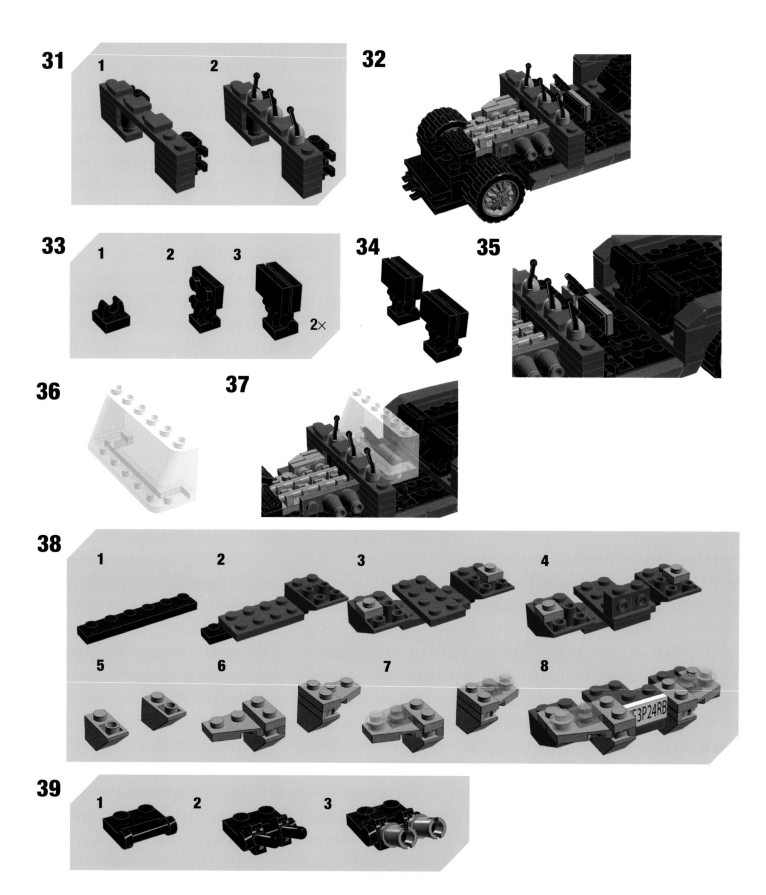

**40**

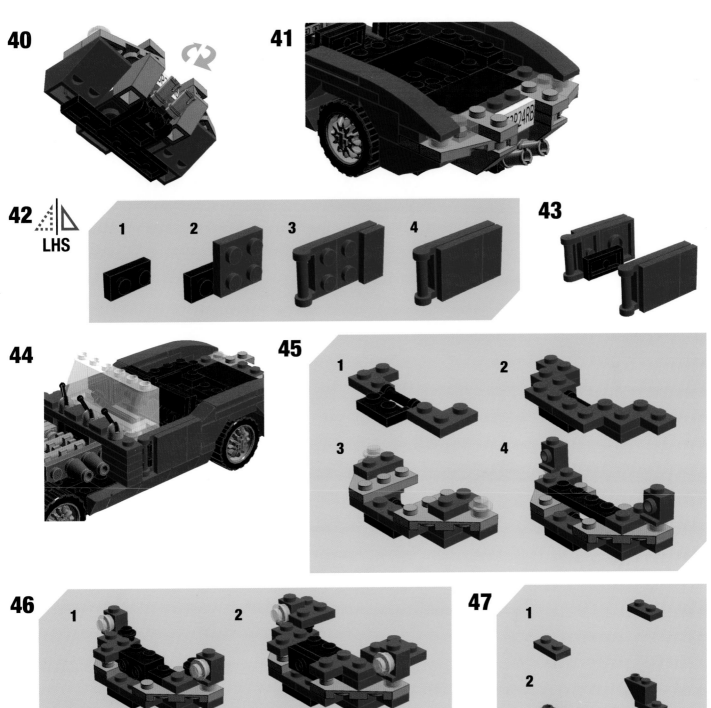

**41**

**42**

LHS

1

2

3

4

**43**

**44**

**45**

1

2

3

4

**46**

1

2

3

4

**47**

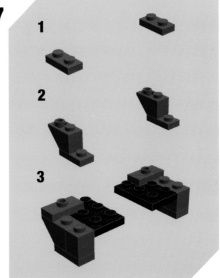

1

2

3

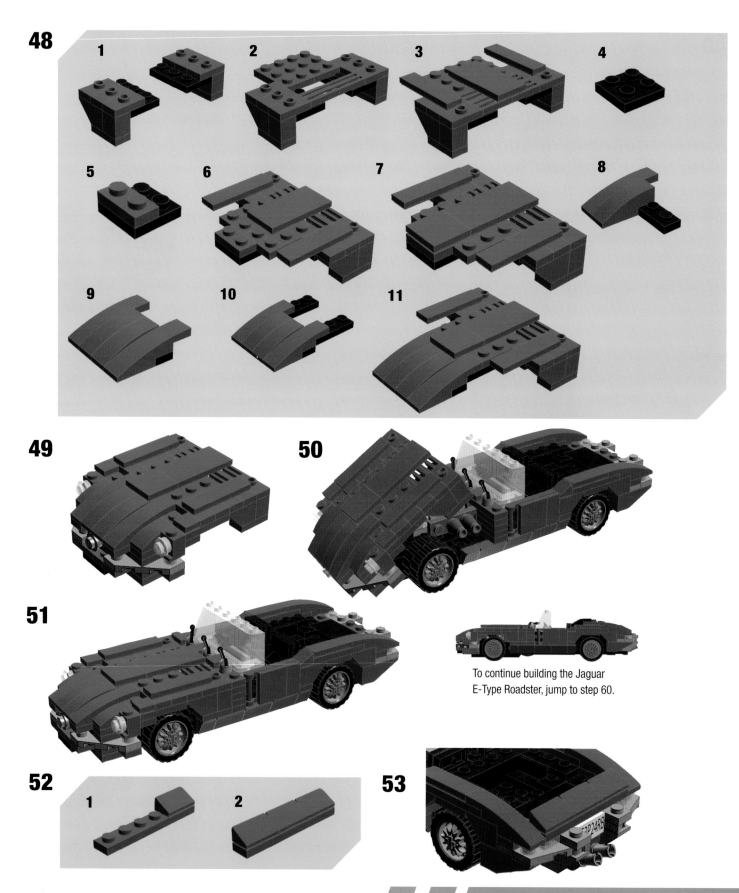

**48**

1 2 3 4

5 6 7 8

9 10 11

**49**

**50**

**51**

To continue building the Jaguar
E-Type Roadster, jump to step 60.

**52**

1 2

**53**

**54**

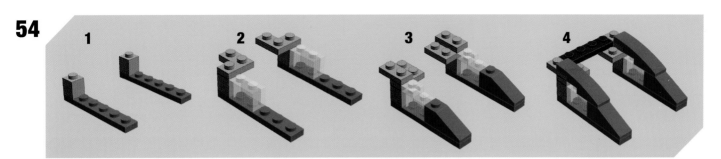

**55**

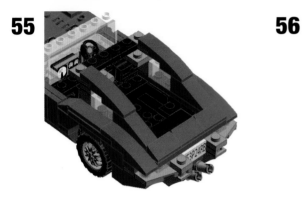

**56**

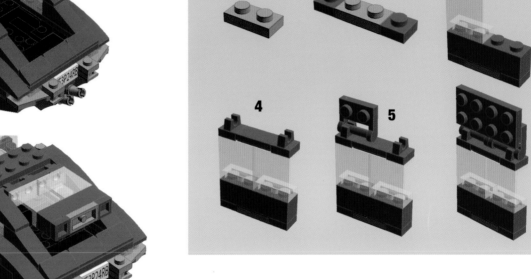

**57**

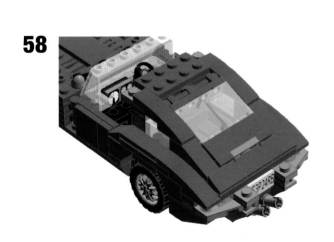

**58**

**59**

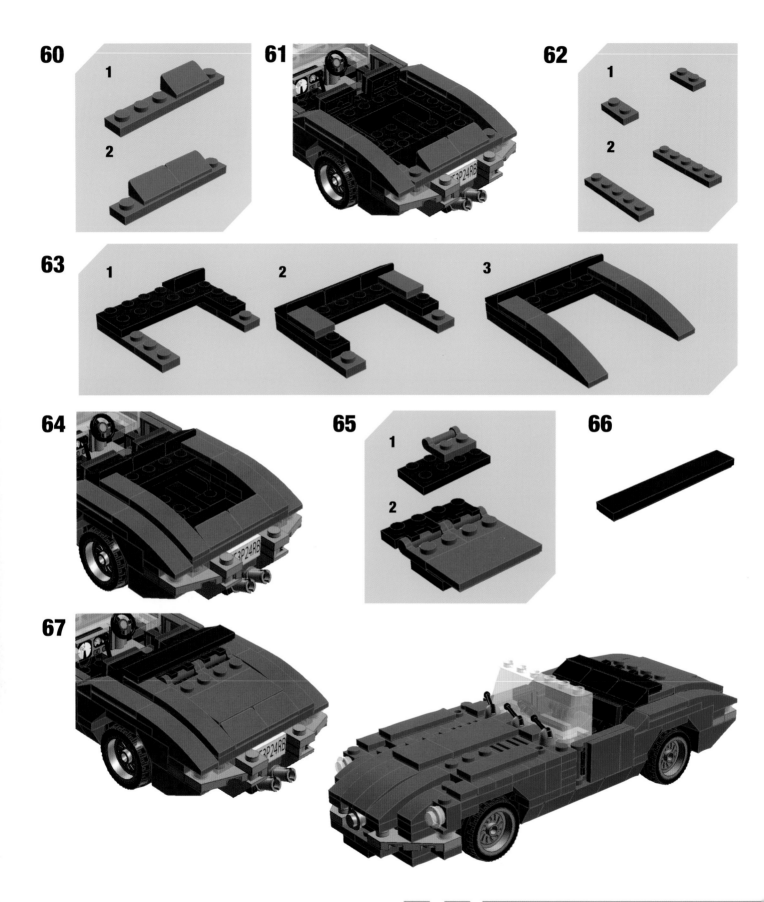

# INTERMEDIATE

S ports cars capture our imagination with their forms, details, sounds, and spirit. This section introduces some of the most revered names in sports car history—each left iconic wheel tracks for others to follow.

Most of the models in Section 2 move to a larger scale—Miniland (1:20)—the scale used in the LEGOLAND® theme parks across the globe. The larger scale allows the scope for introducing more-advanced LEGO® modeling techniques.

Most of these cars include suspension systems, where the wheels move relative to the body via spring systems.

At this scale, the models can also include added details, such as brick-built engines, engine compartments, doors, luggage compartments, and interiors. Though these models include some very specific details, I encourage builders to see them as a basis for creating models personalized to their own tastes.

## 2017 FORD
# F-150 RAPTOR

**M**ix together a half-ton pickup truck, Baja Racer, sports car, and family car, and you pretty much get the Ford F-150 Raptor. I'm not sure who originally came up with the idea, but it has proven popular since its introduction in 2010. The second-generation P552 Raptor shown here was introduced as a 2017 model. Gone was the previous V-8 engine, replaced by a 450-hp (340-kW) version of the 3.5L GTDi EcoBoost V-6—a group of technologies including direct fuel injection and turbocharging, punching out 591 lb-ft (691 Nm) of torque.

Putting all this power to the ground are a 10-speed automatic transmission, dual-ratio electronic transfer case, and AWD with locking front and rear axles. Ford developed an advanced chassis control technology system that selects ratios, throttle maps, transfer case torque distribution, and brake and stability program settings to maximize performance on a large number of different terrains, including tarmac. The goal: to be the fastest pickup truck on any and every track and surface.

As well as all the power and chassis drivetrain technologies, Ford added a wider front and rear track, long travel suspension, FOX-brand shock absorbers, and larger 33-inch tires. Brand imaging for the original 2010 Raptor included a bright-orange truck jumping in the air—no doubt accompanied by a bellowing V-8 roar. Many YouTube videos show customers attempting to repeat the feat, sometimes heading home in an ambulance with the Raptor heading back on a flatbed truck. Although the Raptor is capable, driving any vehicle in this manner is not recommended for one's long-term health.

Many Raptor customers buy two: one stock version for the road and a modified, trailered second truck for off-road racing events such as the Baja series in the US Southwest.

| | |
|---|---|
| **COUNTRY OF ORIGIN:** | USA |
| **PRODUCTION:** | 2017–Present |
| **NUMBER MADE:** | Currently in production |
| **ENGINE:** | 3.5L EcoBoost, 6 cylinders, V |
| **POWER / TORQUE:** | 450 hp (340 kW) / 10 lb-ft (691 Nm) |
| **CONSTRUCTION / DOORS:** | Steel chassis, aluminum body / 4-door pickup |

**This model can also be built in the folowing colors:**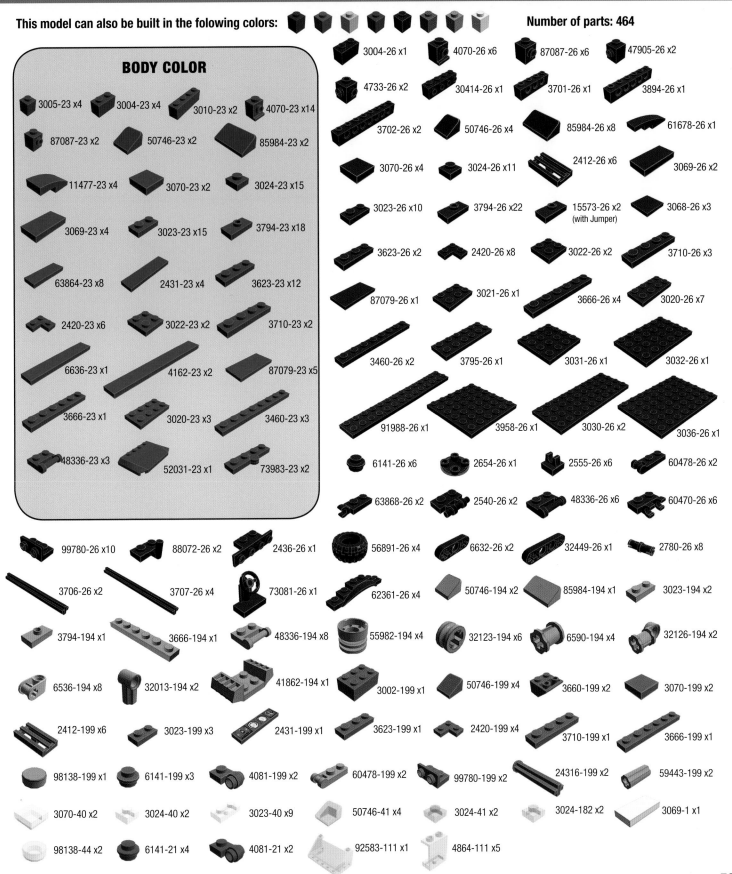

**Number of parts: 464**

**BODY COLOR**

3005-23 x4
3004-23 x4
3010-23 x2
4070-23 x14
87087-23 x2
50746-23 x2
85984-23 x2
11477-23 x4
3070-23 x2
3024-23 x15
3069-23 x4
3023-23 x15
3794-23 x18
63864-23 x8
2431-23 x4
3623-23 x12
2420-23 x6
3022-23 x2
3710-23 x2
6636-23 x1
4162-23 x2
87079-23 x5
3666-23 x1
3020-23 x3
3460-23 x3
48336-23 x3
52031-23 x1
73983-23 x2

3004-26 x1
4070-26 x6
87087-26 x6
47905-26 x2
4733-26 x2
30414-26 x1
3701-26 x1
3894-26 x1
3702-26 x2
50746-26 x4
85984-26 x8
61678-26 x1
3070-26 x4
3024-26 x11
2412-26 x6
3069-26 x2
3023-26 x10
3794-26 x22
15573-26 x2 (with Jumper)
3068-26 x3
3623-26 x2
2420-26 x8
3022-26 x2
3710-26 x3
87079-26 x1
3021-26 x1
3666-26 x4
3020-26 x7
3460-26 x2
3795-26 x1
3031-26 x1
3032-26 x1
91988-26 x1
3958-26 x1
3030-26 x2
3036-26 x1
6141-26 x6
2654-26 x1
2555-26 x6
60478-26 x2
63868-26 x2
2540-26 x2
48336-26 x6
60470-26 x6
99780-26 x10
88072-26 x2
2436-26 x1
56891-26 x4
6632-26 x2
32449-26 x1
2780-26 x8
3706-26 x2
3707-26 x4
73081-26 x1
62361-26 x4
50746-194 x2
85984-194 x1
3023-194 x2
3794-194 x1
3666-194 x1
48336-194 x8
55982-194 x4
32123-194 x6
6590-194 x4
32126-194 x2
6536-194 x8
32013-194 x2
41862-194 x1
3002-199 x1
50746-199 x4
3660-199 x2
3070-199 x2
2412-199 x6
3023-199 x3
2431-199 x1
3623-199 x1
2420-199 x4
3710-199 x1
3666-199 x1
98138-199 x1
6141-199 x3
4081-199 x2
60478-199 x2
99780-199 x2
24316-199 x2
59443-199 x2
3070-40 x2
3024-40 x2
3023-40 x9
50746-41 x4
3024-41 x2
3024-182 x2
3069-1 x1
98138-44 x2
6141-21 x4
4081-21 x2
92583-111 x1
4864-111 x5

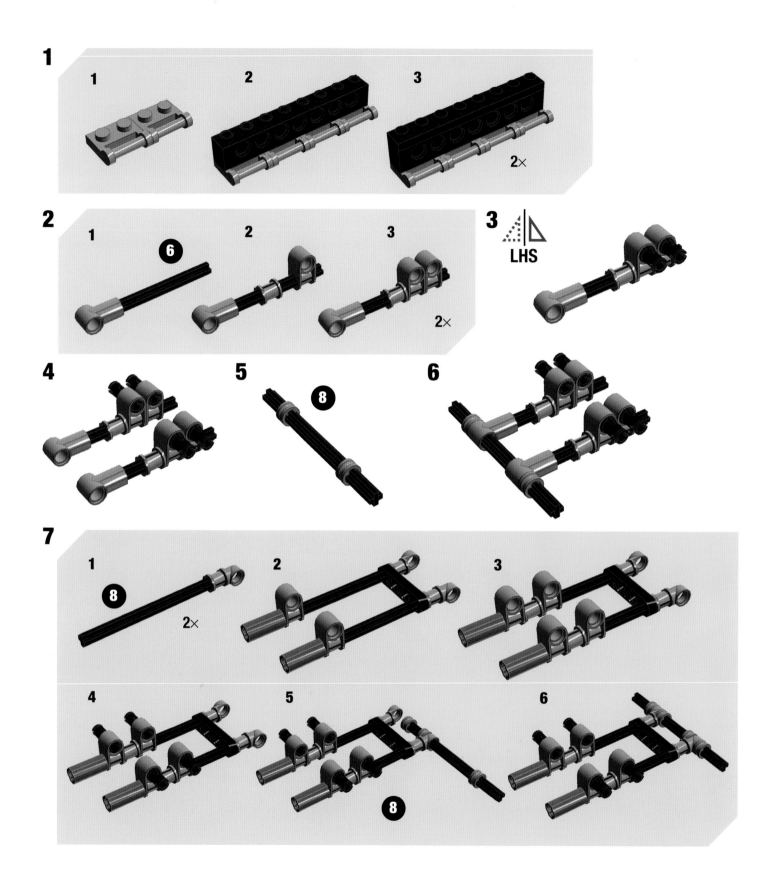

**1**
1    2    3    2×

**2**
1    6    2    3    2×

**3**    LHS

**4**

**5**    8

**6**

**7**
1    8    2×    2    3

4    5    8    6

**8**

**9**

1      2

**10**

**11**

**12**

**13**

**14**

**15**

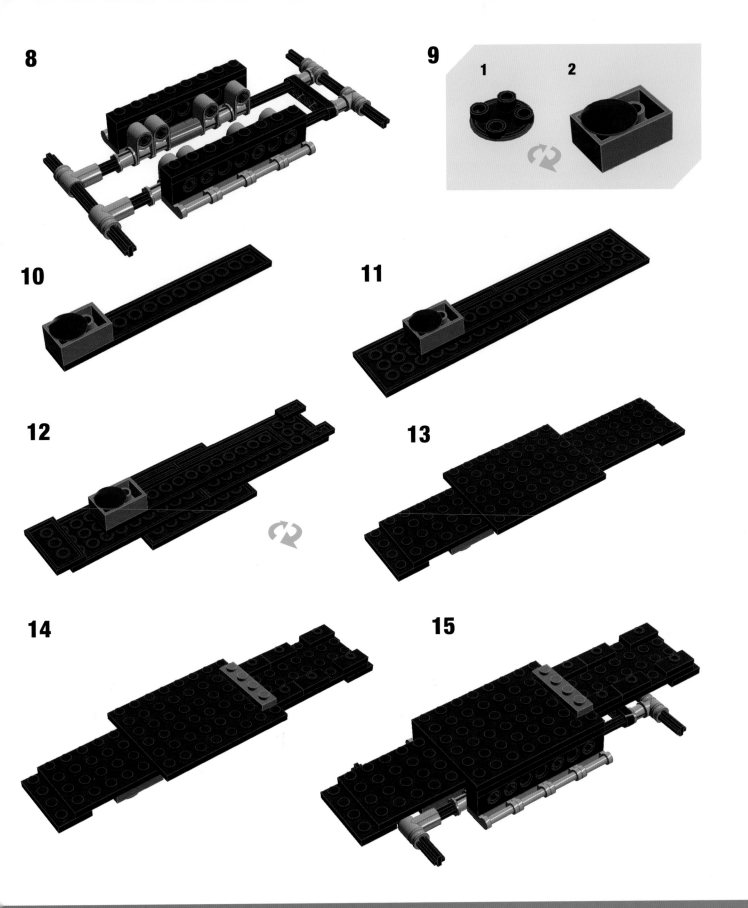

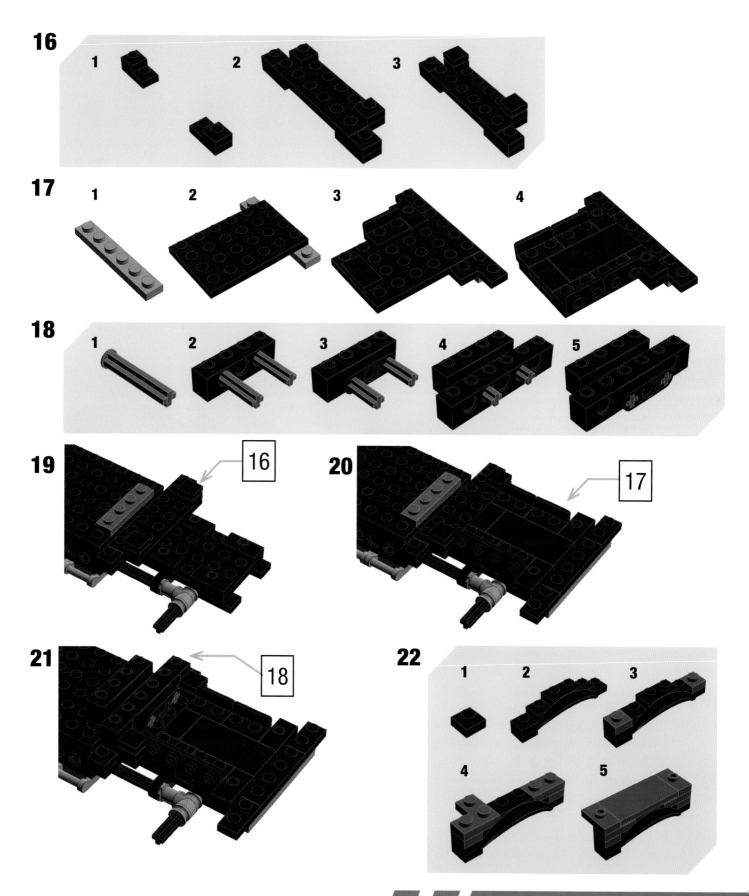

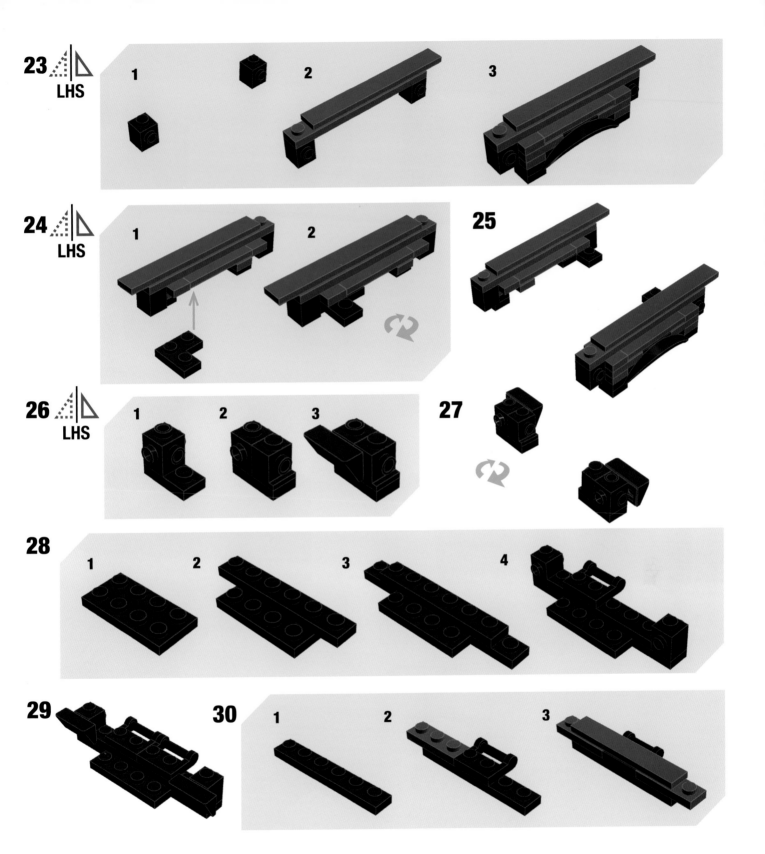

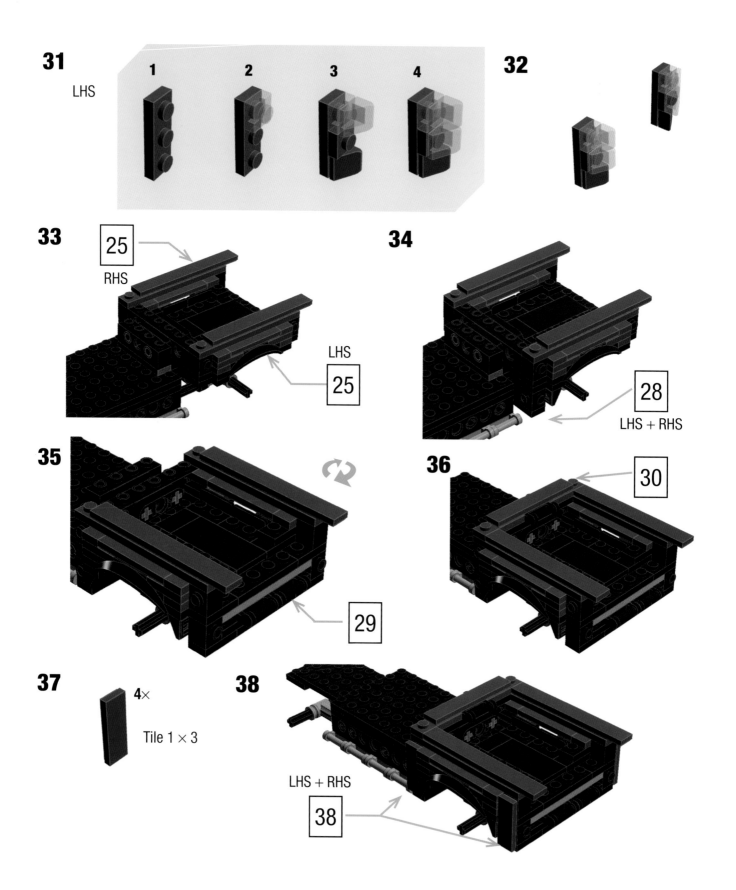

**31**

LHS

1  2  3  4

**32**

**33**

[25]

RHS

LHS
[25]

**34**

[28]
LHS + RHS

**35**

[29]

**36**

[30]

**37**

4×

Tile 1 × 3

**38**

LHS + RHS
[38]

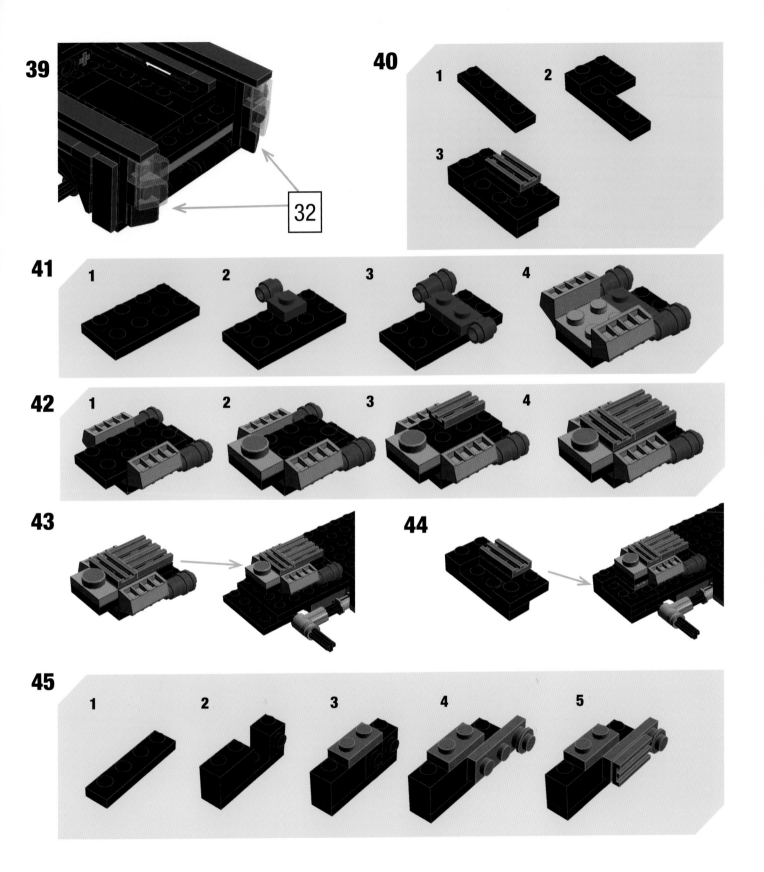

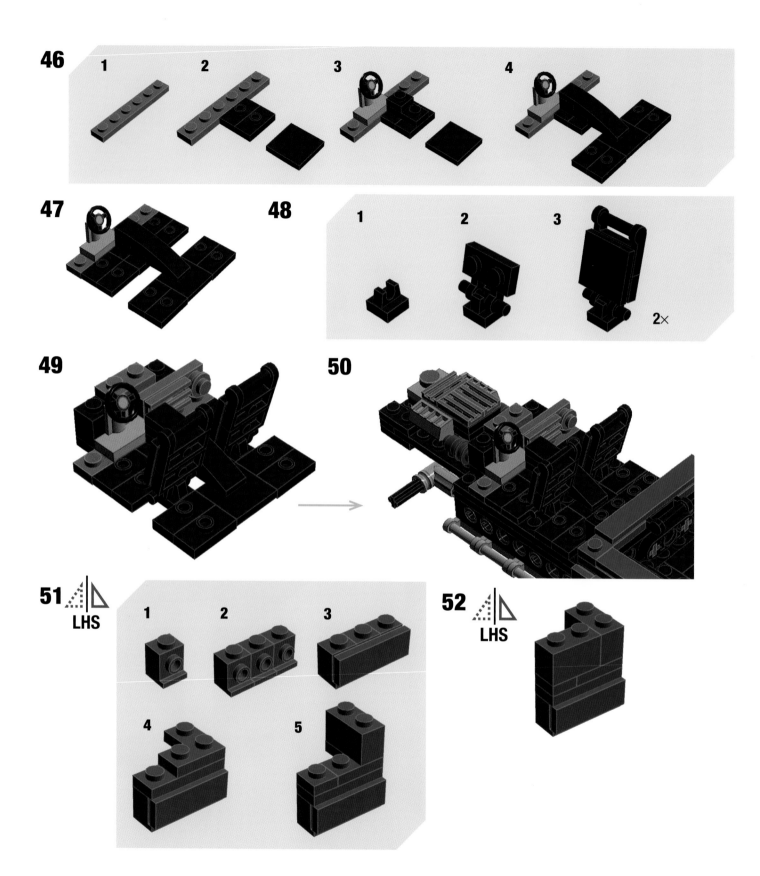

46

1   2   3   4

47   48

1   2   3

2×

49   50

51 LHS

1   2   3

4   5

52 LHS

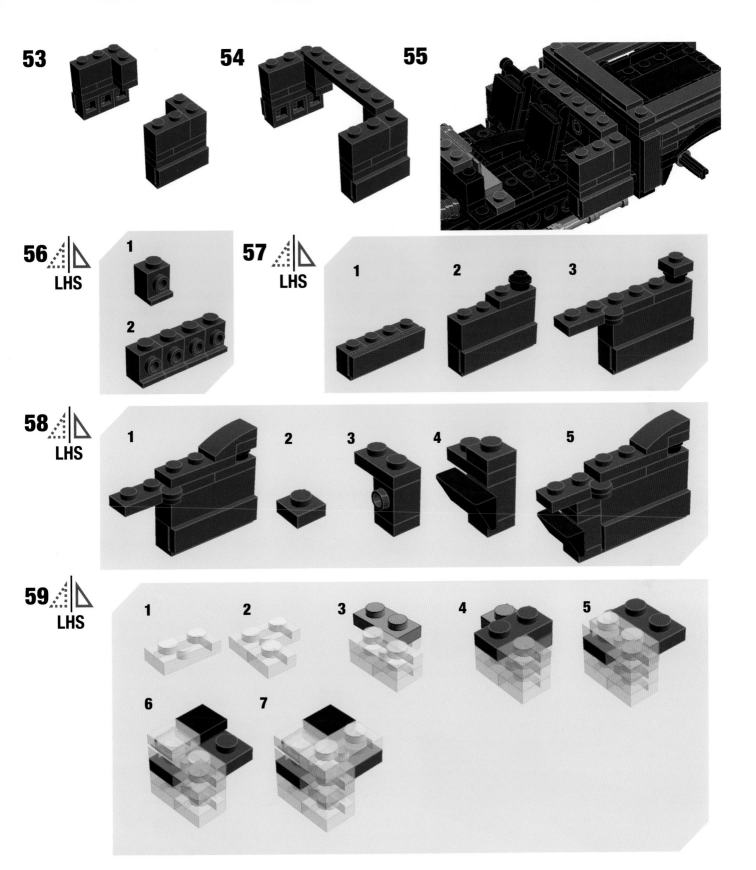

**53**

**54**

**55**

**56** LHS

1

2

**57** LHS

1

2

3

**58** LHS

1

2

3

4

5

**59** LHS

1

2

3

4

5

6

7

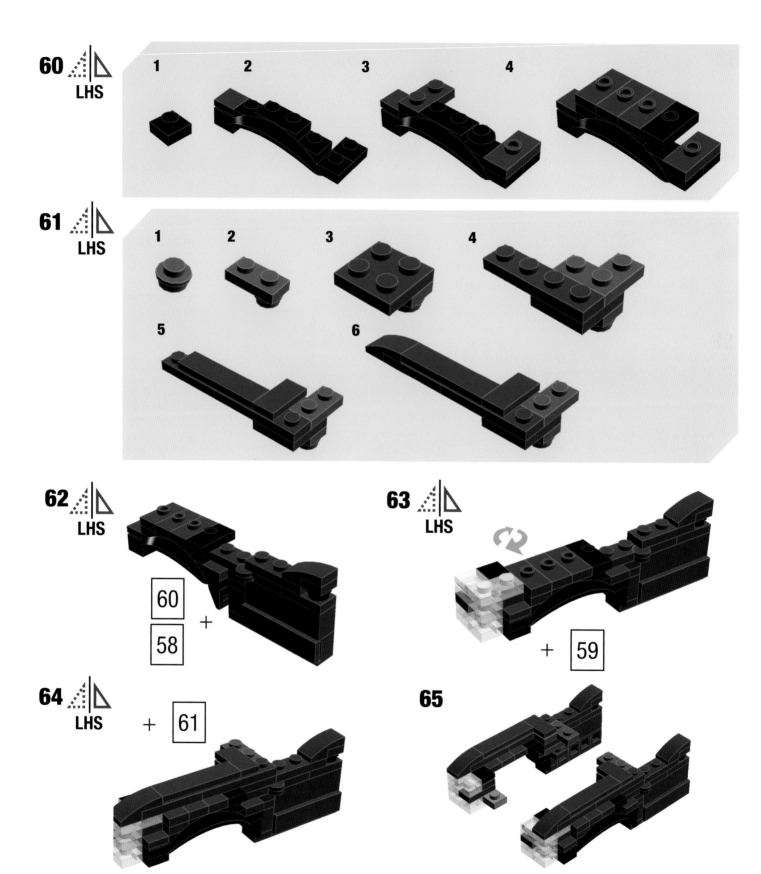

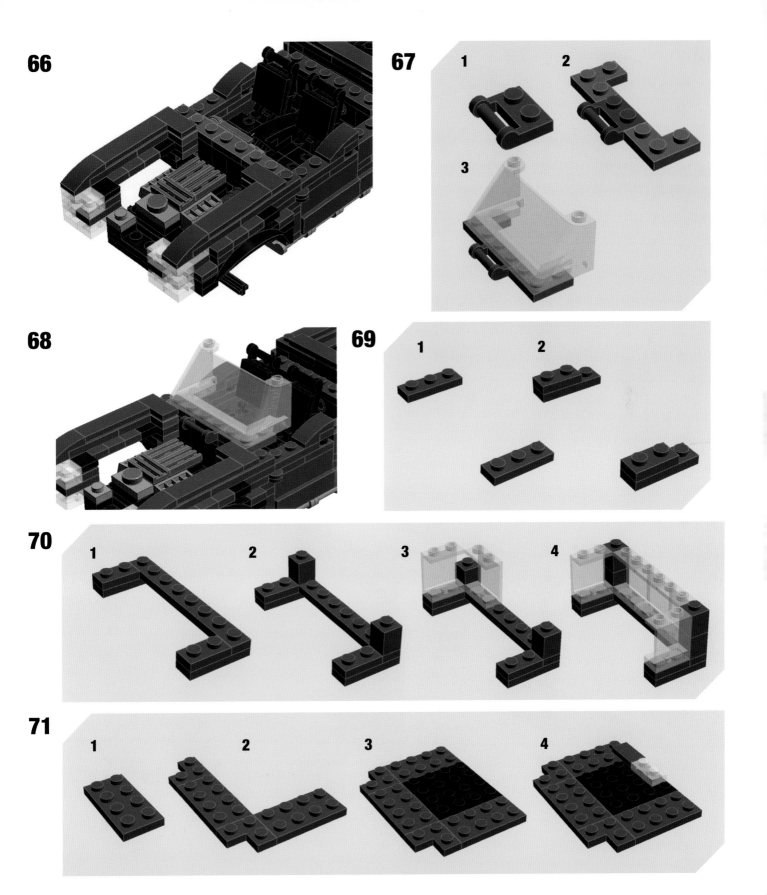

**72**

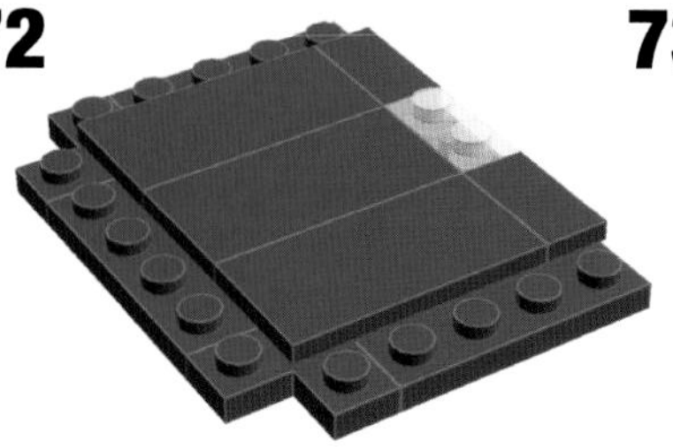

**73**

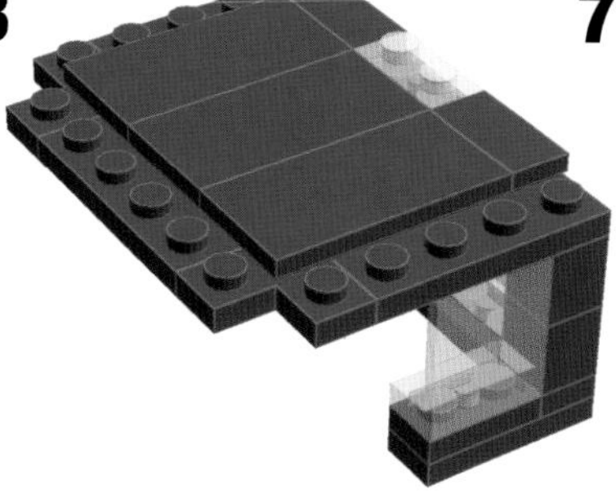

**74**

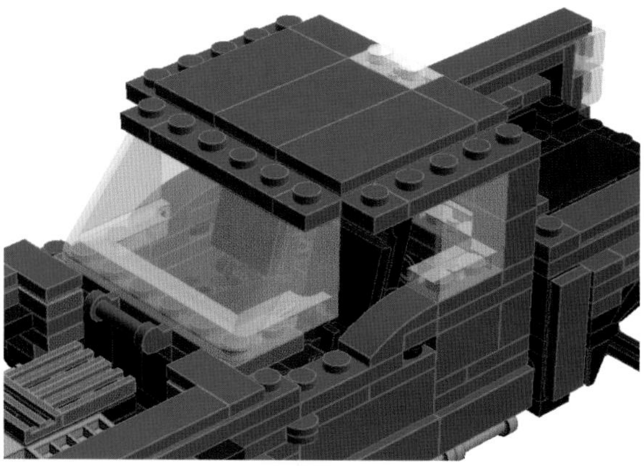

**75**

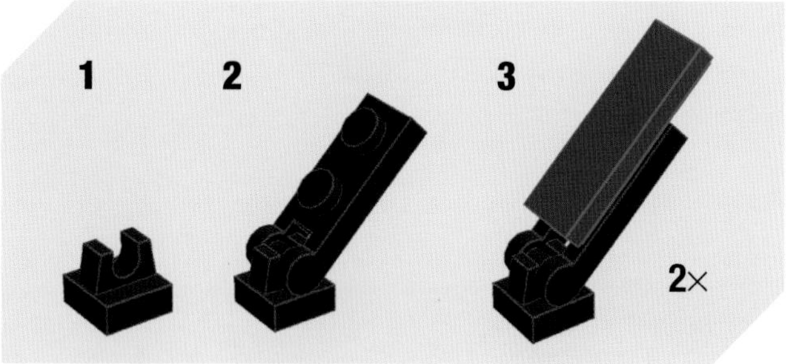

1

2

3

2×

**76**

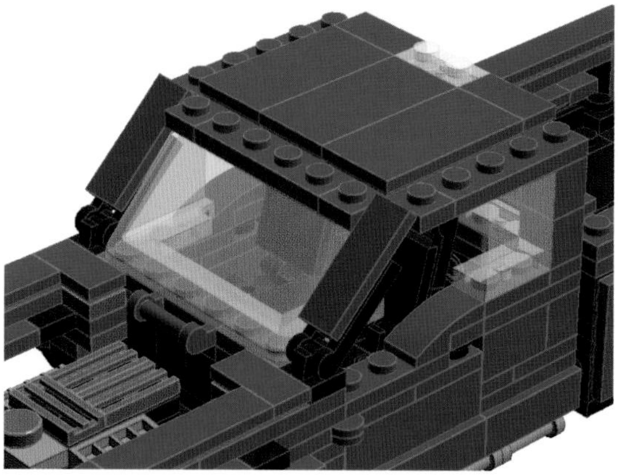

**77**

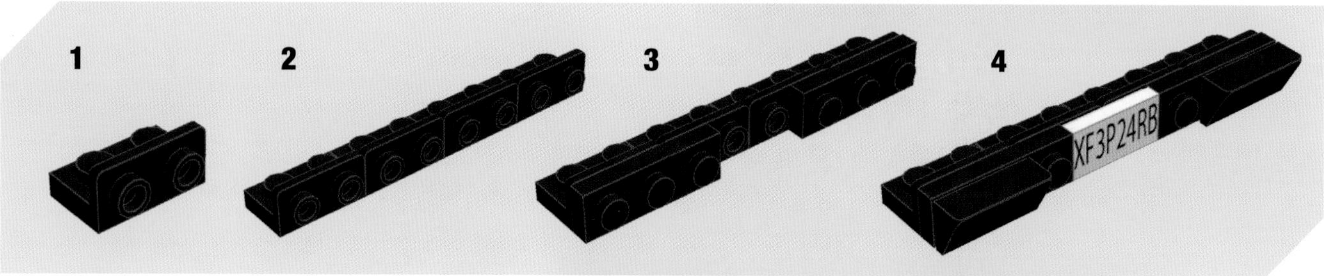

1

2

3

4

XF3P24RB

**78**

XF3P24RB

**79**

F3P24RB

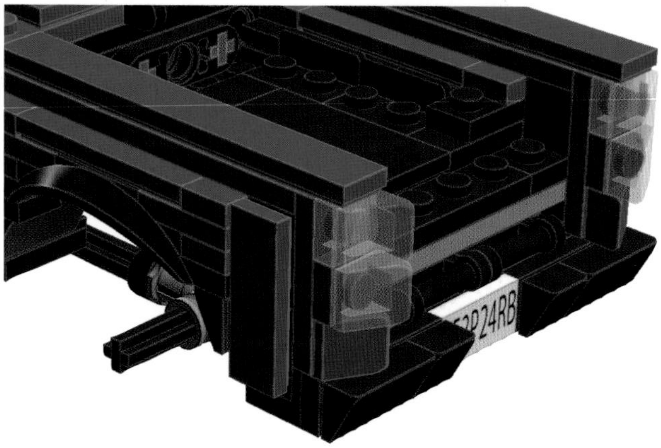

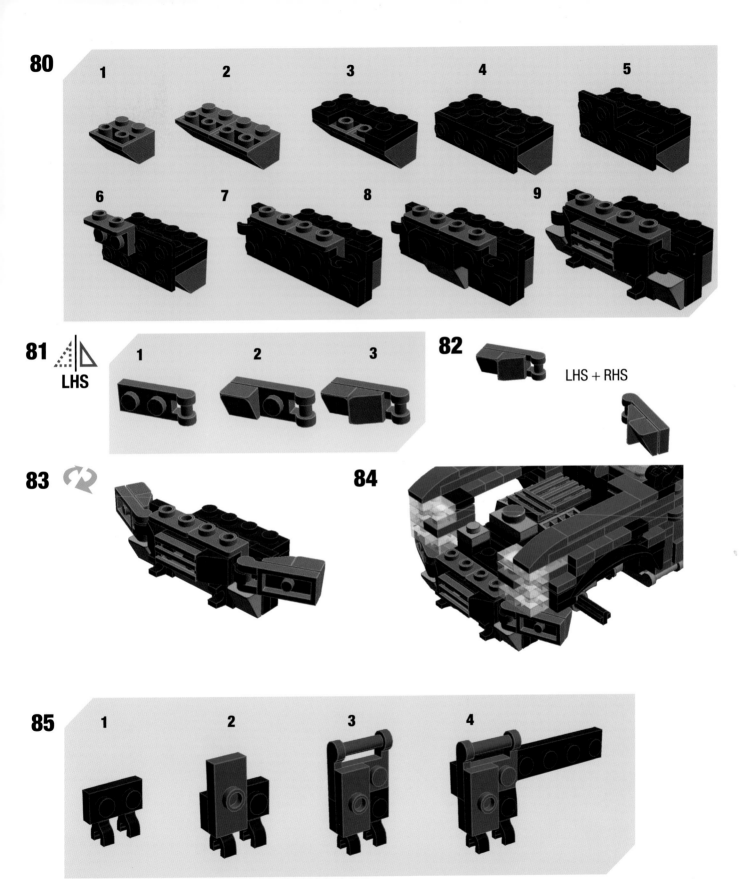

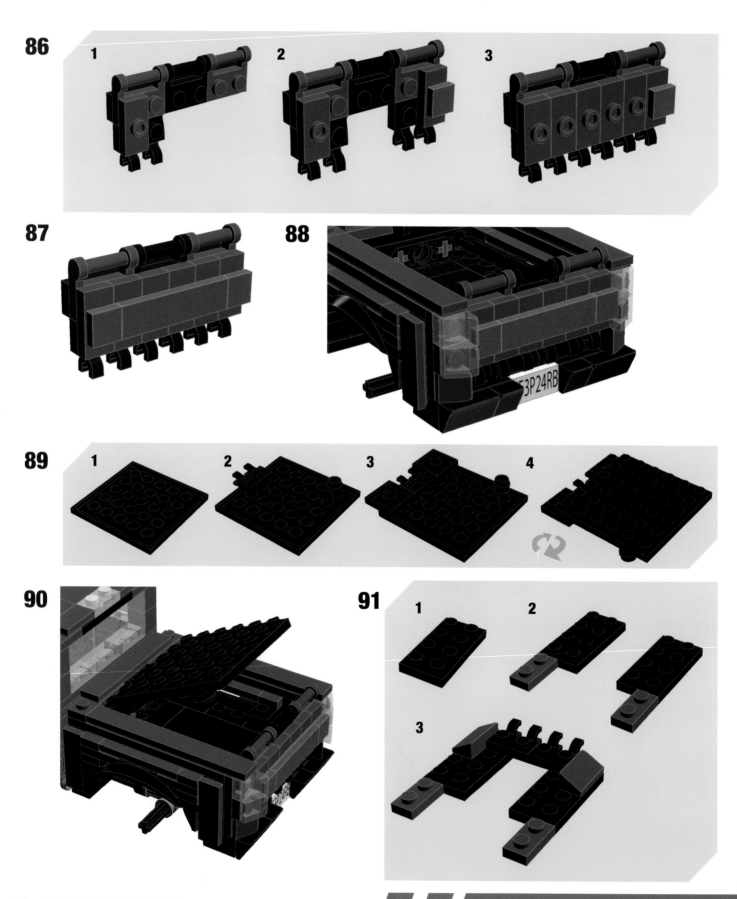

**92**

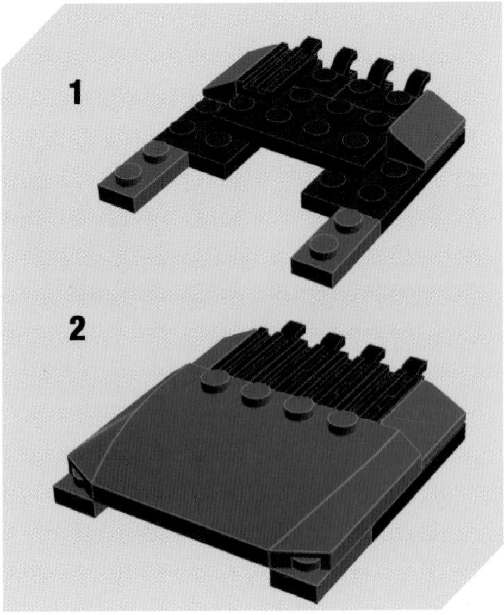

1

2

**93**

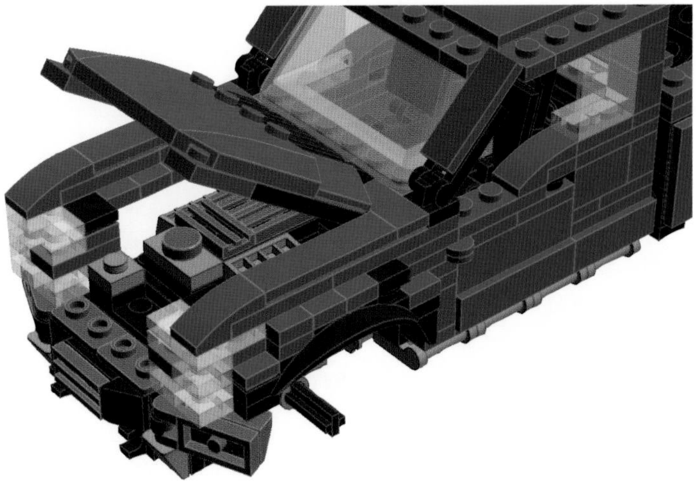

**94**

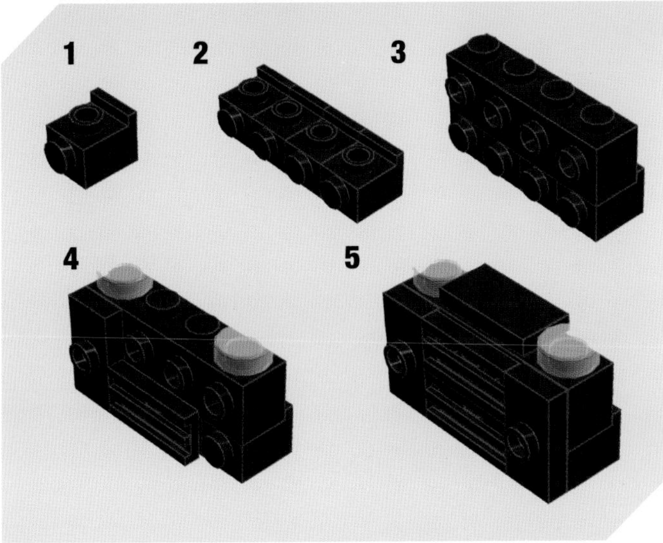

1

2

3

4

5

**95**

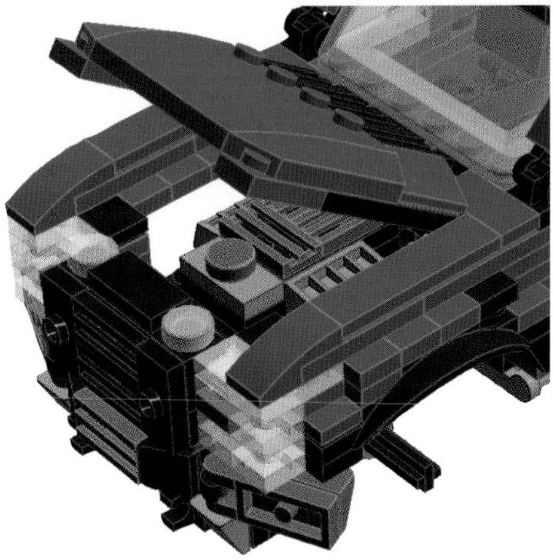

**96**

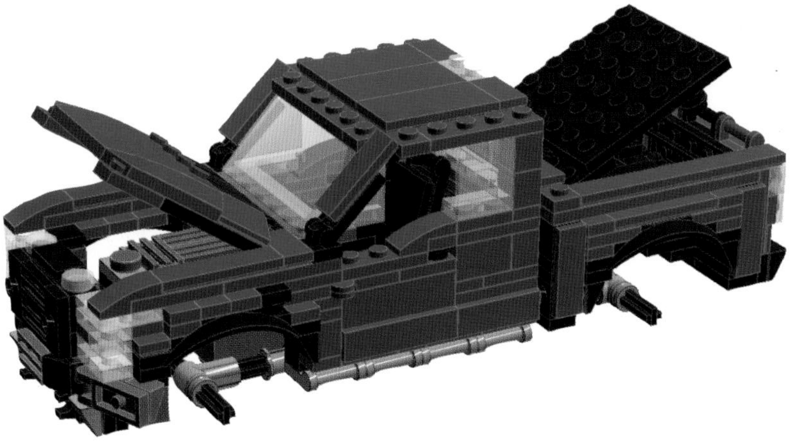

**97**

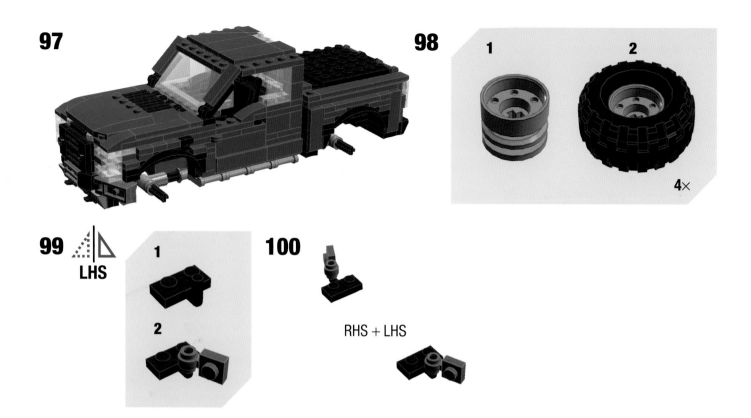

**98**

1    2

4×

**99** LHS

1

2

**100**

RHS + LHS

**101**

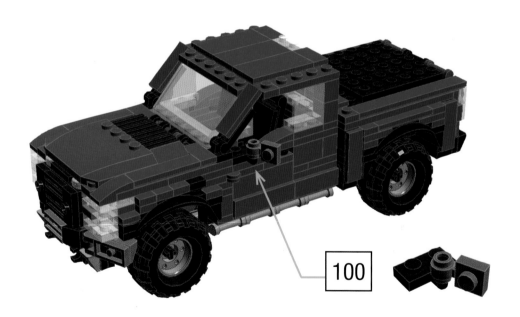

100

# DATSUN
# 240Z COUPE

HL 7639

The S30 Datsun 240Z (also known as the Nissan Fairlady Z in its home market) was not the first Japanese sports car. Nissan, Honda, Toyota, and Mazda had each produced low-volume, domestic-consumption models that were largely ignored by the West. The 240Z was different—mainly in that its intended market was the United States. With 168,584 cars produced over four years, the 240Z marked a major shift in emphasis for the Japanese makers, all of which began to turn their focus across the Pacific.

The 240Z was not overly radical. The engine was a 2.4L inline-six. Tuning was spritely, at 151 bhp. Performance was aided by the 240Z's light weight; the car was small and thus handled very well on independent front and rear suspension. Notably, the 240Z represented an amalgam of contemporary automotive technologies rolled into one vehicle and was built to the high standards that the Japanese were becoming known for.

The US market posed a significant conundrum—big-power V-8s dominated the performance scene in pony cars such as the Mustang and Camaro or muscle cars such as the Charger and GTO. The 240Z's secret lay in its nimble size, classic proportions, and focused two-seat layout. This market had been substantially owned by the Europeans—UK makers in particular—after World War II, but poor build quality and lack of investment in new technologies had meant that they easily fell to the Z's charm and performance. As a comparison, a Porsche 911 of the era also had engine of 2.4L and was little faster.

In 1974, the 240Z received an increase in engine capacity to 2.6L, and in 1978 (in the United States only), it increased to 2.9L as a result of pollution regulations. At the same time, the car also received a slightly longer 2+2 version, losing some of the design balance. The build model is a special 2.0L twin-cam engine JDM Fairlady Z432R rally special, which was sold in orange paint with a black engine cover.

| | |
|---|---|
| **COUNTRY OF ORIGIN:** | Japan |
| **PRODUCTION:** | 1970–1973 |
| **NUMBER MADE:** | 168,584 |
| **LAYOUT / DRIVE:** | Front engine / Rear-wheel drive |
| **ENGINE:** | 2,393 cc, 6 cylinders, inline |
| **POWER / TORQUE:** | 151 bhp (113 kW) / 146 lb-ft (198 Nm) |
| **CONSTRUCTION / DOORS:** | Steel monocoque / 2-door coupe |

This model can also be built in the folowing colors: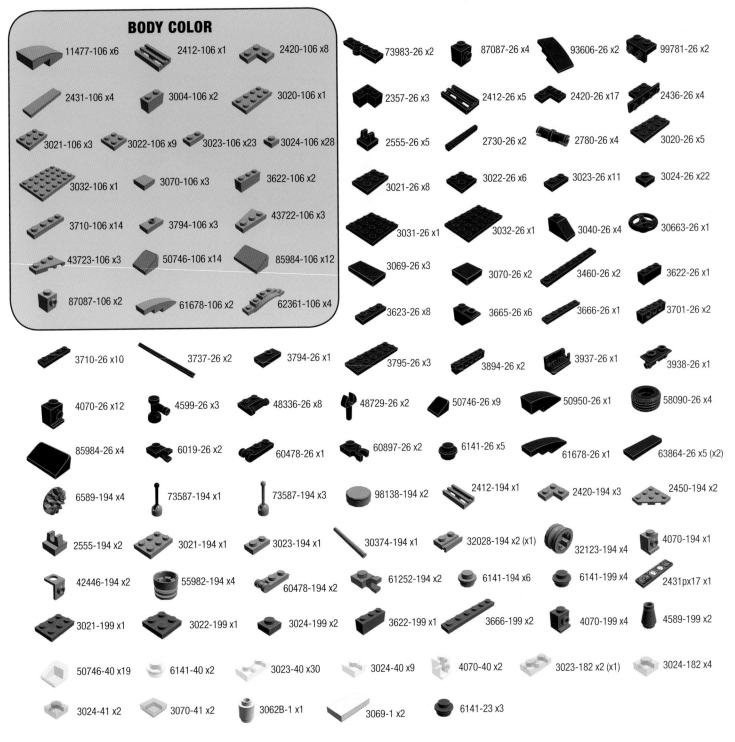

**Number of parts: 499**

## BODY COLOR

| | | |
|---|---|---|
| 11477-106 x6 | 2412-106 x1 | 2420-106 x8 |
| 2431-106 x4 | 3004-106 x2 | 3020-106 x1 |
| 3021-106 x3 | 3022-106 x9 | 3023-106 x23 · 3024-106 x28 |
| 3032-106 x1 | 3070-106 x3 | 3622-106 x2 |
| 3710-106 x14 | 3794-106 x3 | 43722-106 x3 |
| 43723-106 x3 | 50746-106 x14 | 85984-106 x12 |
| 87087-106 x2 | 61678-106 x2 | 62361-106 x4 |

| | | | |
|---|---|---|---|
| 73983-26 x2 | 87087-26 x4 | 93606-26 x2 | 99781-26 x2 |
| 2357-26 x3 | 2412-26 x5 | 2420-26 x17 | 2436-26 x4 |
| 2555-26 x5 | 2730-26 x2 | 2780-26 x4 | 3020-26 x5 |
| 3021-26 x8 | 3022-26 x6 | 3023-26 x11 | 3024-26 x22 |
| 3031-26 x1 | 3032-26 x1 | 3040-26 x4 | 30663-26 x1 |
| 3069-26 x3 | 3070-26 x2 | 3460-26 x2 | 3622-26 x1 |
| 3623-26 x8 | 3665-26 x6 | 3666-26 x1 | 3701-26 x2 |
| 3710-26 x10 | 3737-26 x2 | 3794-26 x1 | 3795-26 x3 · 3894-26 x2 · 3937-26 x1 · 3938-26 x1 |
| 4070-26 x12 | 4599-26 x3 | 48336-26 x8 | 48729-26 x2 · 50746-26 x9 · 50950-26 x1 · 58090-26 x4 |
| 85984-26 x4 | 6019-26 x2 | 60478-26 x1 | 60897-26 x2 · 6141-26 x5 · 61678-26 x1 · 63864-26 x5 (x2) |
| 6589-194 x4 | 73587-194 x1 | 73587-194 x3 | 98138-194 x2 · 2412-194 x1 · 2420-194 x3 · 2450-194 x2 |
| 2555-194 x2 | 3021-194 x1 | 3023-194 x1 | 30374-194 x1 · 32028-194 x2 (x1) · 32123-194 x4 · 4070-194 x1 |
| 42446-194 x2 | 55982-194 x4 | 60478-194 x2 | 61252-194 x2 · 6141-194 x6 · 6141-199 x4 · 2431px17 x1 |
| 3021-199 x1 | 3022-199 x1 | 3024-199 x2 | 3622-199 x1 · 3666-199 x2 · 4070-199 x4 · 4589-199 x2 |
| 50746-40 x19 | 6141-40 x2 | 3023-40 x30 | 3024-40 x9 · 4070-40 x2 · 3023-182 x2 (x1) · 3024-182 x4 |
| 3024-41 x2 | 3070-41 x2 | 3062B-1 x1 | 3069-1 x2 · 6141-23 x3 |

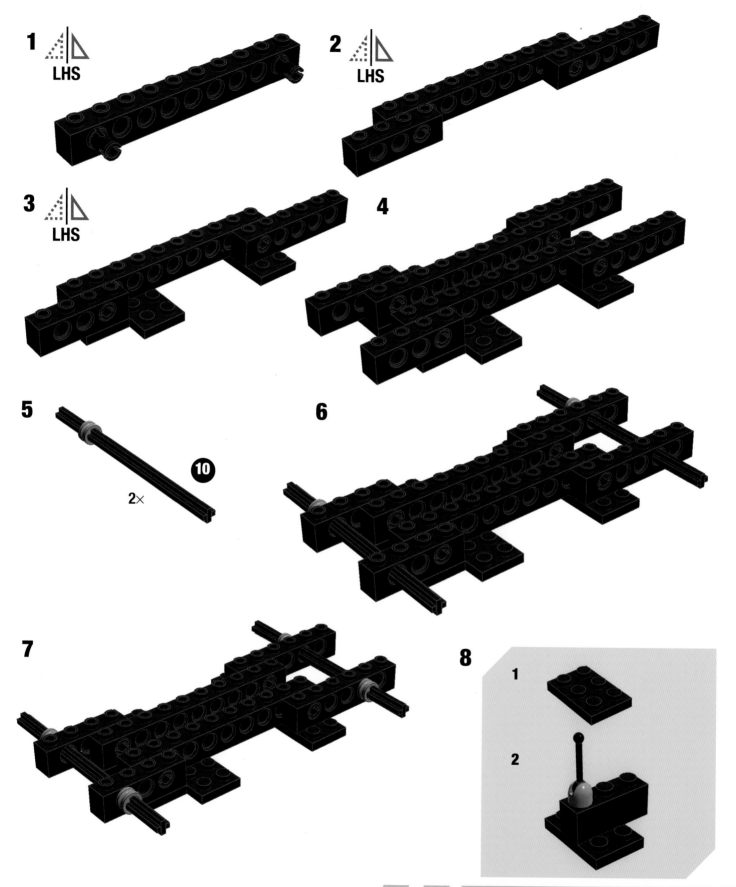

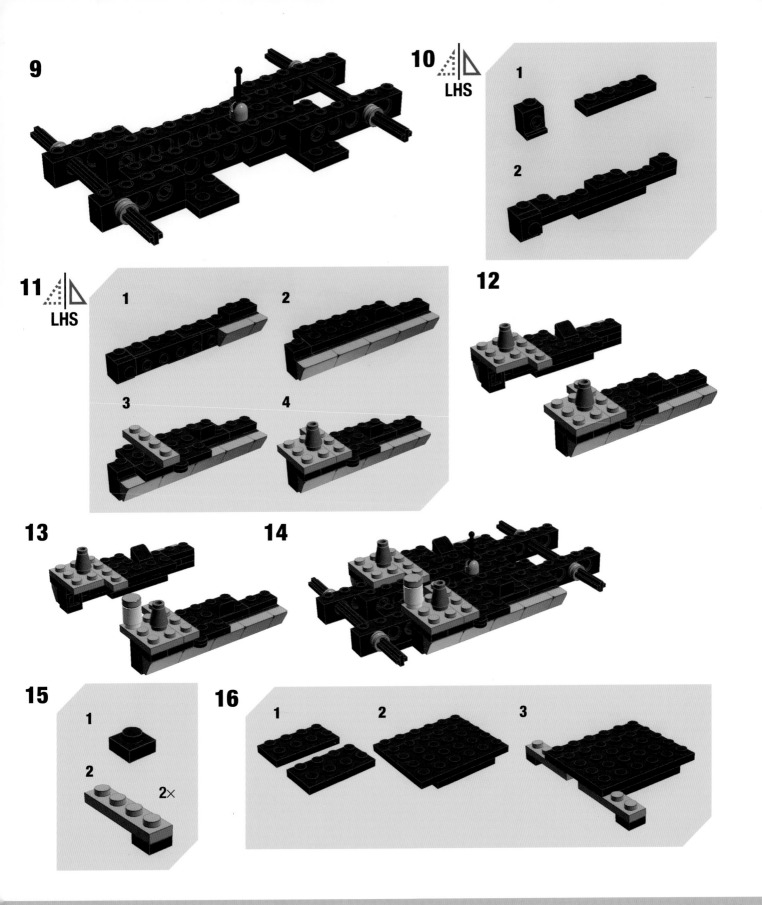

**9**

**10** LHS

1

2

**11** LHS

1    2

3    4

**12**

**13**

**14**

**15**

1

2    2×

**16**

1    2    3

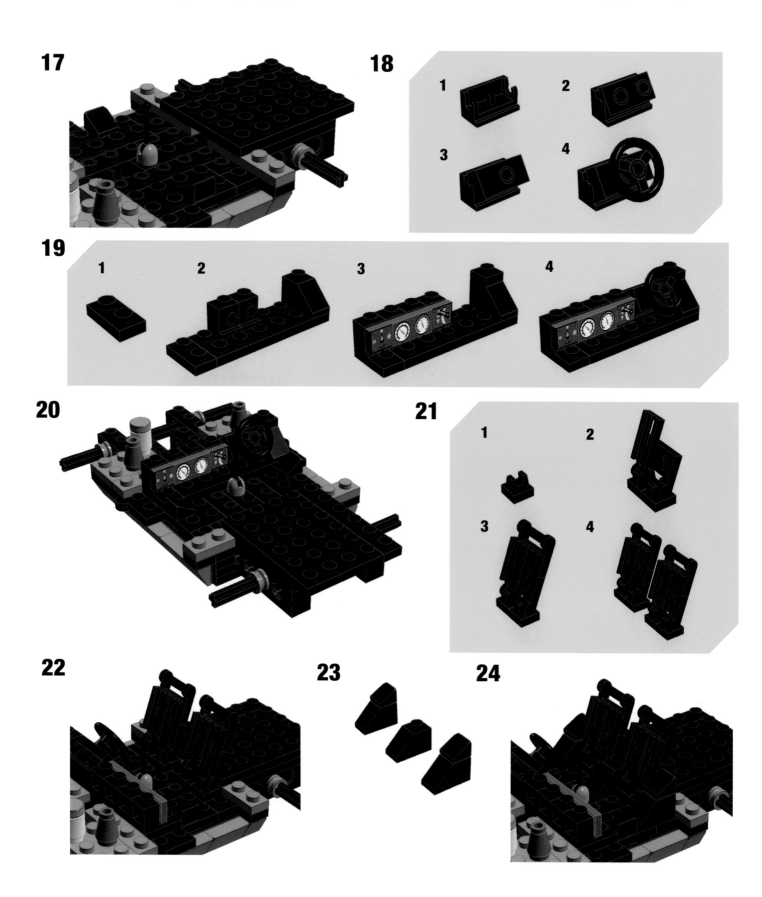

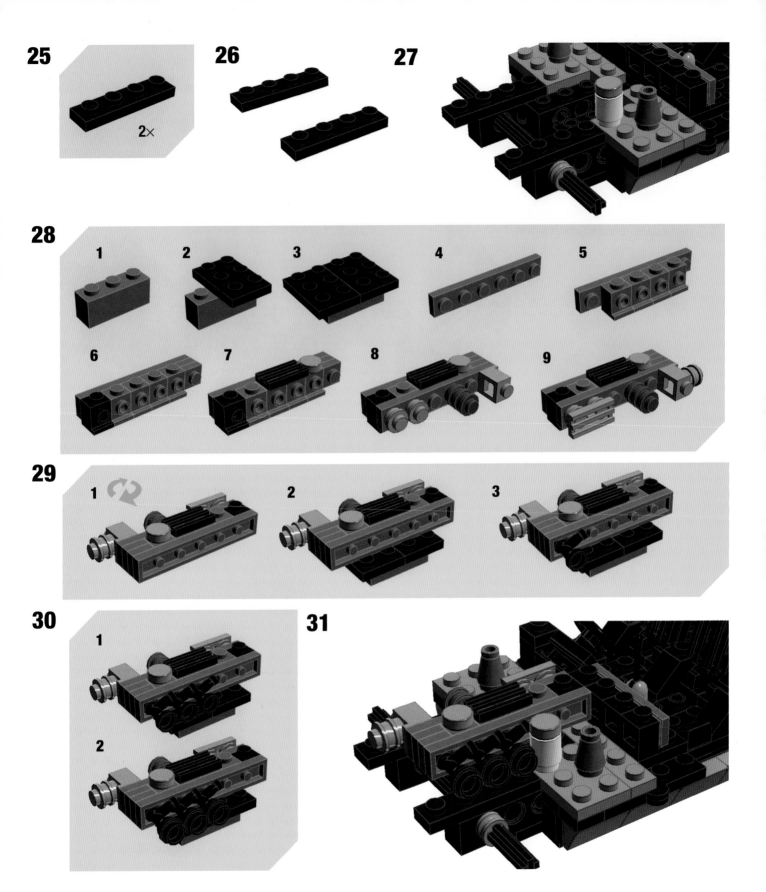

**25**

**26**

**27**

**28**

1  2  3  4  5

6  7  8  9

**29**

1  2  3

**30**

1

2

**31**

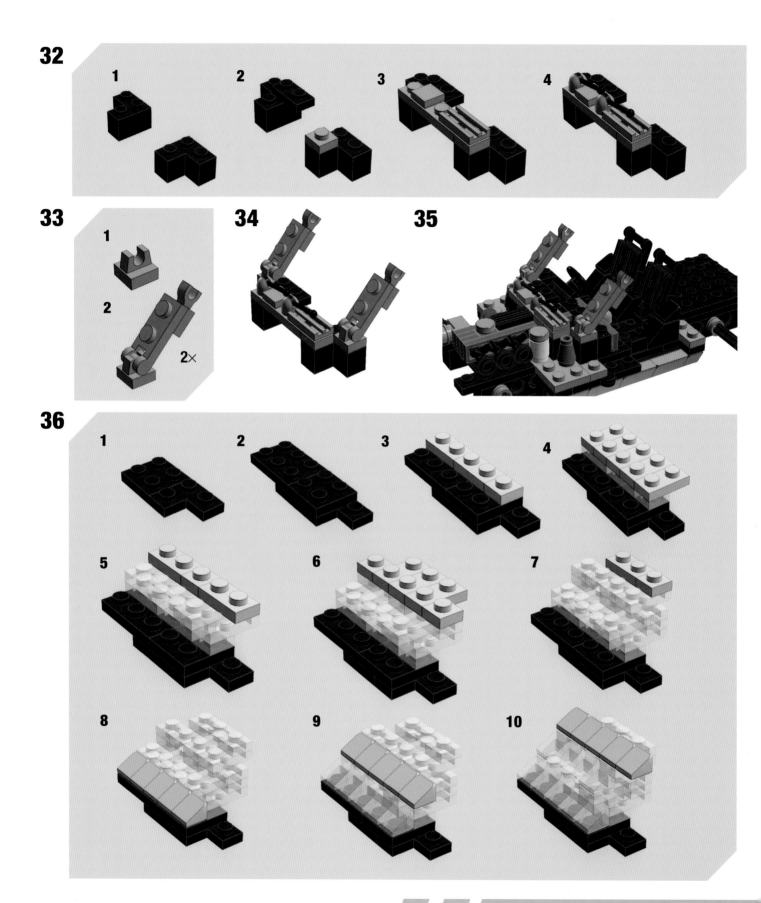

**37**

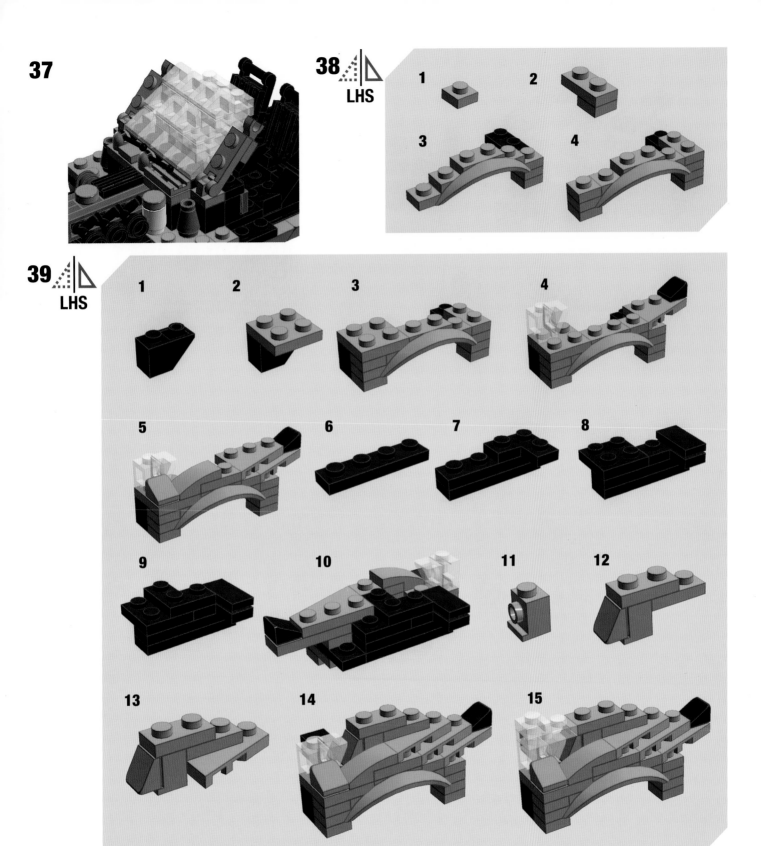

**38** LHS

1
2
3
4

**39** LHS

1
2
3
4
5
6
7
8
9
10
11
12
13
14
15

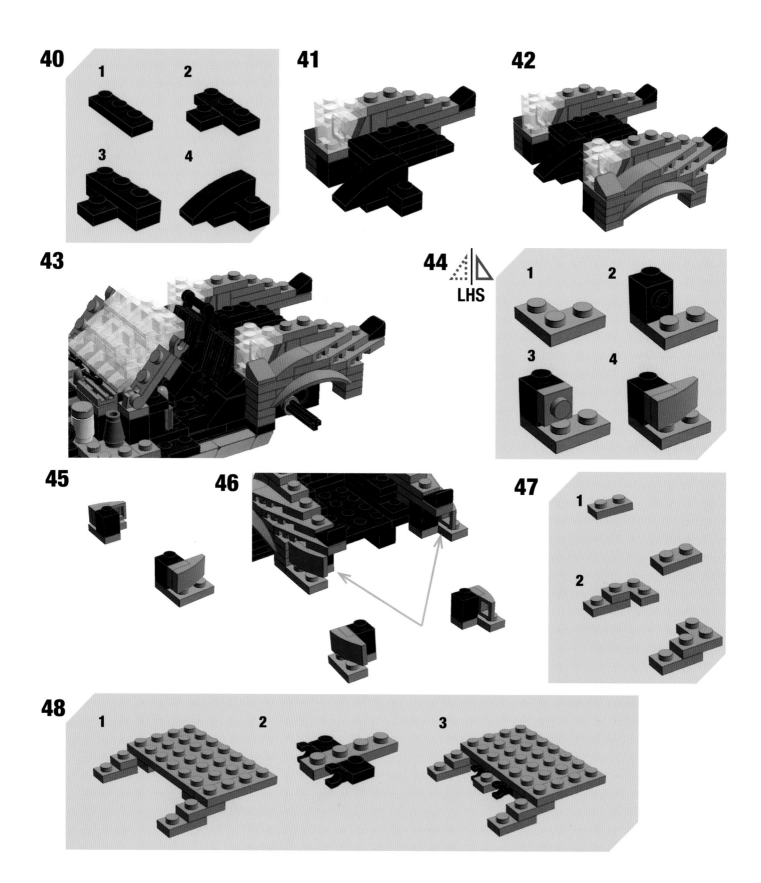

**49**

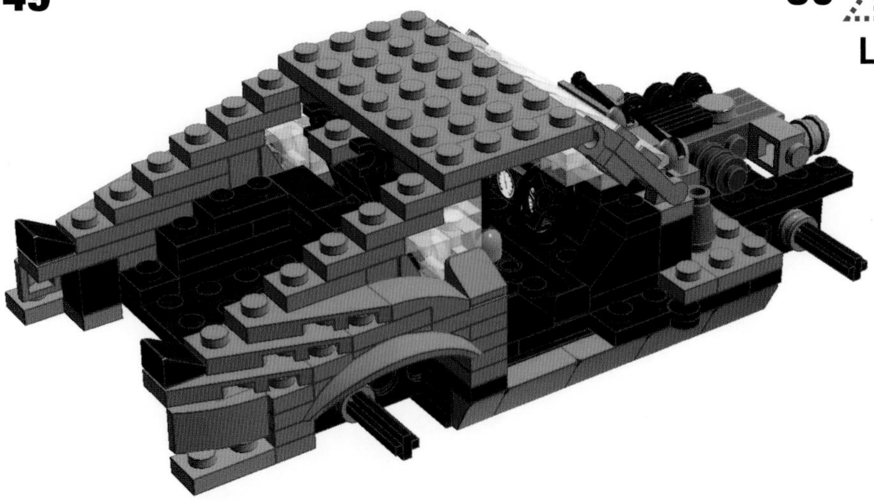

**50** LHS

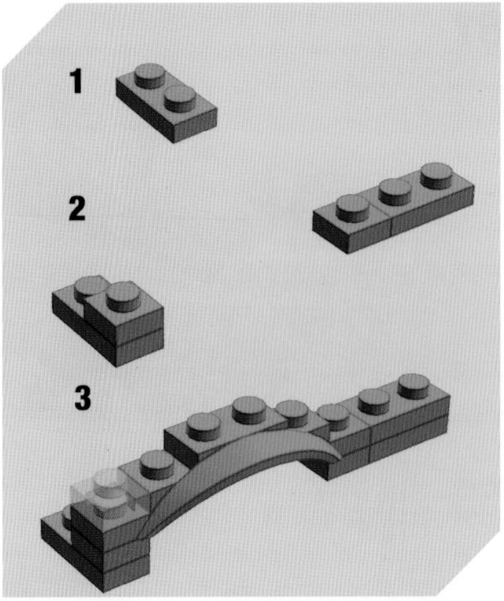

1

2

3

**51** LHS

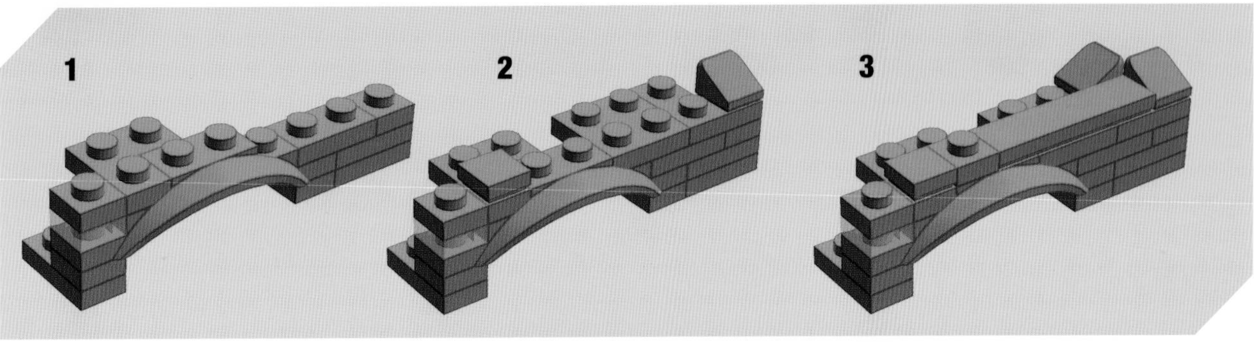

1

2

3

**52** LHS

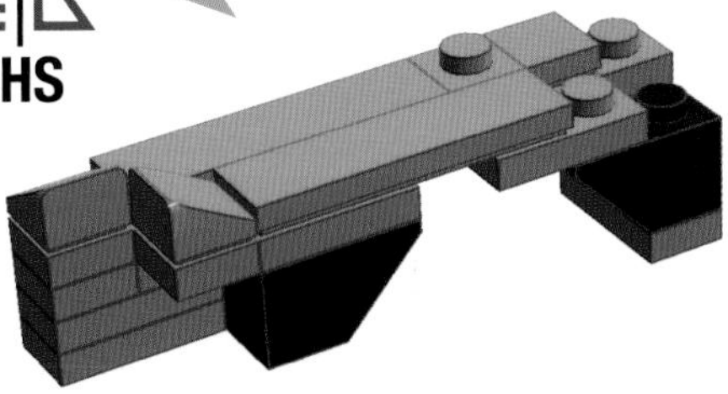

**53** LHS

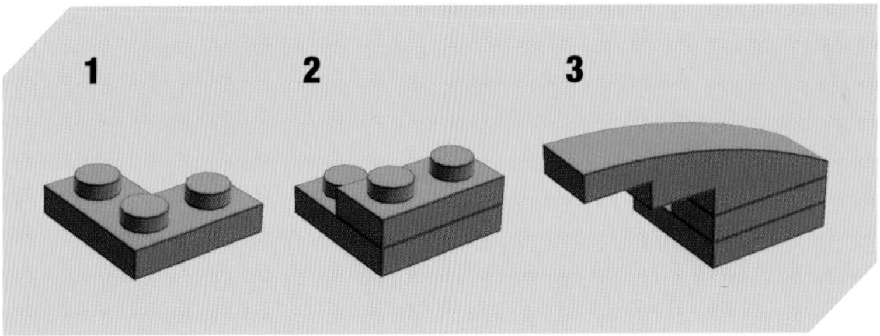

1

2

3

**54** LHS

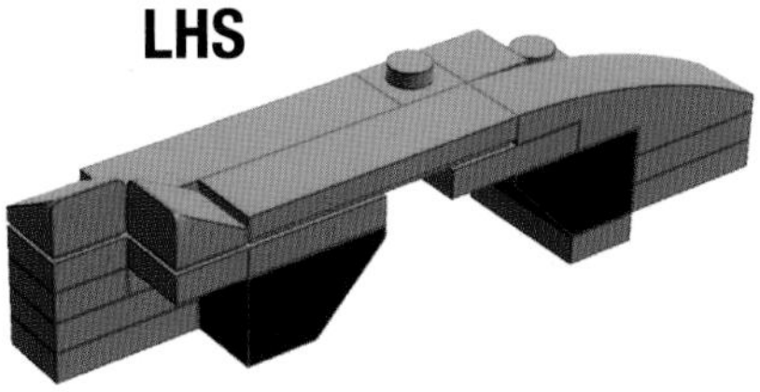

**55** LHS

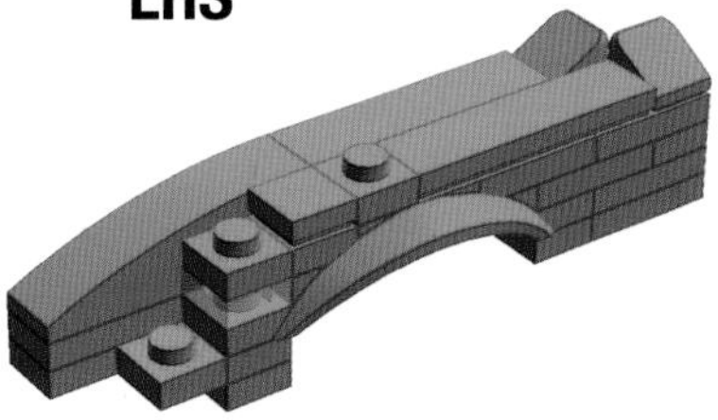

**56**

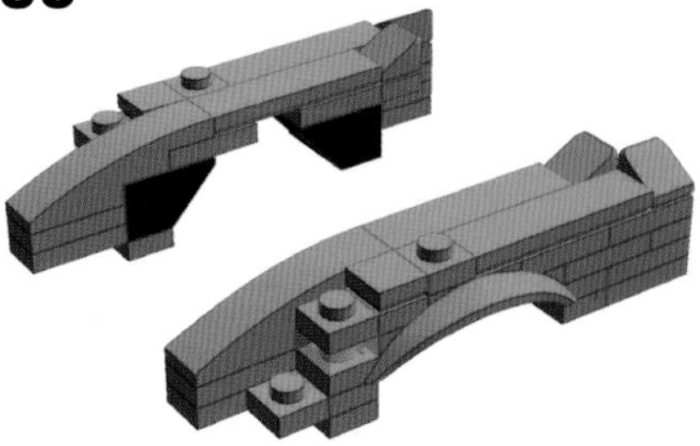

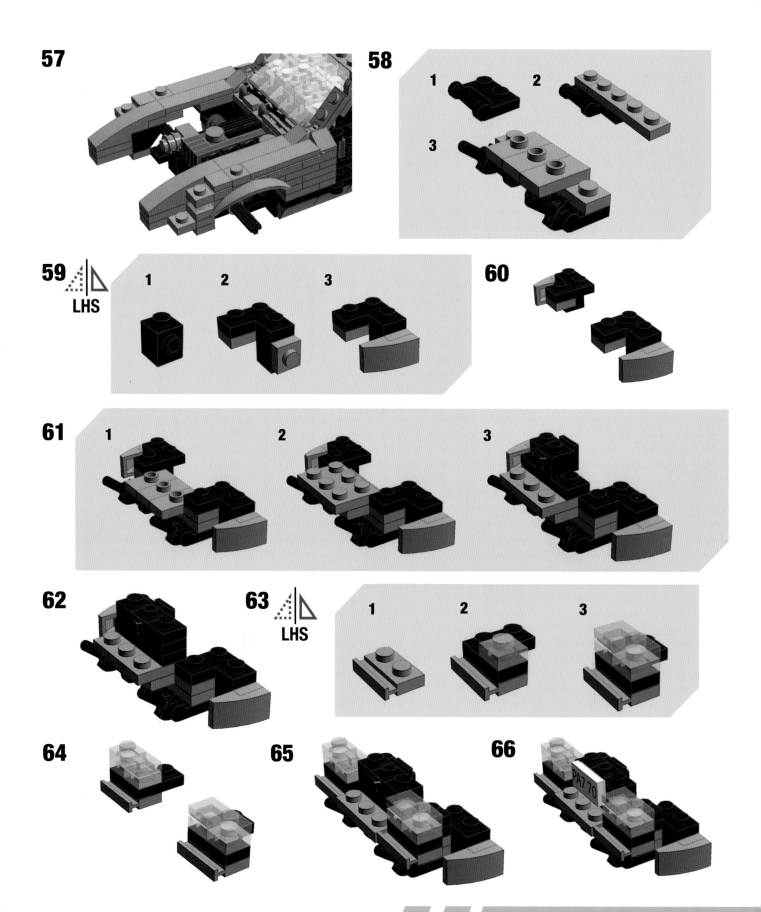

**57**

**58**
1    2
3

**59** LHS
1    2    3

**60**

**61**
1    2    3

**62**

**63** LHS
1    2    3

**64**

**65**

**66**
PA7 70

**67**

**68**

1

2

2×

**69**

**70** ↻

**71**

1

2

3

4

5

6

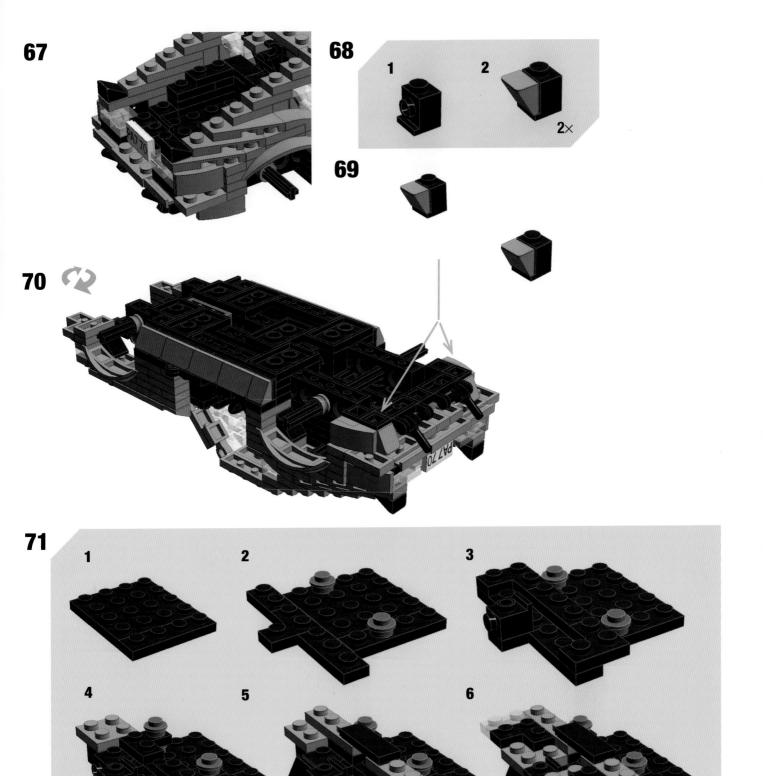

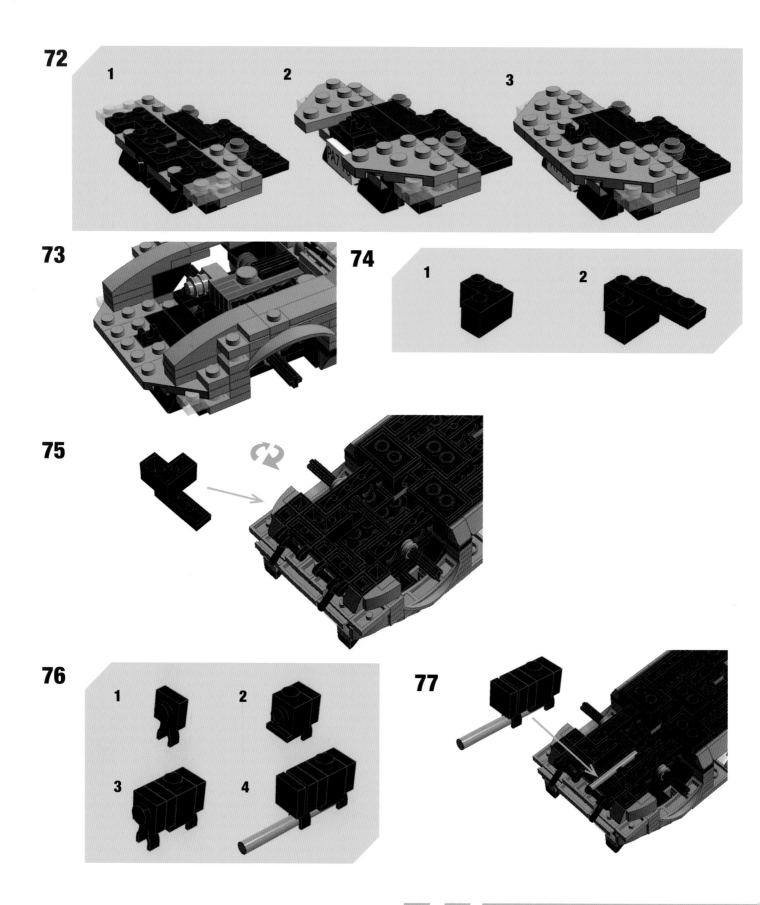

**78**

**79**

**80**
1

2

3

2×

**81**

**82**

**83** LHS

1

2

3

4

**84**

**85**

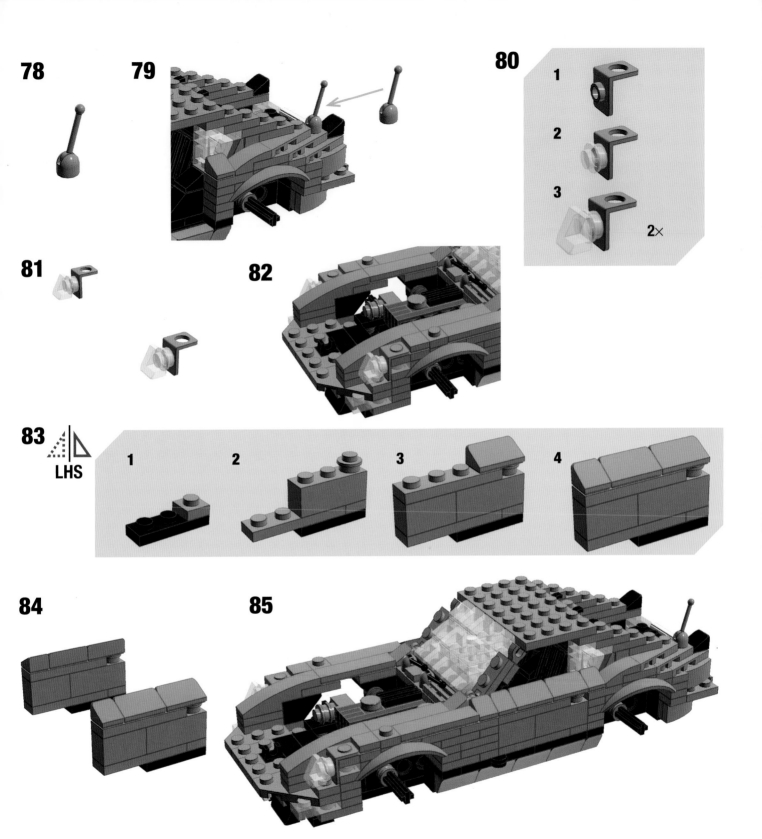

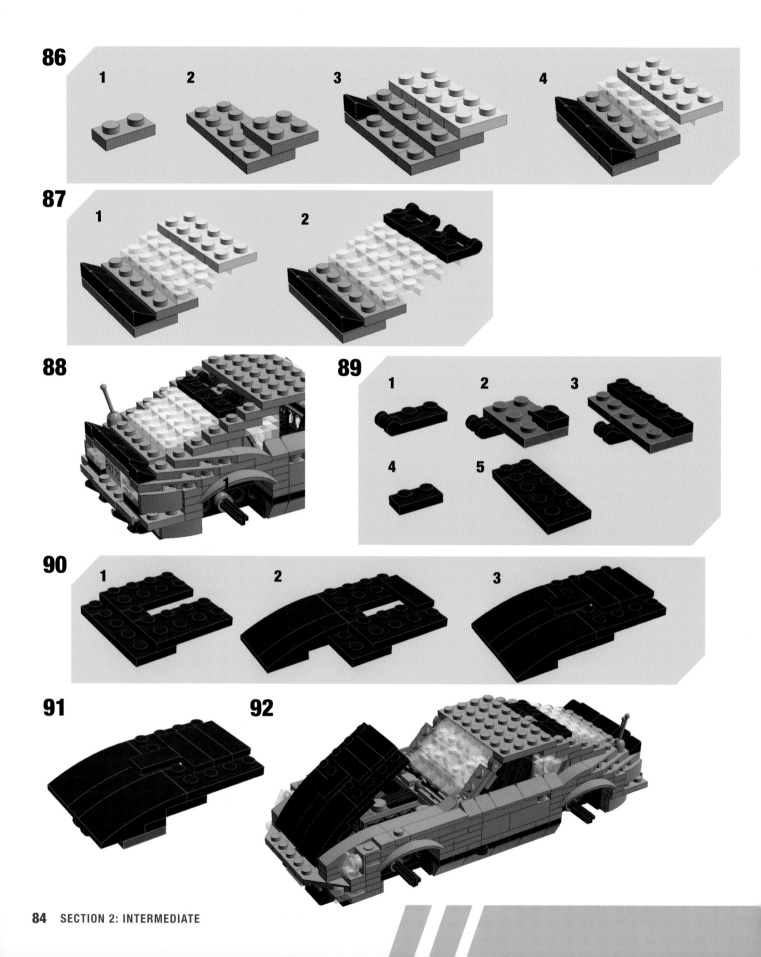

**86**

1 2 3 4

**87**

1 2

**88**

1

**89**

1 2 3

4 5

**90**

1 2 3

**91** **92**

**93**

1

2

2×

**94**

**95**

1

2

4×

**96**

**97**

4×

**98**

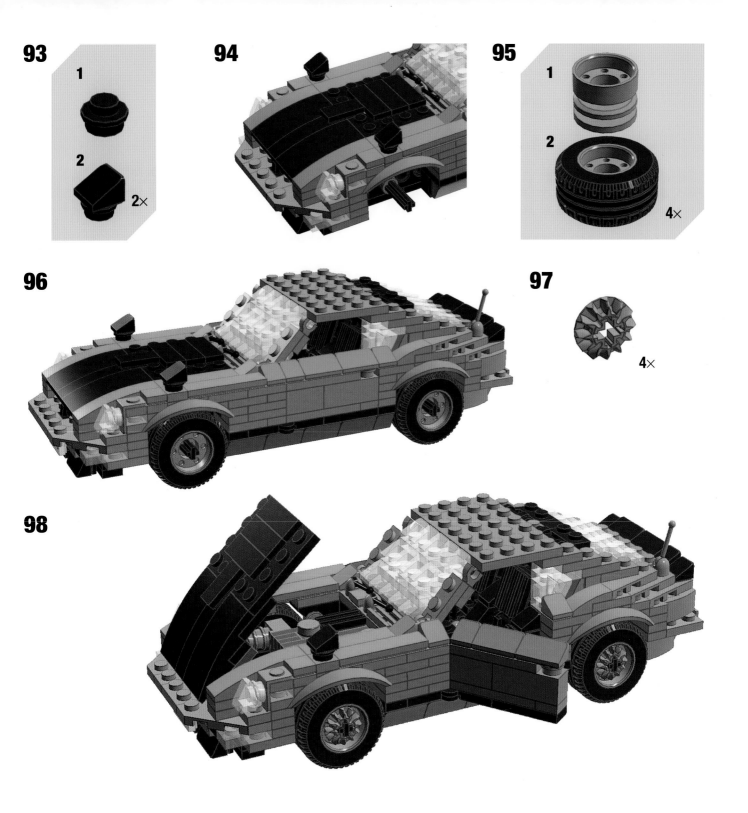

# 250 GT SWB CALIFORNIA SPYDER

There are fast Ferraris and there are beautiful Ferraris. When the two are combined, a legend is usually born. The Ferrari 250 GT SWB California Spyder is such a car. This legend was reincarnated in popular culture in the 1986 film *Ferris Bueller's Day Off*—a replica based on an MG that suffered an unfortunate fate!

The Ferrari 250 line had enjoyed half a decade of development by the time of the 250 SWB Spyder. The car featured an uprated 3.0L V-12 engine with 276 bhp (206 kW), nearly as much power as the Le Mans racing and FIA GT championship–winning 250 GTO. The 250 line actually refers to the swept-volume cubic capacity of each of the V-12's cylinders. The SWB chassis was based on the 250 GT SWB road racer, one of the last of the breed of racing cars that were also produced as road cars.

The beauty came in the form of the open-top Spyder bodywork. This was fitted to the 2,400mm wheelbase frame, a 200mm reduction on the earlier road car. The car was built in both steel- and aluminum-bodied versions, and the latter were also used as race cars. The car's styling typifies the period—a long hood housing the engine, Borrani wire wheels, egg-crate grille, fender grilles to help keep the engine bay cool, and a thin-chrome-rimmed, swept-back windscreen. Most cars were fitted with blade-like chrome bumpers, often removed for track work.

For all these reasons and more, the car was popular with celebrities—actors, singers, racers, and others. The pedigree of both car and owners ensures that today, as cars become available for sale, many change hands in excess of $10 million, making the 250 GT SWB Spyder one of the most valuable and coveted of all classic cars.

| | |
|---|---|
| **COUNTRY OF ORIGIN:** | Italy |
| **PRODUCTION:** | 1960–63 |
| **NUMBER MADE:** | 55 |
| **LAYOUT / DRIVE:** | Front engine / Rear-wheel drive |
| **ENGINE:** | 2,953 cc, 12 cylinders, V |
| **POWER / TORQUE:** | 276 bhp (206 kW) / 206 lb-ft (280 Nm) |
| **CONSTRUCTION / DOORS:** | Tubular steel / 2-door Spyder |

## BODY COLOR

11153-21 x2  11477-21 x2  2420-21 x10

2431-21 x2  3009-21 x2  3020-21 x2

3021-21 x4  3023-21 x13  3024-21 x22

3068-21 x4  3069-21 x12  3070-21 x4

3623-21 x4  3666-21 x2  3710-21 x7

3794-21 x14  3795-21 x1  4070-21 x4

43722-21 x4  43723-21 x4  4477-21 x2

48336-21 x4  50746-21 x8  60470-21 x4

6091-21 x10  6141-21 x3  6191-21 x2

6231-21 x2  62361-21 x4  63864-21 x4

6636-21 x2  73983-21 x2  87079-21 x1

93606-21 x3  98138-21 x1  99780-21 x1

12825-194 x2  2450-194 x2  2555-194 x1  30162-194 x3

3020-194 x1  3024-194 x1  30374-194 x2  30377-194 x1

3069-194 x2  3070-194 x1  32028-194 x2  32123-194 x11

3623-194 x2  3666-194 x1  43722-194 x1  43723-194 x1

4510-194 x2  55982-194 x4  60478-194 x2  6589-194 x6

6590-194 x2  6632-194 x1  73587-194 x3  87079-194 x1

85984-26 x5  99780-26 x2  2420-26 x4  2431-26 x3

2540-26 x1  2555-26 x2  2780-26 x3  3957-26 x1

3020-26 x4  3021-26 x2  3022-26 x4  3023-26 x18

3024-26 x3  3032-26 x1  3034-26 x2  3035-26 x1

30374-26 x2  3040-26 x1  30663-26 x1  3069-26 x3

3070-26 x3  32062-26 x2  32073-26 x1  3460-26 x3

3700-26 x3  3701-26 x2  3702-26 x2  3705-26 x1

3623-26 x12  3665-26 x2  3666-26 x7

3706-26 x2  3707-26 x2  3710-26 x5  3794-26 x2  3795-26 x3  3894-26 x2  3937-26 x6

3938-26 x6  4070-26 x14  4081-26 x2  4519-26 x2  48729-26 x1  50746-26 x5  58090-26 x4

59443-26 x1  6019-26 x3  6091-26 x4  6141-26 x4  63868-26 x4  6558-26 x2  6636-26 x1

2431-199 x1  2654-199 x1  3070-199 x2  32013-199 x4  32034-199 x2  3666-199 x1  3710-199 x1

4085-199 x3  61409-199 x2  63864-199 x2  6553-199 x4  6587-199 x2  6632-199 x4  30162-194 x2

6141-315 x2  6636-315 x1  3022-24 x2  3023-40 x2  4176-40 x1  50746-40 x2  6141-182 x2

6141-41 x4  6141-44 x2  3024-41 x2  3069-1 x1

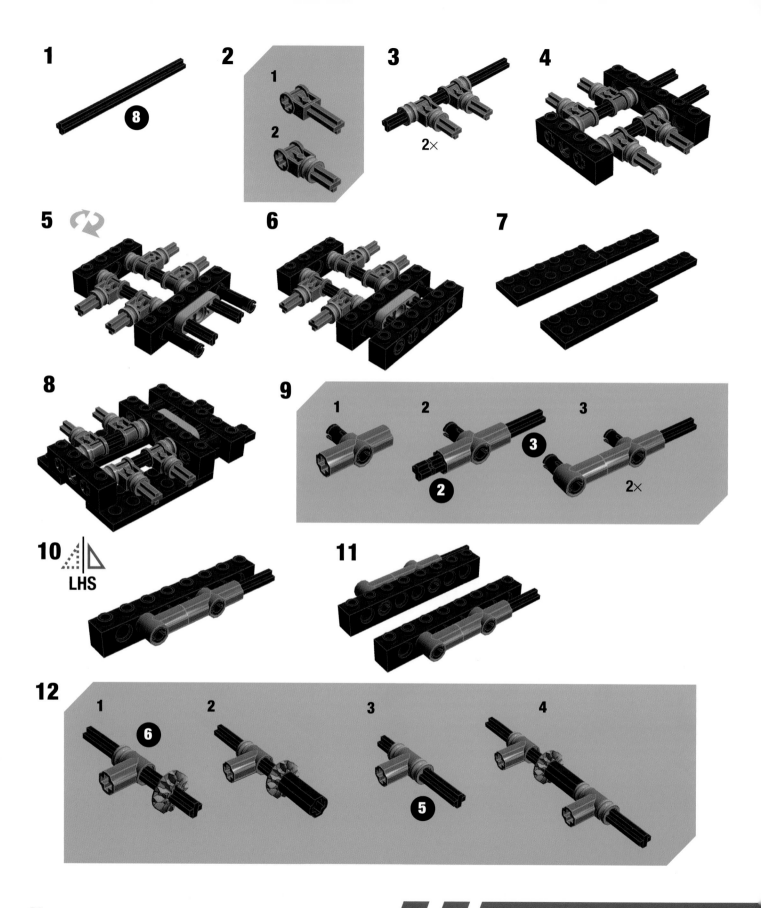

**1**

**8**

**2**

1

2

**3**

2×

**4**

**5**

**6**

**7**

**8**

**9**

1

2

3

3

2

**2×**

**10** LHS

**11**

**12**

1

**6**

2

3

**5**

4

**13**

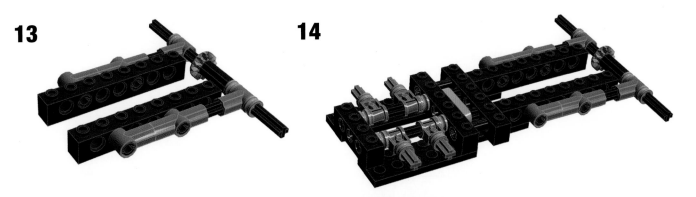

**14**

**15**

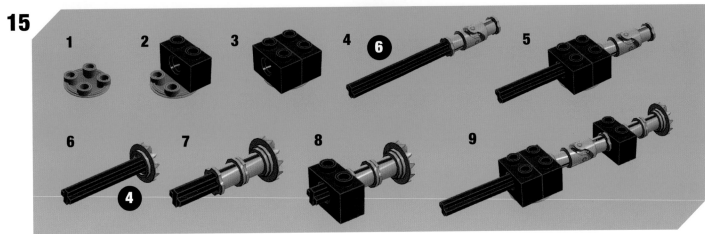

1  2  3  4  **6**  5

6  **4**  7  8  9

**16**

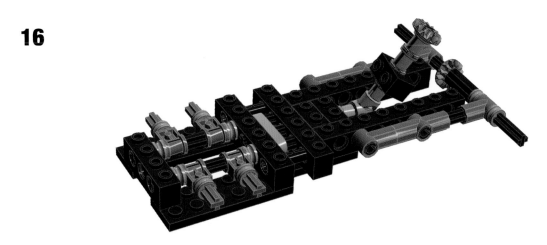

**17**

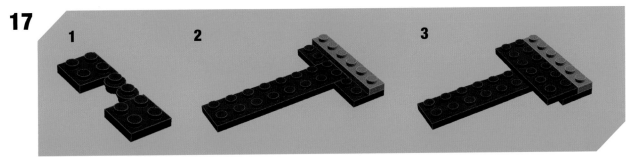

1  2  3

**18**

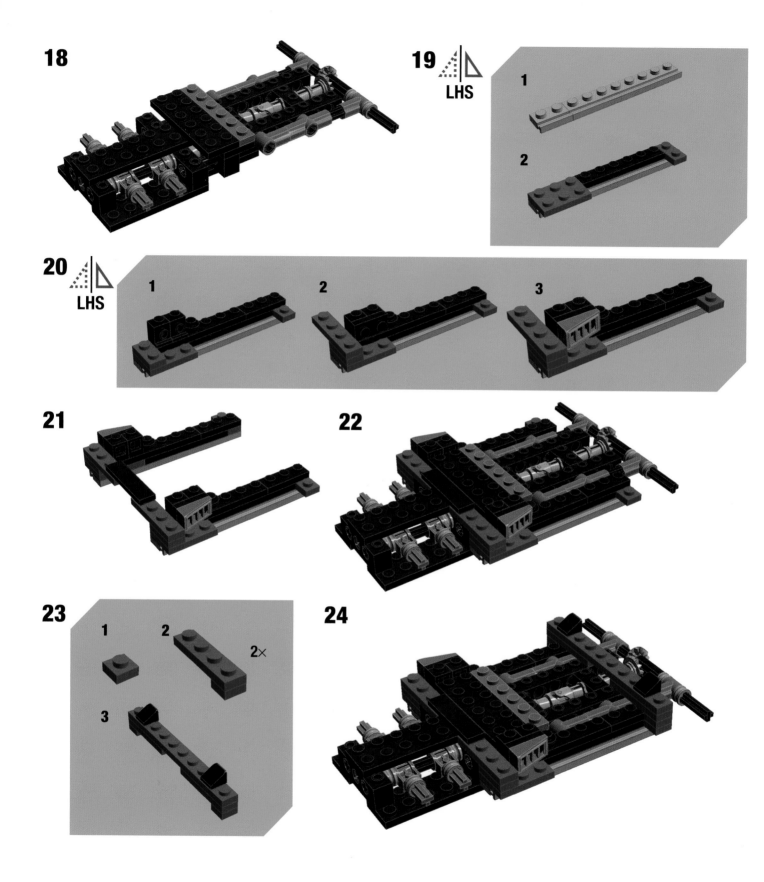

**19** LHS

1

2

**20** LHS

1

2

3

**21**

**22**

**23**

1

2

2×

3

**24**

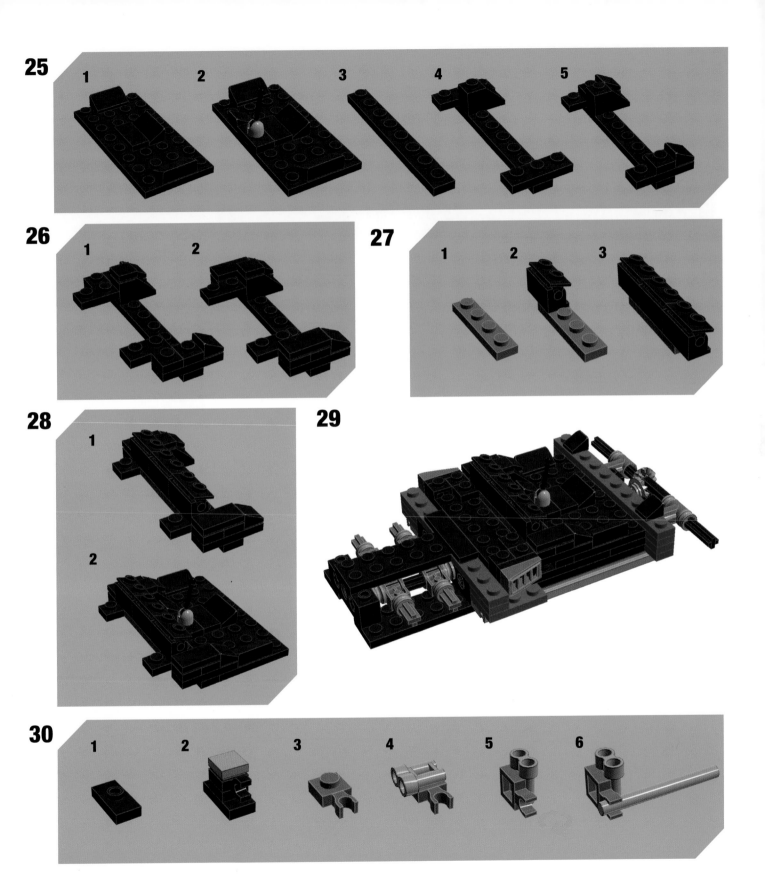

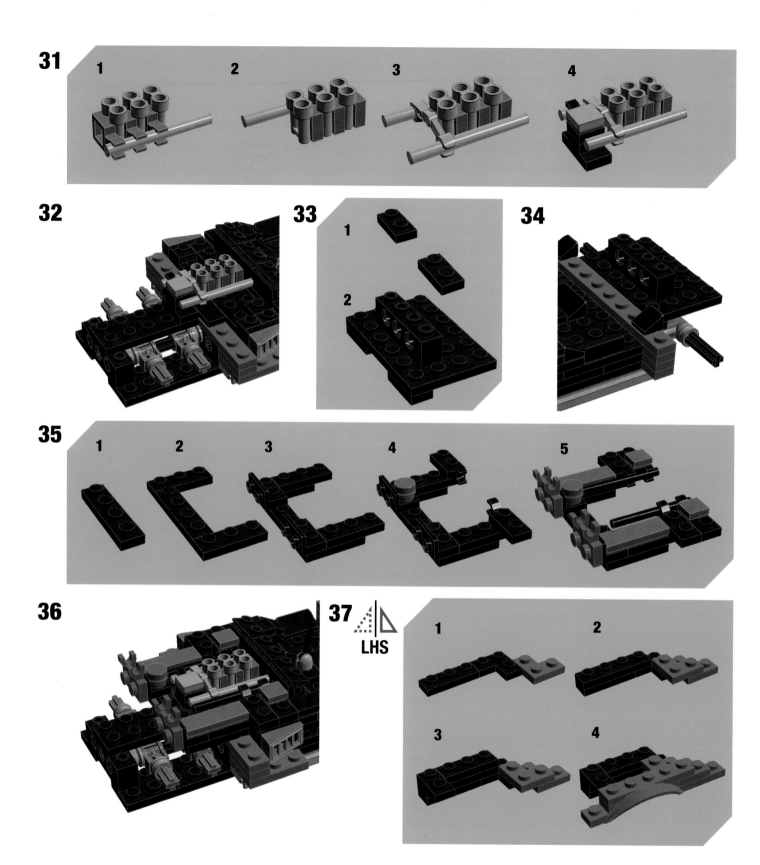

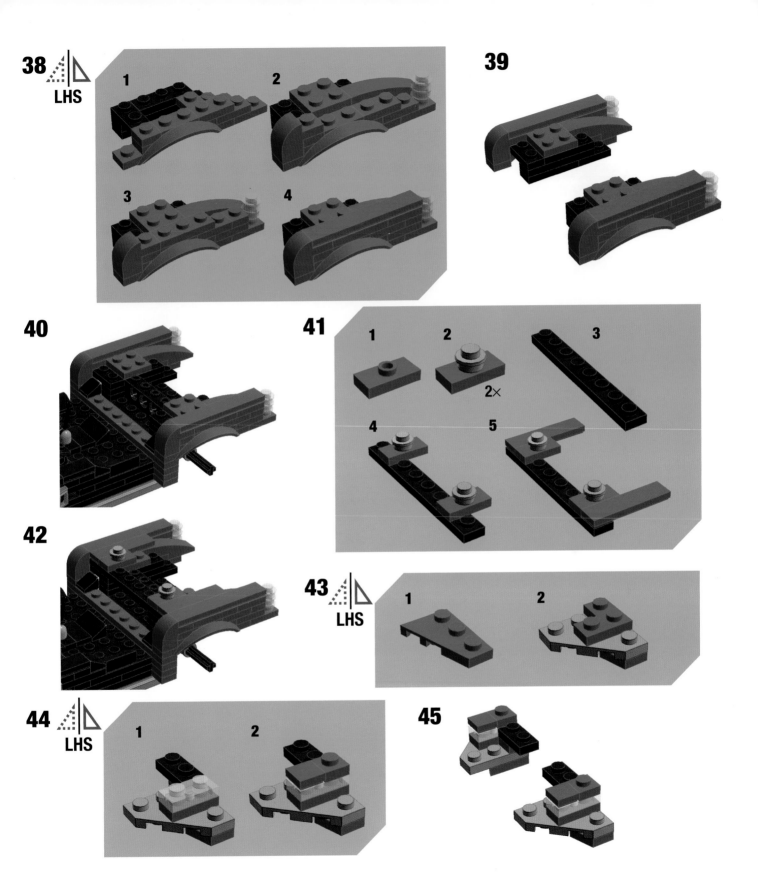

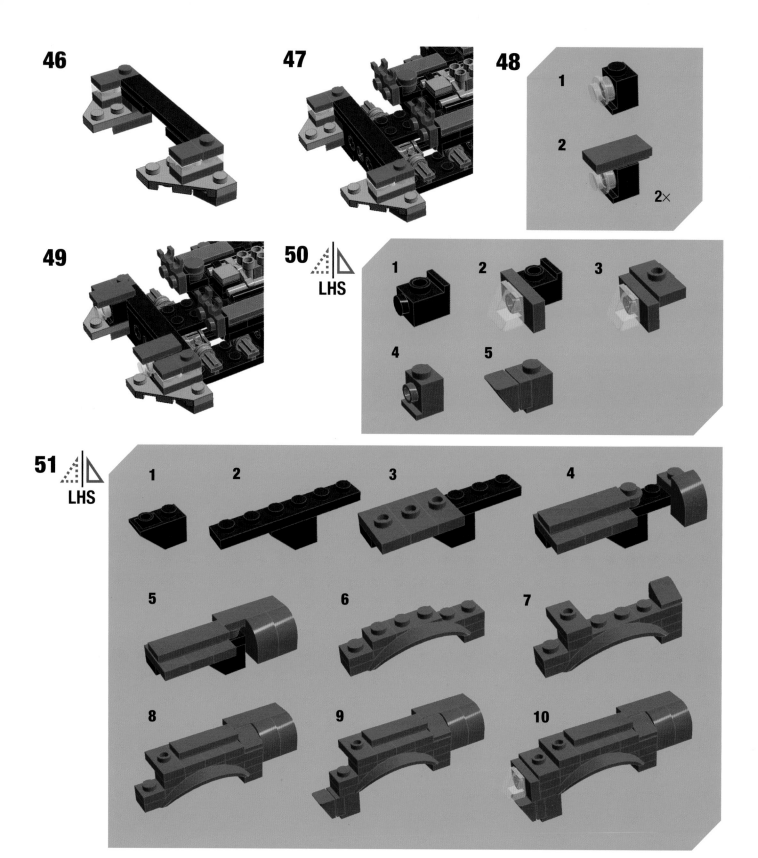

**46**

**47**

**48**
1
2
2×

**49**

**50** LHS
1 2 3
4 5

**51** LHS
1 2 3 4
5 6 7
8 9 10

**52**

LHS

**53**

**54**

**55**

1

2

3

4

**56**

**57**

1

2

3

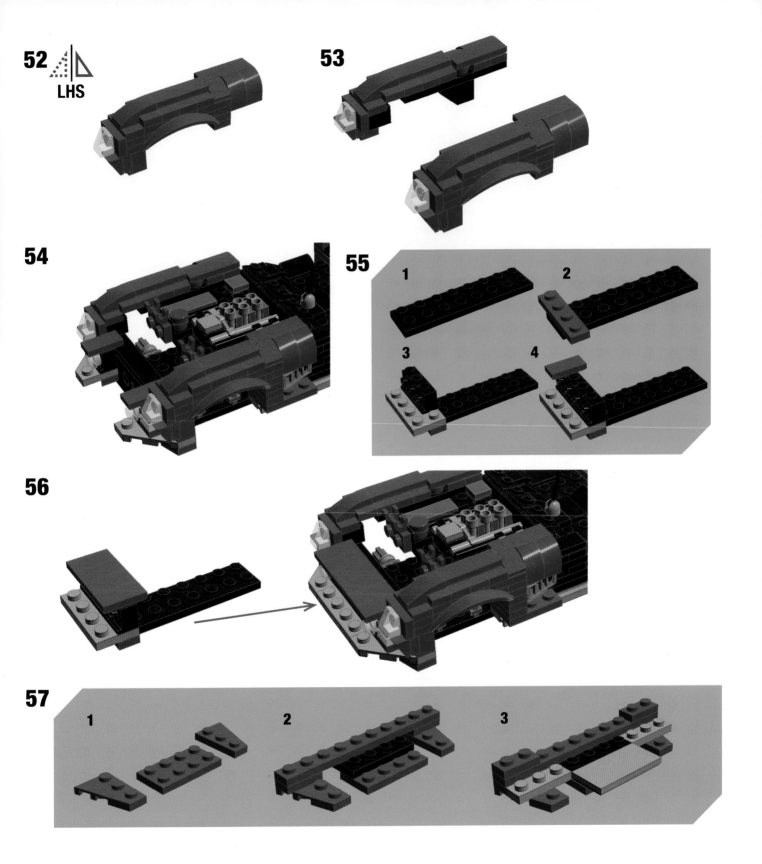

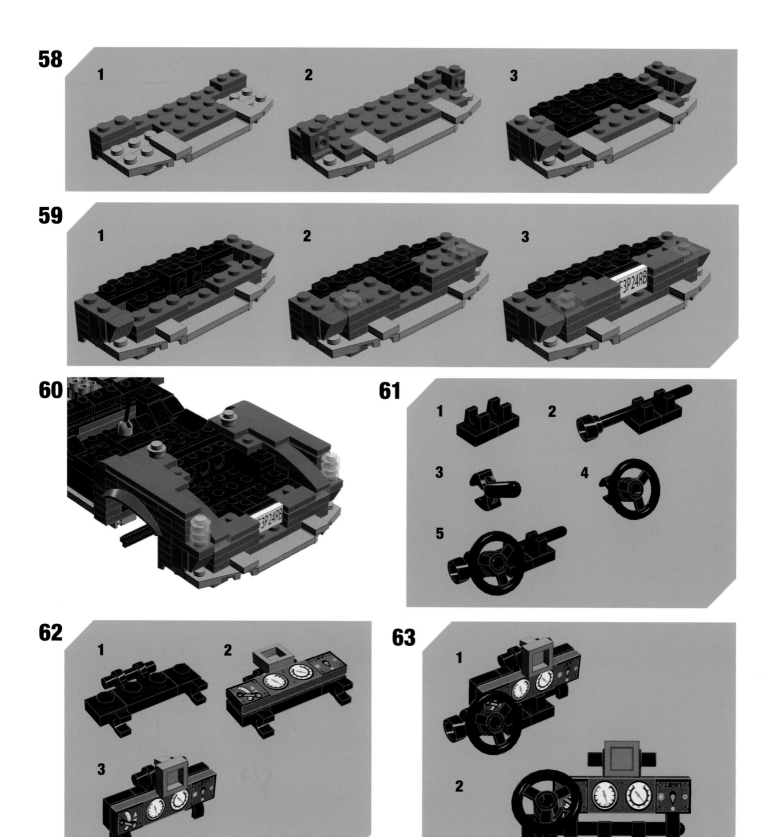

**64**

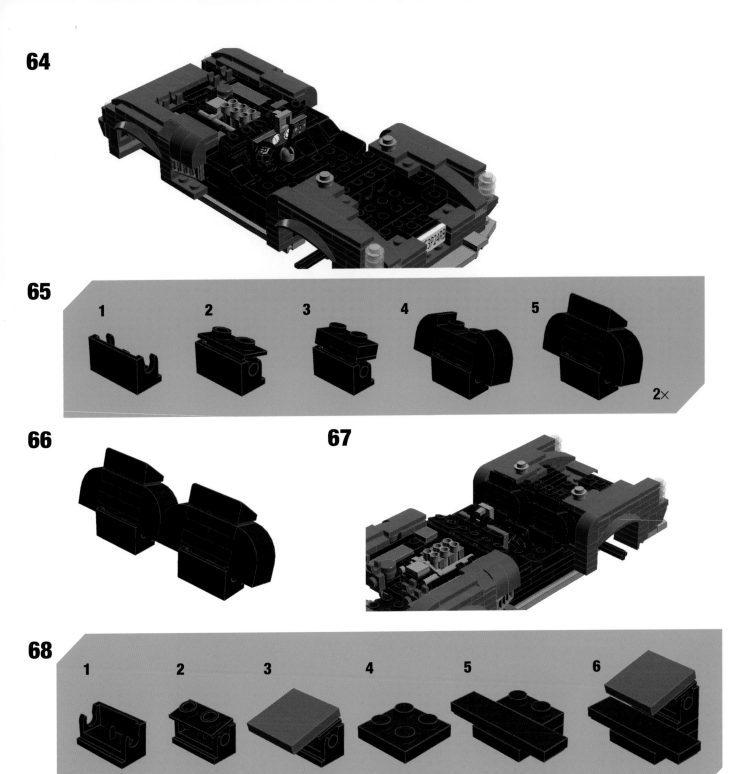

**65**

1

2

3

4

5

2×

**66**

**67**

**68**

1

2

3

4

5

6

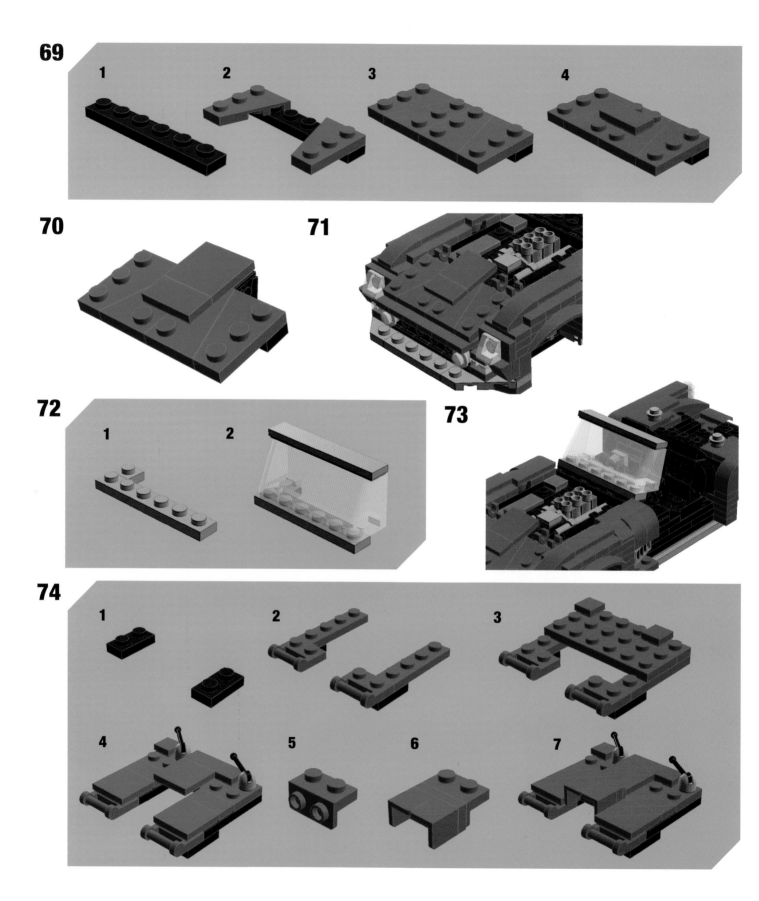

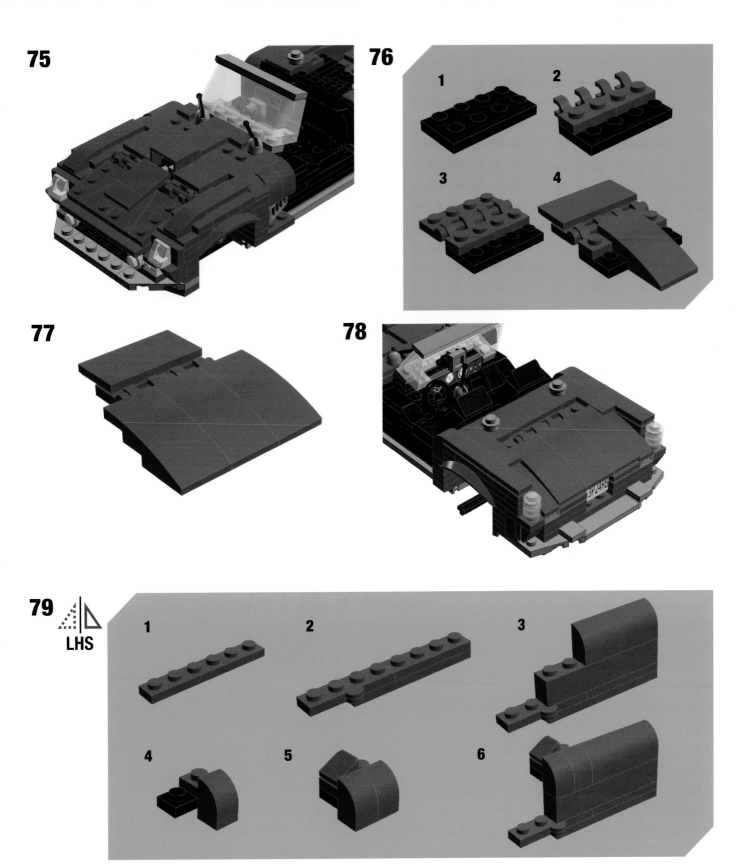

**80**

**81**

**82**

2×

**83**

**84**

1    2

2×

**85**

**86**

1

2

4×

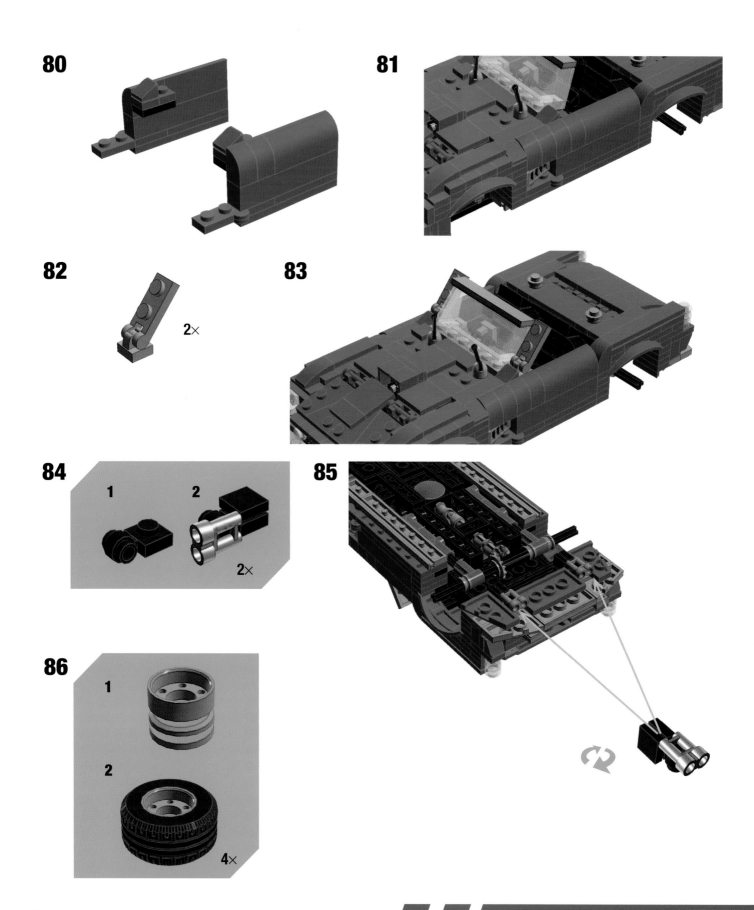

**87**

**88**
1  2  3
2×

**89**
4×

**90**

**91**

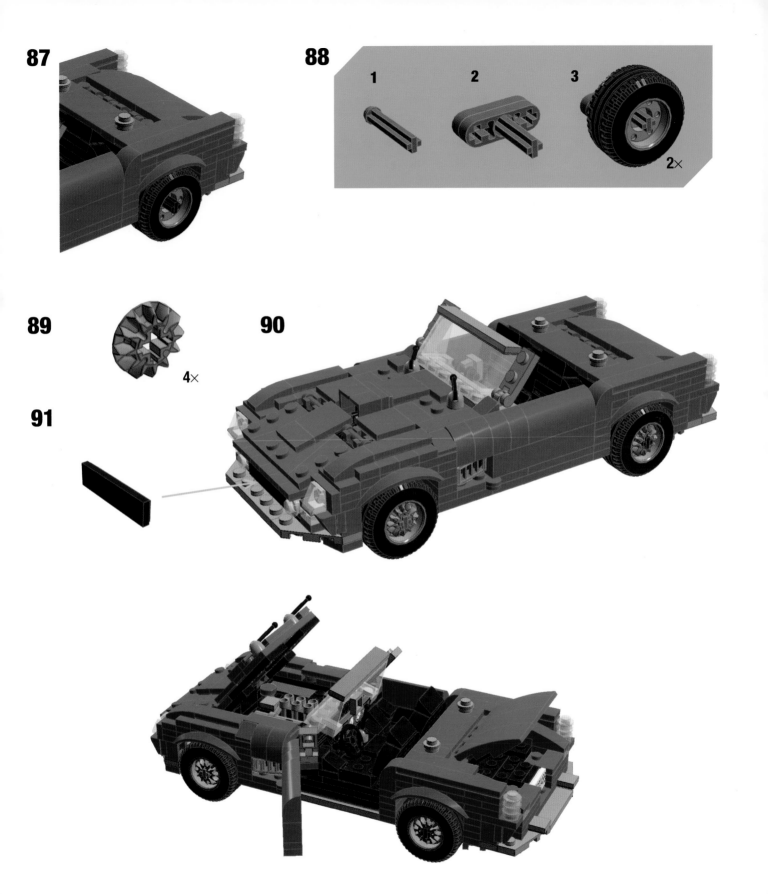

# i8 HYBRID COUPE

The future of the twenty-first-century supercar starts here. Anyone who thought that a supercar needed 8 or more cylinders and should burn gasoline at 10 mpg or worse (when cruising) is soundly rebuked by this high-performance coupe from BMW. The i8 has only 3 cylinders in its mid-mounted 1.5L engine, yet it produces a solid 231 PS (170 kW), augmented by a 131 PS (96 kW) Synchronous Electric Hybrid Drive. The characteristics of each propulsion system complement one another—the electric drive produces instantaneous low-speed torque (184 lb-ft/250 Nm), progressively transferring torque demand to the gasoline-powered internal-combustion engine as speed increases.

The performance is brisk: 0 to 62 mph (0 to 100 km/h) in 4.4 seconds and a top speed of 155 mph (250 km/h). The hybrid drive alone allows 120-km/h cruising in electric mode, aided, no doubt, by an impressive coefficient of aerodynamic drag ($C_d$) of 0.26. The acceleration is also aided by a low vehicle weight of 3,274 lb. (1,485 kg), the result of focused system selection and weight-saving measures, such as the aluminum-alloy subframes attached to the carbon-fiber-reinforced plastic (CFRP) composite body. One compromise normally imposed by a hybrid drivetrain is the large and heavy battery; the i8 uses a 7.1-kWh lithium-ion battery, permitting an all-electric (zero emissions) range of 23 miles (37 km) as calculated by the European NEDC cycle. The US EPA test reduces this by approximately 35 percent.

Supercars are nothing without a little drama. The preceding BMW Vision EfficientDynamics show car of 2009 showed off a dramatic form, including a new interpretation of butterfly doors. All these elements translated largely intact to the i8 production car, down to the contrasting color "blades" along the sill line and air-guide vanes on the tail of the car.

The BMW i8 marks the start of a new line of BMW models; a follow-up city car, the BMW i3, was launched later in the year, deploying the same technology set in a more practical everyday form.

| | |
|---|---|
| **COUNTRY OF ORIGIN:** | Germany |
| **PRODUCTION:** | 2014–Present |
| **NUMBER MADE:** | Currently in production (2014: 1,741, 2015: 5,456) |
| **LAYOUT / DRIVE:** | Mid engine / All-wheel drive |
| **ENGINE:** | 1,499 cc, 3 cylinders, inline, turbocharged |
| **POWER / TORQUE (GASOLINE MOTOR):** | 231 PS (170 kW) / 236 lb-ft (320 Nm) |
| **POWER / TORQUE (HYBRID SYNCHRONOUS MOTOR):** | 131 PS (96 kW) / 184 lb-ft (250 Nm) |
| **CONSTRUCTION / DOORS:** | Aluminum-alloy spaceframe, carbon-fiber body / 2-door |

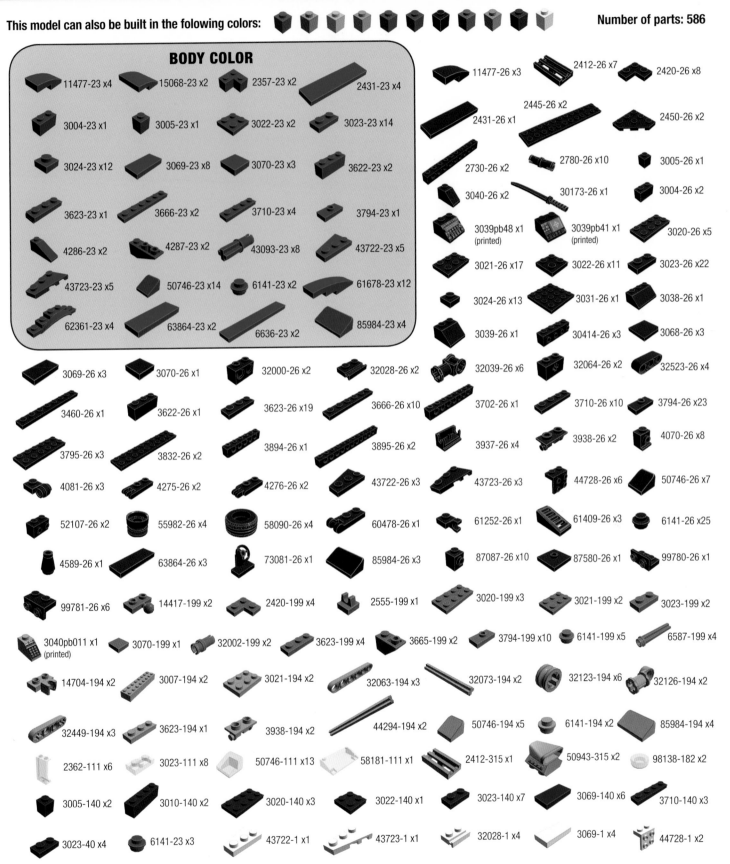

**Number of parts: 586**

### BODY COLOR

11477-23 x4    15068-23 x2    2357-23 x2    2431-23 x4

3004-23 x1    3005-23 x1    3022-23 x2    3023-23 x14

3024-23 x12    3069-23 x8    3070-23 x3    3622-23 x2

3623-23 x1    3666-23 x2    3710-23 x4    3794-23 x1

4286-23 x2    4287-23 x2    43093-23 x8    43722-23 x5

43723-23 x5    50746-23 x14    6141-23 x2    61678-23 x12

62361-23 x4    63864-23 x2    6636-23 x2    85984-23 x4

11477-26 x3    2412-26 x7    2420-26 x8

2445-26 x2

2431-26 x1    2450-26 x2

2730-26 x2    2780-26 x10    3005-26 x1

3040-26 x2    30173-26 x1    3004-26 x2

3039pb48 x1 (printed)    3039pb41 x1 (printed)    3020-26 x5

3021-26 x17    3022-26 x11    3023-26 x22

3024-26 x13    3031-26 x1    3038-26 x1

3039-26 x1    30414-26 x3    3068-26 x3

3069-26 x3    3070-26 x1    32000-26 x2    32028-26 x2    32039-26 x6    32064-26 x2    32523-26 x4

3460-26 x1    3622-26 x1    3623-26 x19    3666-26 x10    3702-26 x1    3710-26 x10    3794-26 x23

3795-26 x3    3832-26 x2    3894-26 x1    3895-26 x2    3937-26 x4    3938-26 x2    4070-26 x8

4081-26 x3    4275-26 x2    4276-26 x2    43722-26 x3    43723-26 x3    44728-26 x6    50746-26 x7

52107-26 x2    55982-26 x4    58090-26 x4    60478-26 x1    61252-26 x1    61409-26 x3    6141-26 x25

4589-26 x1    63864-26 x3    73081-26 x1    85984-26 x3    87087-26 x10    87580-26 x1    99780-26 x1

99781-26 x6    14417-199 x2    2420-199 x4    2555-199 x1    3020-199 x3    3021-199 x2    3023-199 x2

3040pb011 x1 (printed)    3070-199 x1    32002-199 x2    3623-199 x4    3665-199 x2    3794-199 x10    6141-199 x5    6587-199 x4

14704-194 x2    3007-194 x2    3021-194 x2    32063-194 x3    32073-194 x2    32123-194 x6    32126-194 x2

32449-194 x3    3623-194 x1    3938-194 x2    44294-194 x2    50746-194 x5    6141-194 x2    85984-194 x4

2362-111 x6    3023-111 x8    50746-111 x13    58181-111 x1    2412-315 x1    50943-315 x2    98138-182 x2

3005-140 x2    3010-140 x2    3020-140 x3    3022-140 x1    3023-140 x7    3069-140 x6    3710-140 x3

3023-40 x4    6141-23 x3    43722-1 x1    43723-1 x1    32028-1 x4    3069-1 x4    44728-1 x2

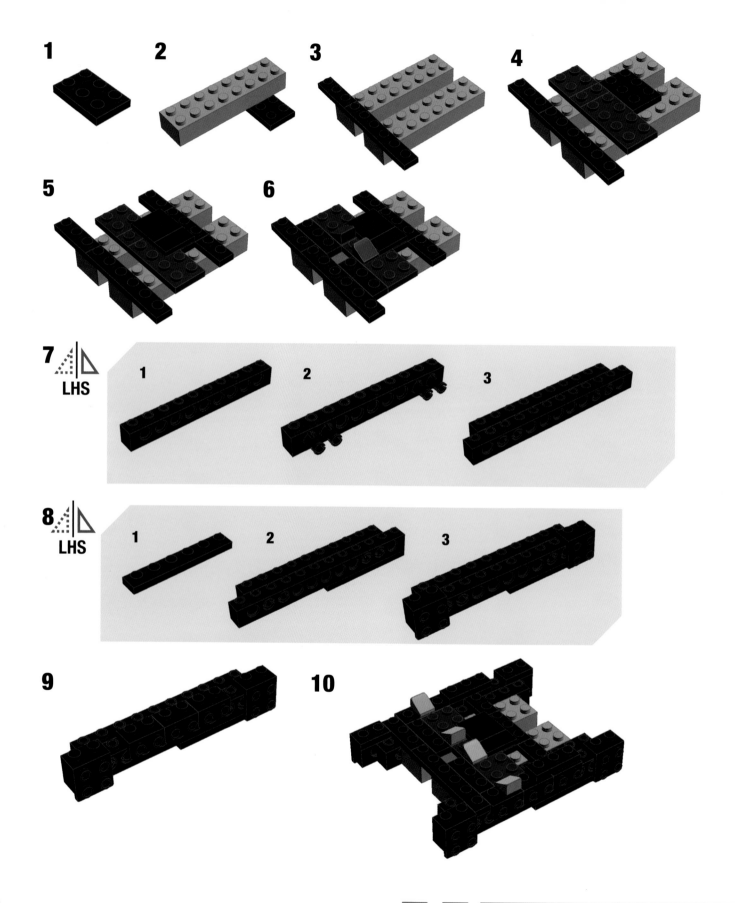

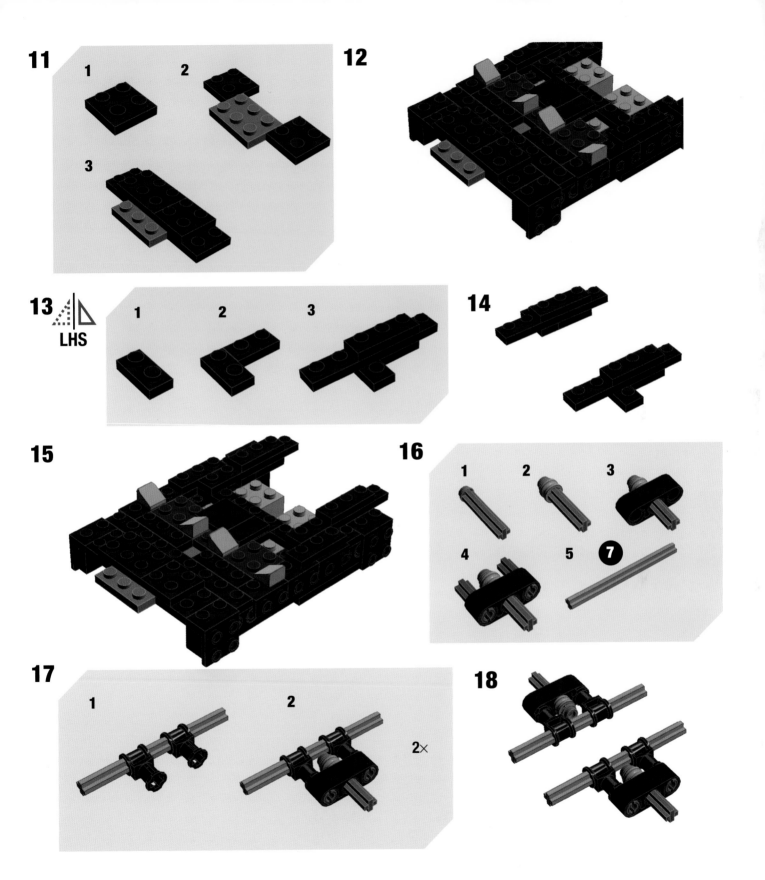

**19**

**20**

**21**

**22**

**23**

1

2

3

**24**

**25**

**26**

1

2

3

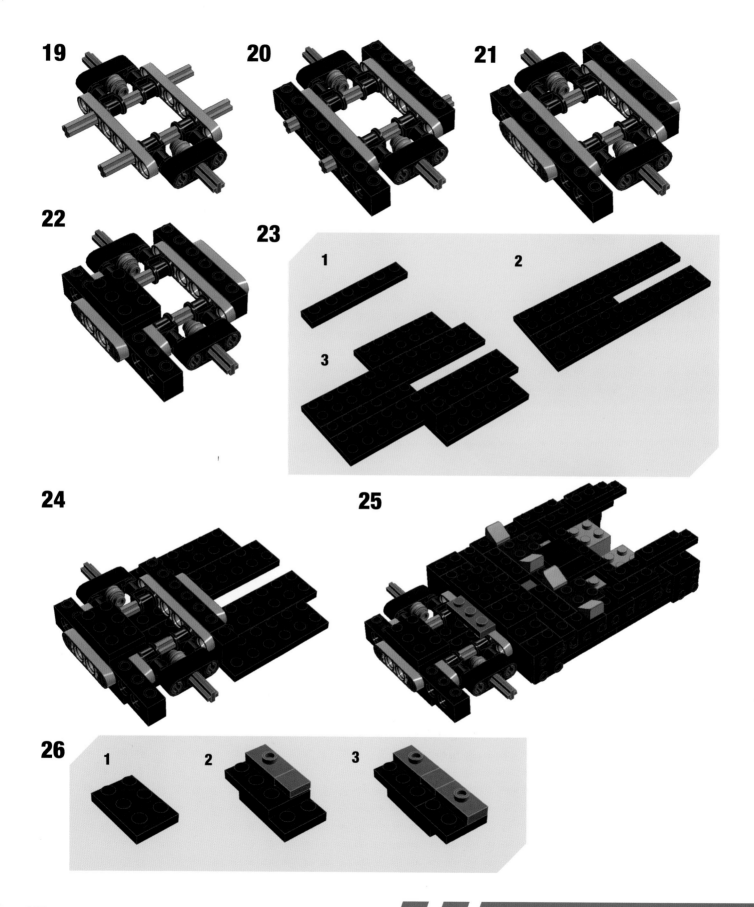

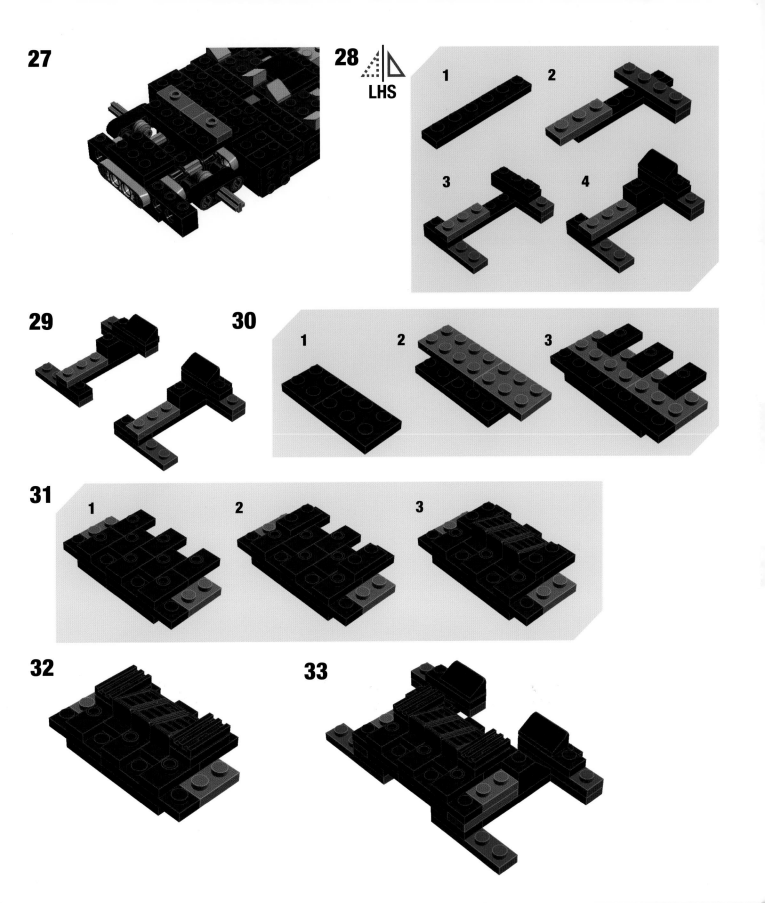

**27**

**28** LHS
1
2
3
4

**29**

**30**
1
2
3

**31**
1
2
3

**32**

**33**

**34**

**35**

1   2

3

**36**

1   2

**37**

1

2

**38**

**39**

**40**

1   2   3   4   5   6

2×

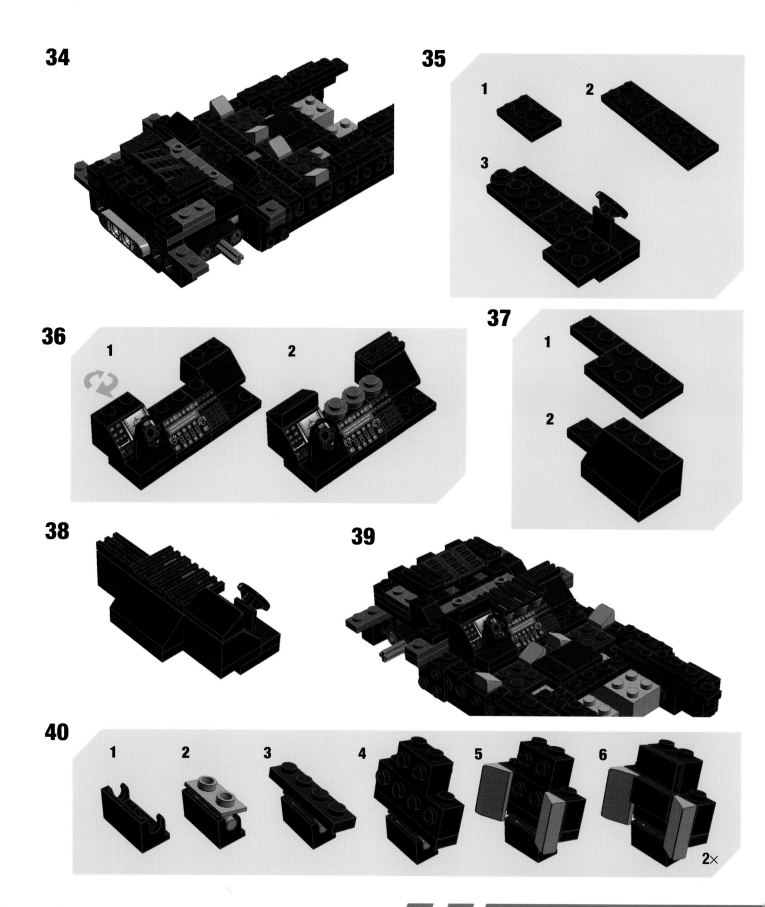

**41**

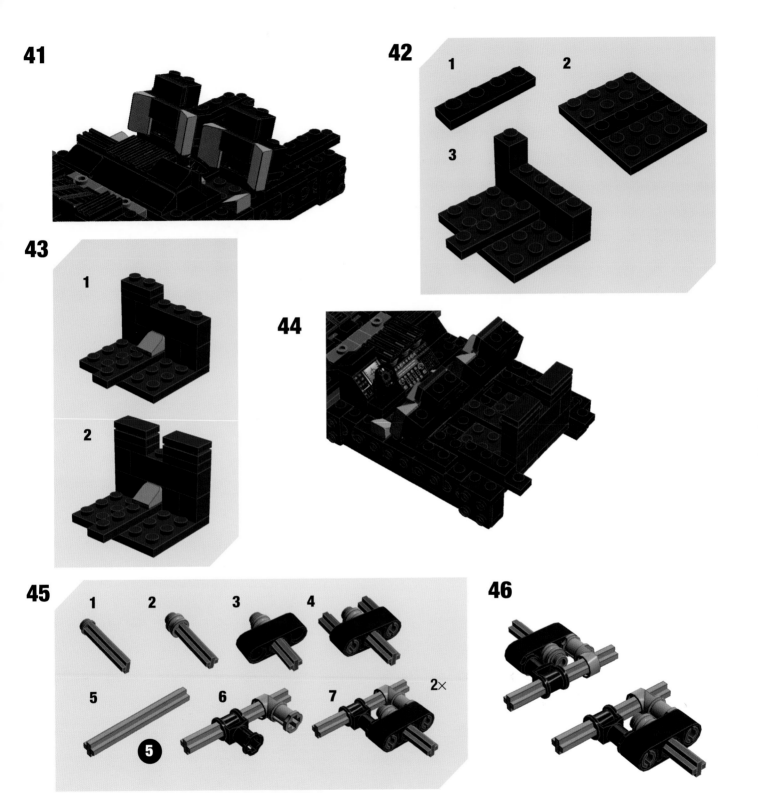

**42**

1

2

3

**43**

1

2

**44**

**45**

1 2 3 4

5 6 7 2×

5

**46**

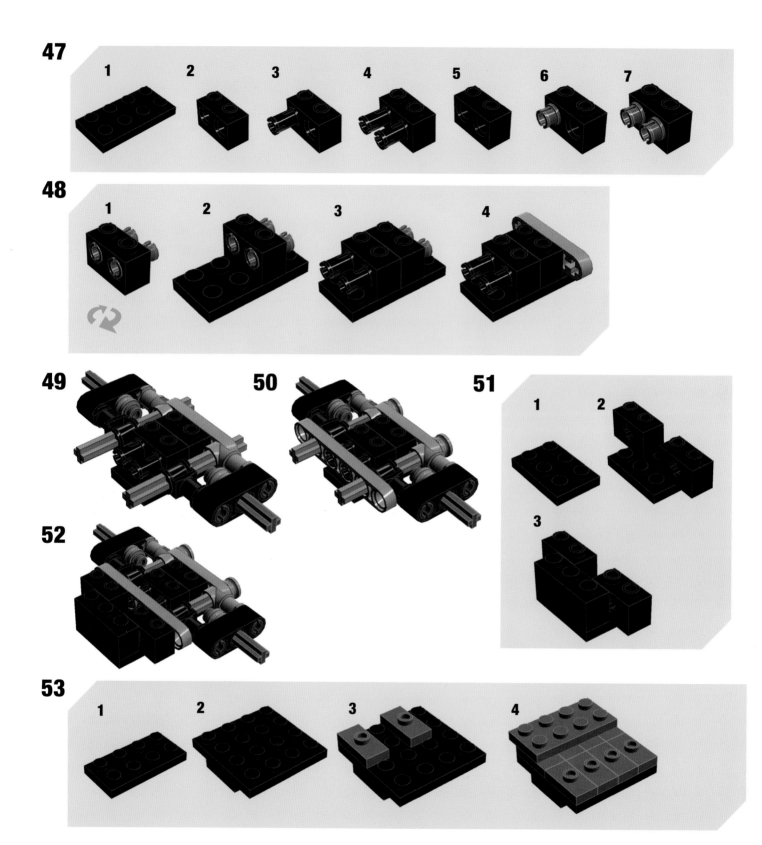

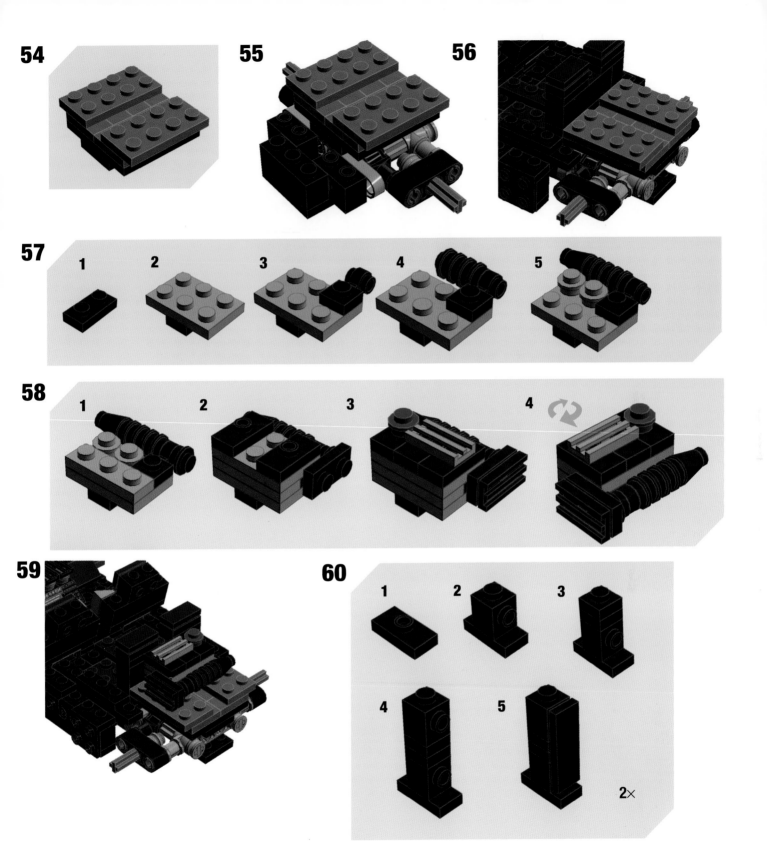

**54**

**55**

**56**

**57**
1   2   3   4   5

**58**
1   2   3   4

**59**

**60**
1   2   3

4   5

2×

**61**

**62**

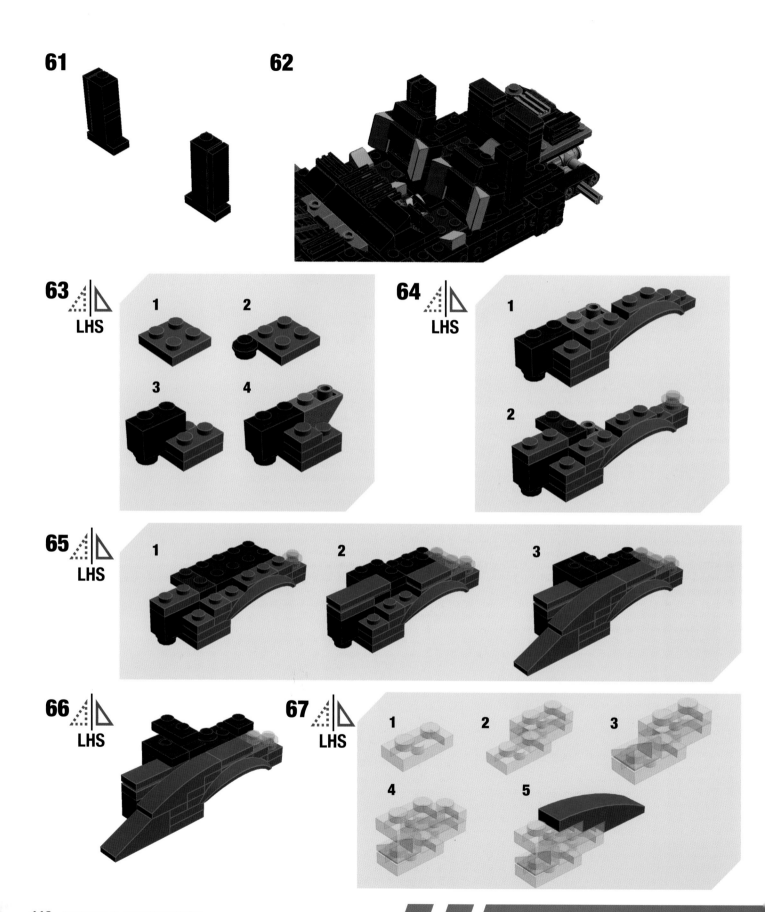

**63** LHS
1
2
3
4

**64** LHS
1
2

**65** LHS
1
2
3

**66** LHS

**67** LHS
1
2
3
4
5

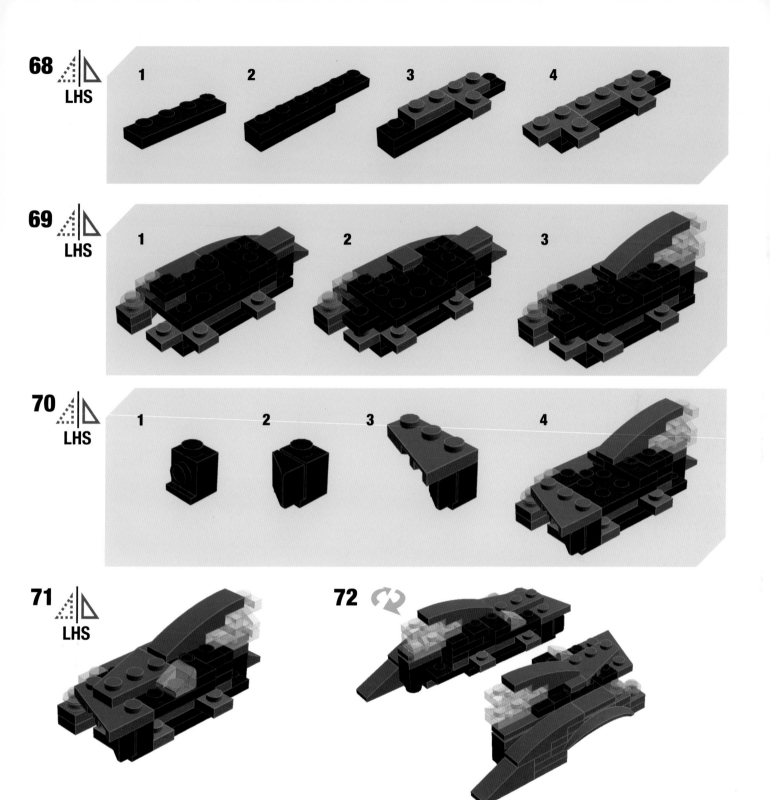

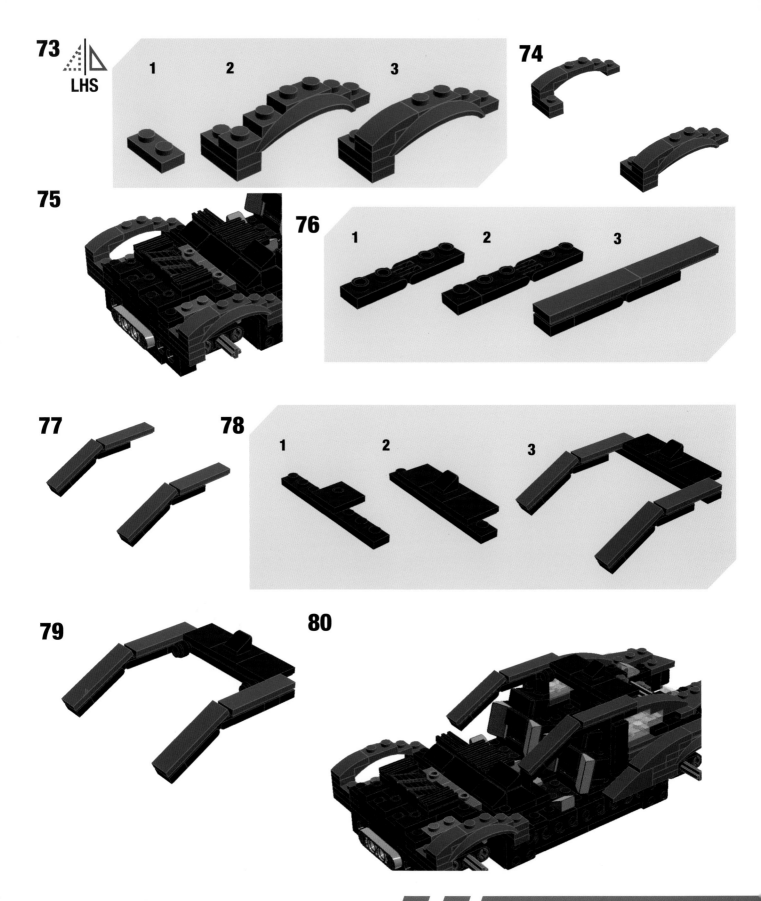

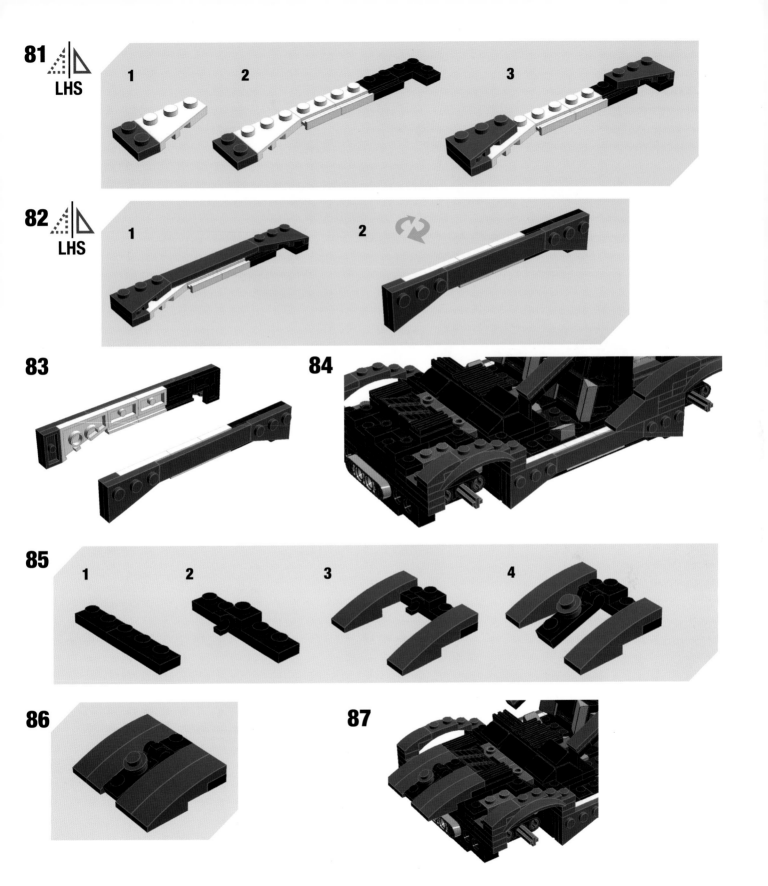

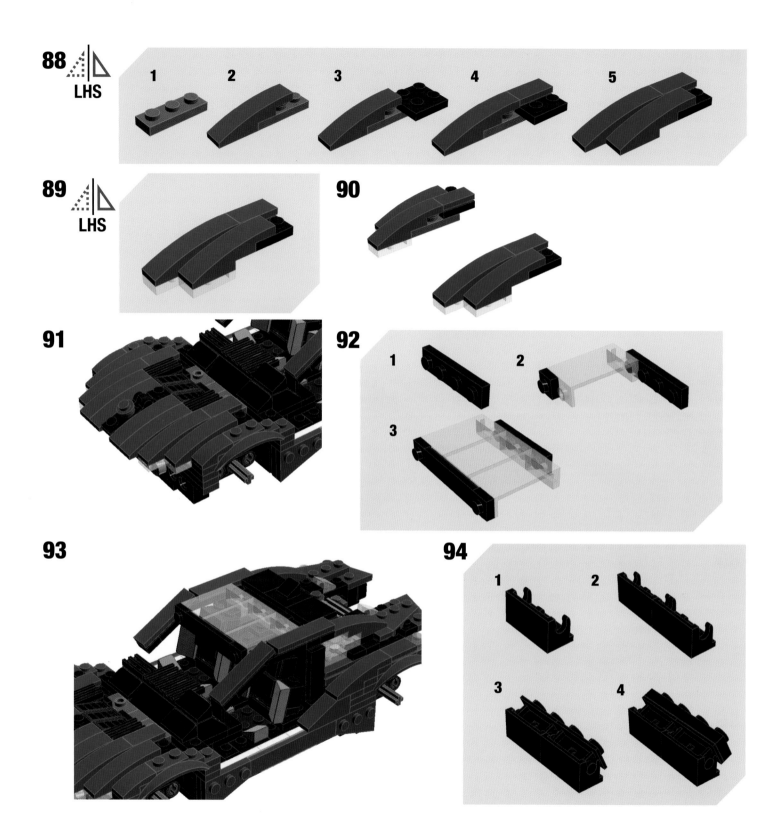

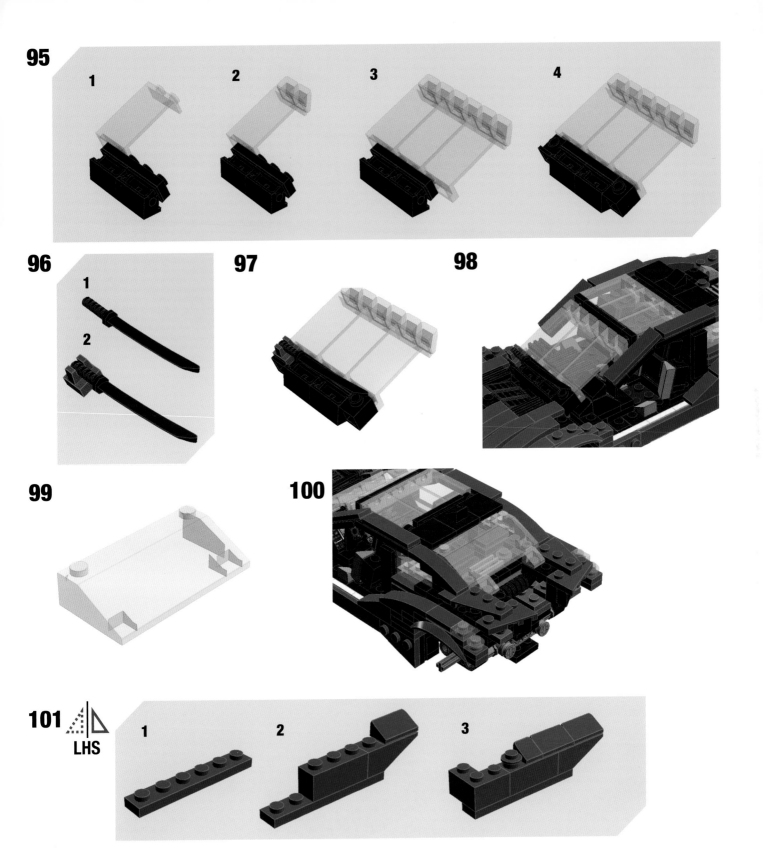

**95**  1  2  3  4

**96**  1  2

**97**  **98**

**99**  **100**

**101**  LHS  1  2  3

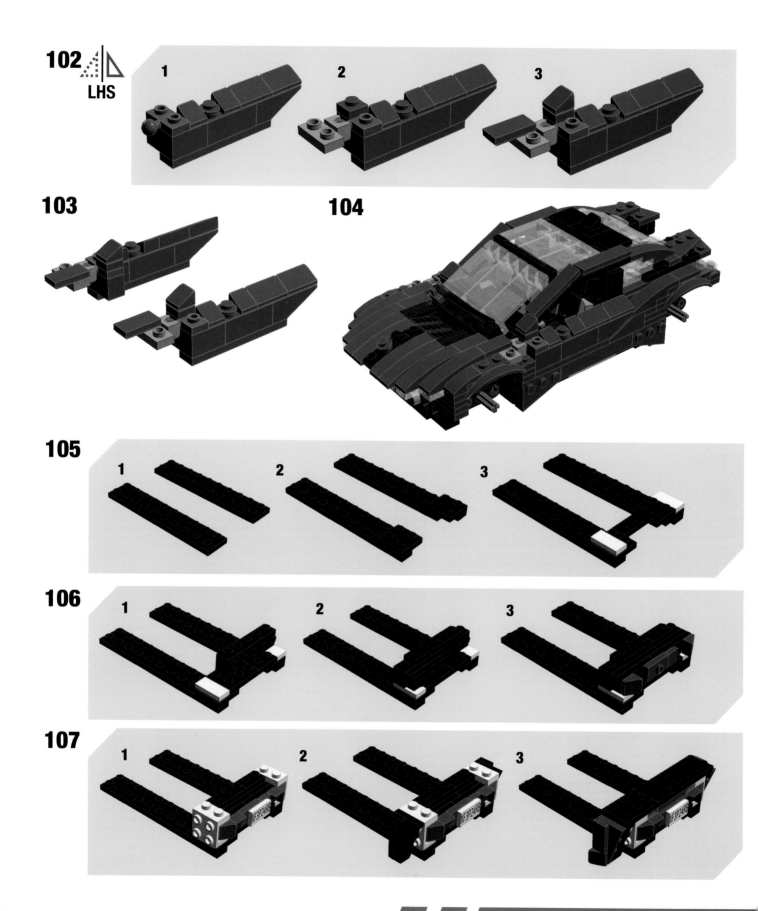

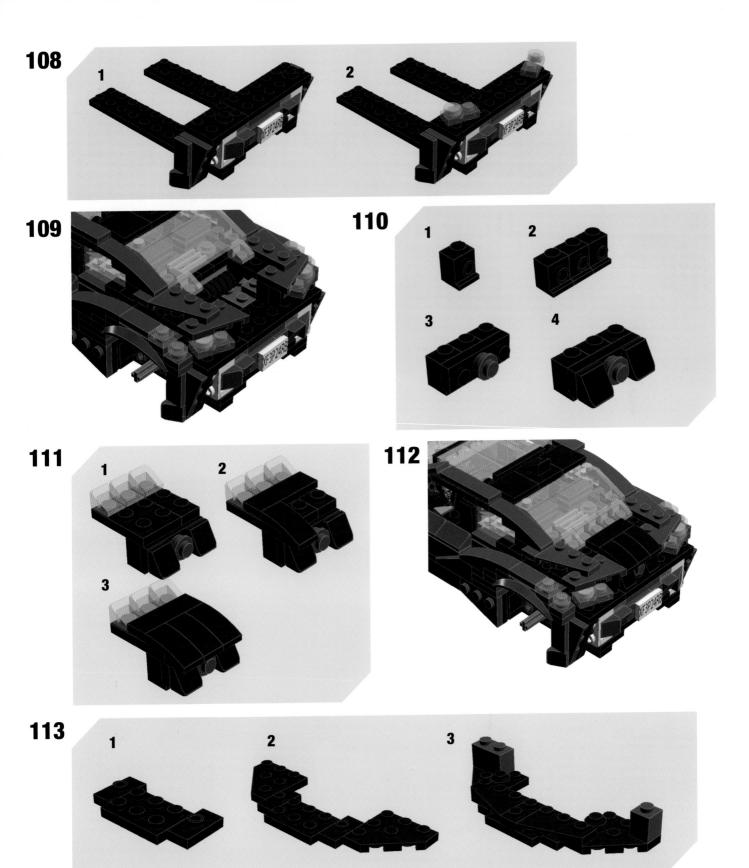

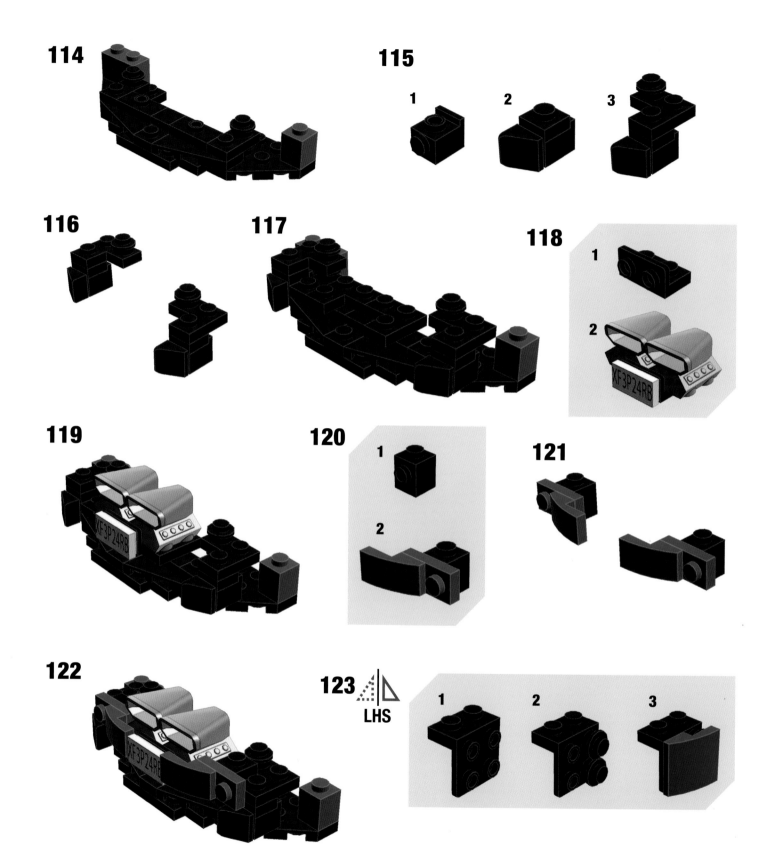

**114**

**115**

1

2

3

**116**

**117**

**118**

1

2

XF3P24RB

**119**

XF3P24RB

**120**

1

2

**121**

**122**

XF3P24RB

**123** LHS

1

2

3

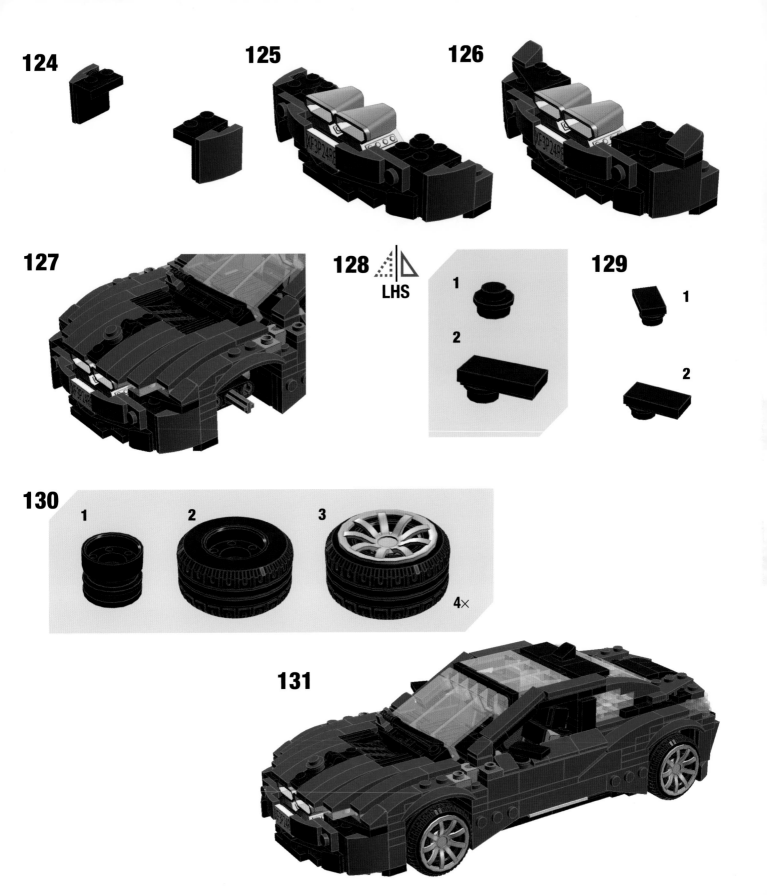

**124**

**125**

**126**

**127**

**128** LHS
1
2

**129**
1
2

**130**
1
2
3
4×

**131**

# 911 CARRERA 2.7 RS

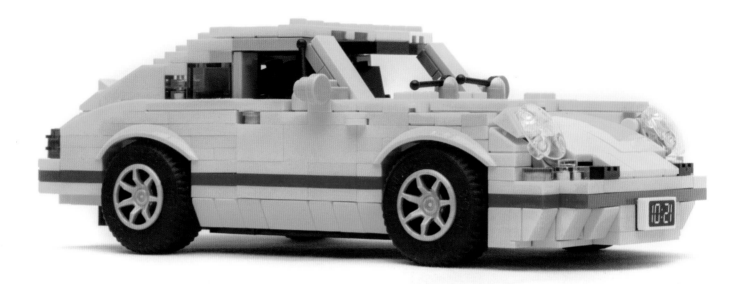

The Porsche 911 has the most-recognized sports car silhouette—partly because it has been produced continually from 1963 to today and also because of its 6-cylinder, horizontally opposed engine mounted longitudinally behind the rear axle. The shape was an evolution of the earlier 356 model. The new distinction for the 2.7 RS was the addition of the small "ducktail" spoiler mounted to the engine cover.

Ten years of continued evolution led to the most coveted of collector 911s, the 1973 RS. This model had the perfect blend of poise and performance. The car was a lightweight at 2,150 lb. (975 kg), making the most of the 2.7L engine's output of 210 hp (155 kW). The Carrera 2.7 RS was built by Porsche to homologate the car for FIA Group 4 racing (five hundred units required). The car derived its name from the Carrera Panamericana, a famous road race through Mexico where racing Porsches had many victories during the 1950s.

Further evolution of the 2.7 RS occurred in 1974 with the RSR—the engine gained another 121 cc (to 2.808L), producing 300 hp (220 kW).

From 1974 onward, all 911 road cars gained US-style impact bumpers, adding weight, and though the engines increased in capacity, emission regulations reduced power output and response. The 1973 2.7 RS is considered the finest of the breed.

Porsche intended to replace the 911 with water-cooled, front-engined models, notably the luxurious V-8 grand tourer Porsche 928 of 1977, but for many enthusiasts, the 911 was *the* Porsche. The classic 911 shape remained until the Porsche 996–generation model 911 in 1998.

**COUNTRY OF ORIGIN:** Germany

**PRODUCTION:** 1973

**NUMBER MADE:** 1,580

**LAYOUT / DRIVE:** Rear engine / Rear-wheel drive

**ENGINE:** 2.7L, 6 cylinders, horizontally opposed

**POWER / TORQUE:** 210 hp (155 kW) / 188 lb-ft (255 Nm)

**CONSTRUCTION / DOORS:** Monocoque / 2 doors

This model can also be built in the folowing colors:
Number of parts: 442

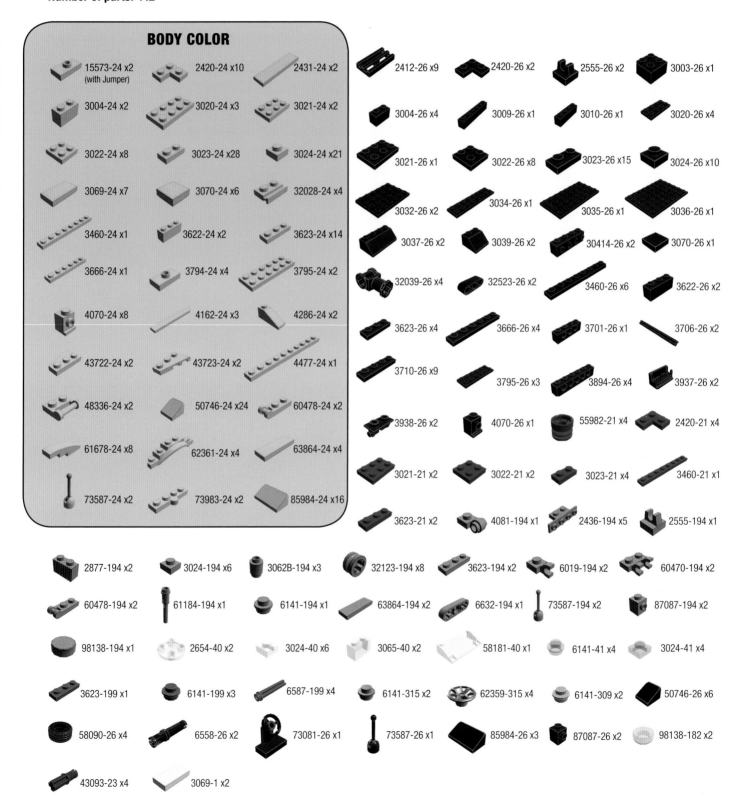

**BODY COLOR**

15573-24 x2 (with Jumper)
2420-24 x10
2431-24 x2
3004-24 x2
3020-24 x3
3021-24 x2
3022-24 x8
3023-24 x28
3024-24 x21
3069-24 x7
3070-24 x6
32028-24 x4
3460-24 x1
3622-24 x2
3623-24 x14
3666-24 x1
3794-24 x4
3795-24 x2
4070-24 x8
4162-24 x3
4286-24 x2
43722-24 x2
43723-24 x2
4477-24 x1
48336-24 x2
50746-24 x24
60478-24 x2
61678-24 x8
62361-24 x4
63864-24 x4
73587-24 x2
73983-24 x2
85984-24 x16

2412-26 x9
2420-26 x2
2555-26 x2
3003-26 x1
3004-26 x4
3009-26 x1
3010-26 x1
3020-26 x4
3021-26 x1
3022-26 x8
3023-26 x15
3024-26 x10
3032-26 x2
3034-26 x1
3035-26 x1
3036-26 x1
3037-26 x2
3039-26 x2
30414-26 x2
3070-26 x1
32039-26 x4
32523-26 x2
3460-26 x6
3622-26 x2
3623-26 x4
3666-26 x4
3701-26 x1
3706-26 x2
3710-26 x9
3795-26 x3
3894-26 x4
3937-26 x2
3938-26 x2
4070-26 x1
55982-21 x4
2420-21 x4
3021-21 x2
3022-21 x2
3023-21 x4
3460-21 x1
3623-21 x2
4081-194 x1
2436-194 x5
2555-194 x1

2877-194 x2
3024-194 x6
3062B-194 x3
32123-194 x8
3623-194 x2
6019-194 x2
60470-194 x2
60478-194 x2
61184-194 x1
6141-194 x1
63864-194 x2
6632-194 x1
73587-194 x2
87087-194 x2
98138-194 x1
2654-40 x2
3024-40 x6
3065-40 x2
58181-40 x1
6141-41 x4
3024-41 x4
3623-199 x1
6141-199 x3
6587-199 x4
6141-315 x2
62359-315 x4
6141-309 x2
50746-26 x6
58090-26 x4
6558-26 x2
73081-26 x1
73587-26 x1
85984-26 x3
87087-26 x2
98138-182 x2
43093-23 x4
3069-1 x2

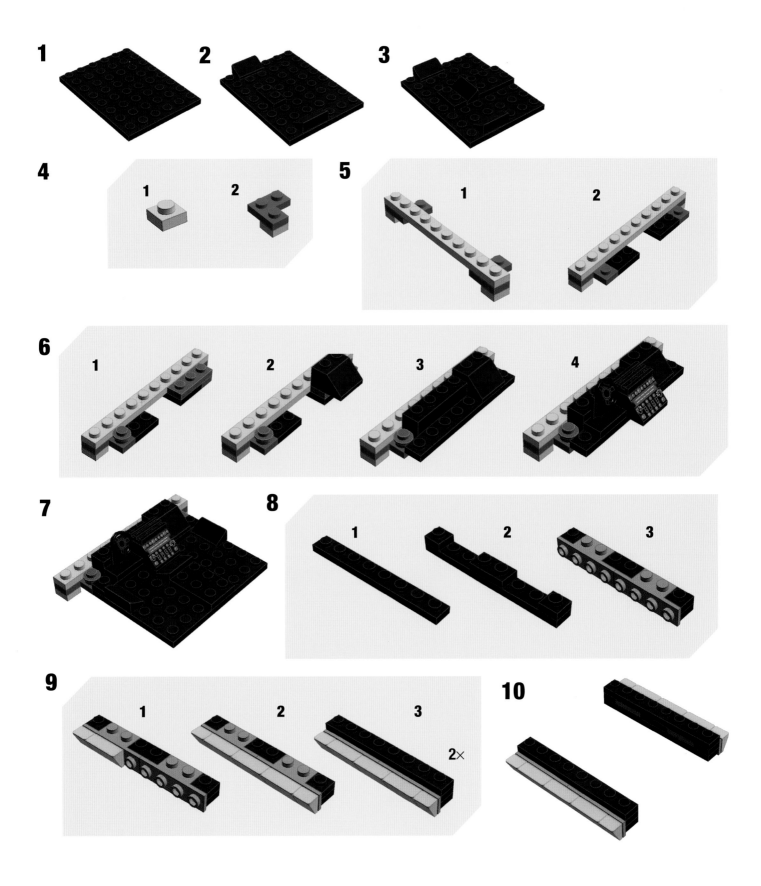

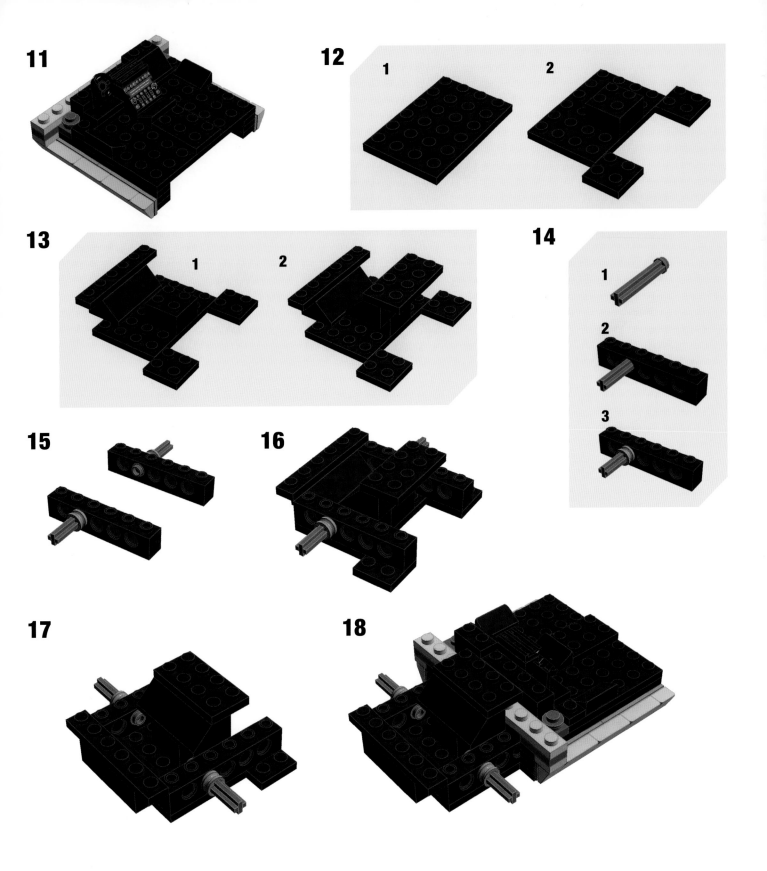

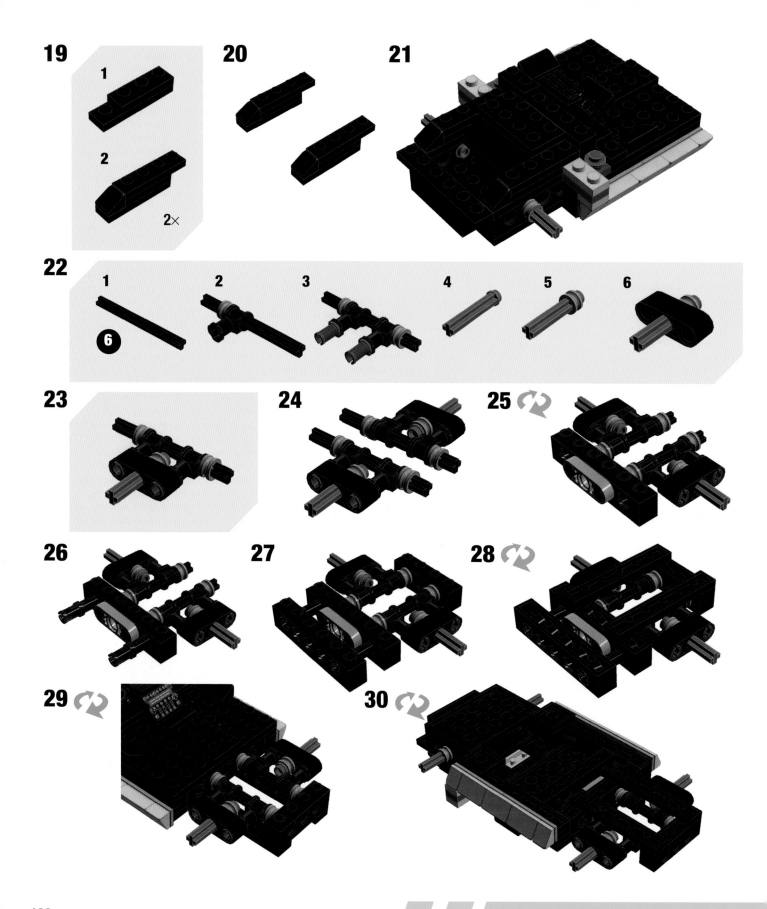

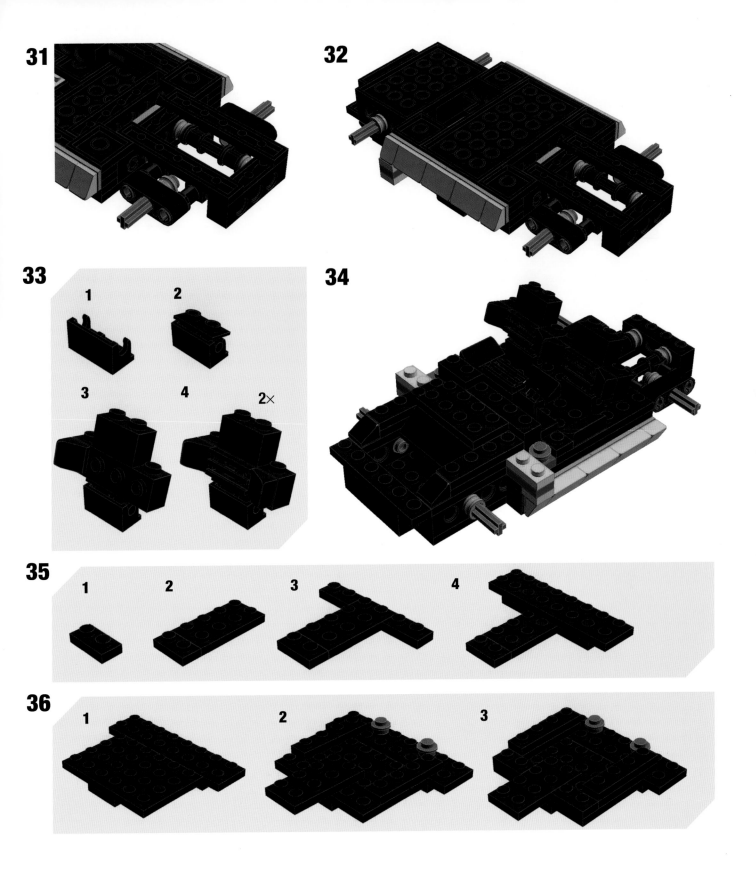

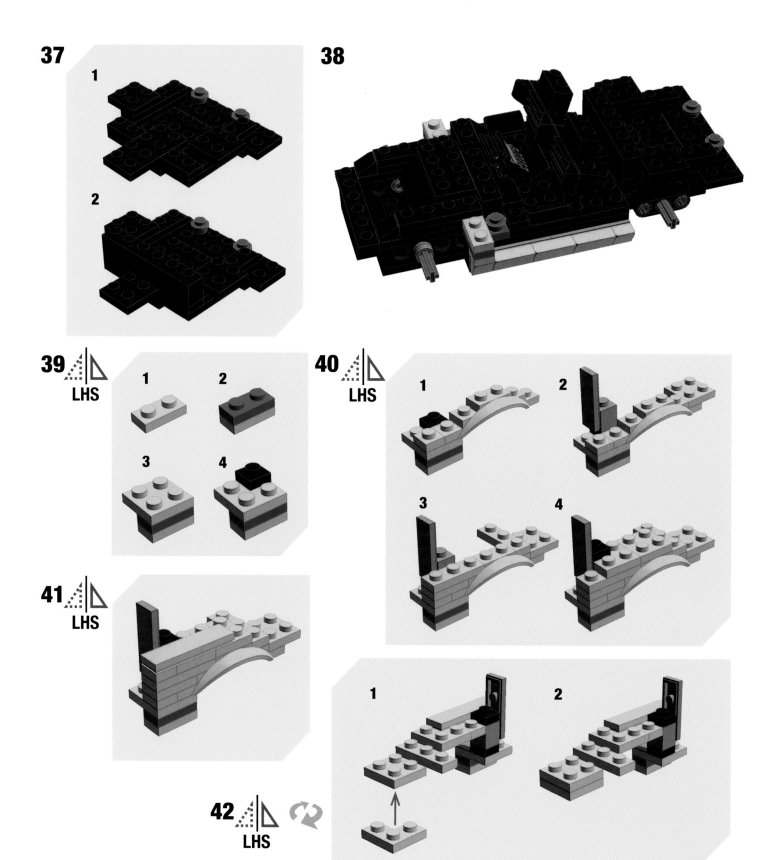

**37**

1

2

**38**

**39** LHS

1 2

3 4

**40** LHS

1 2

3 4

**41** LHS

**42** LHS

1

2

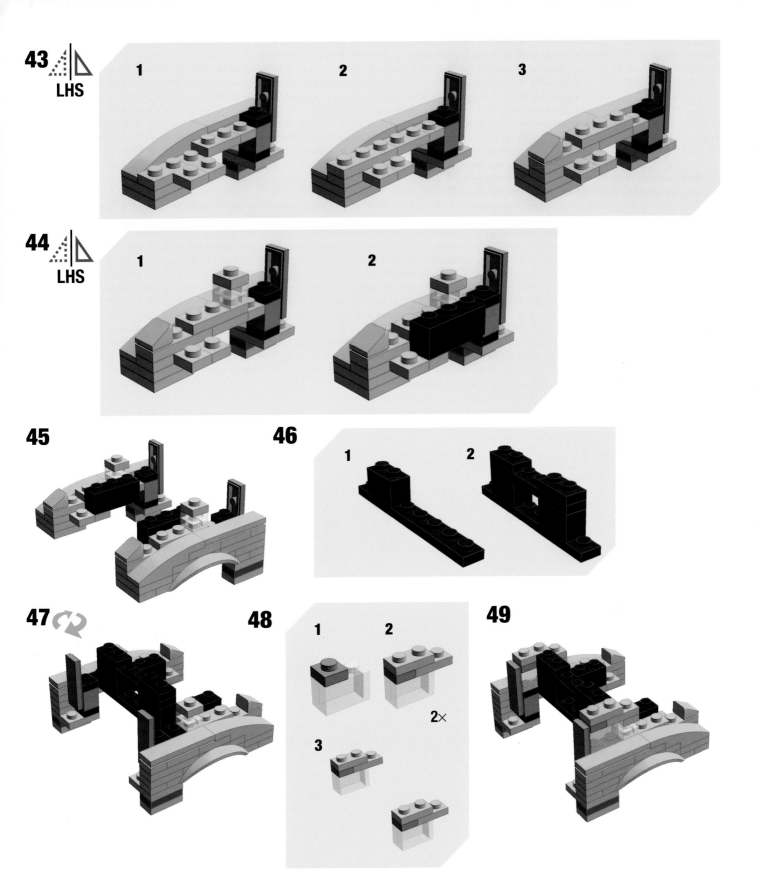

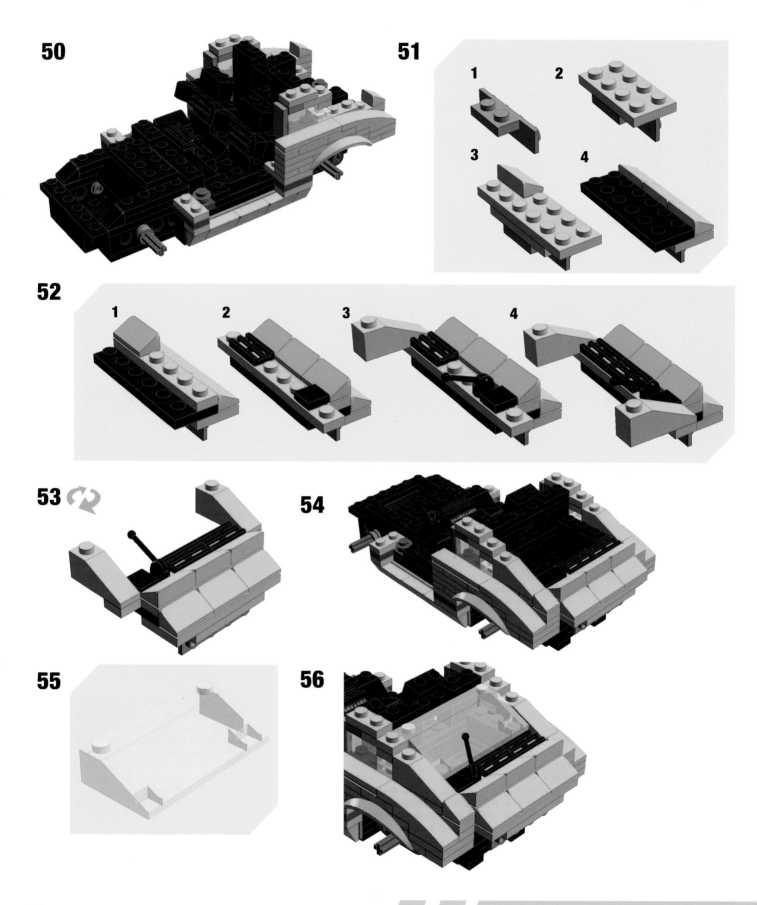

**50** **51**

1 2

3 4

**52**

1 2 3 4

**53** **54**

**55** **56**

**57**

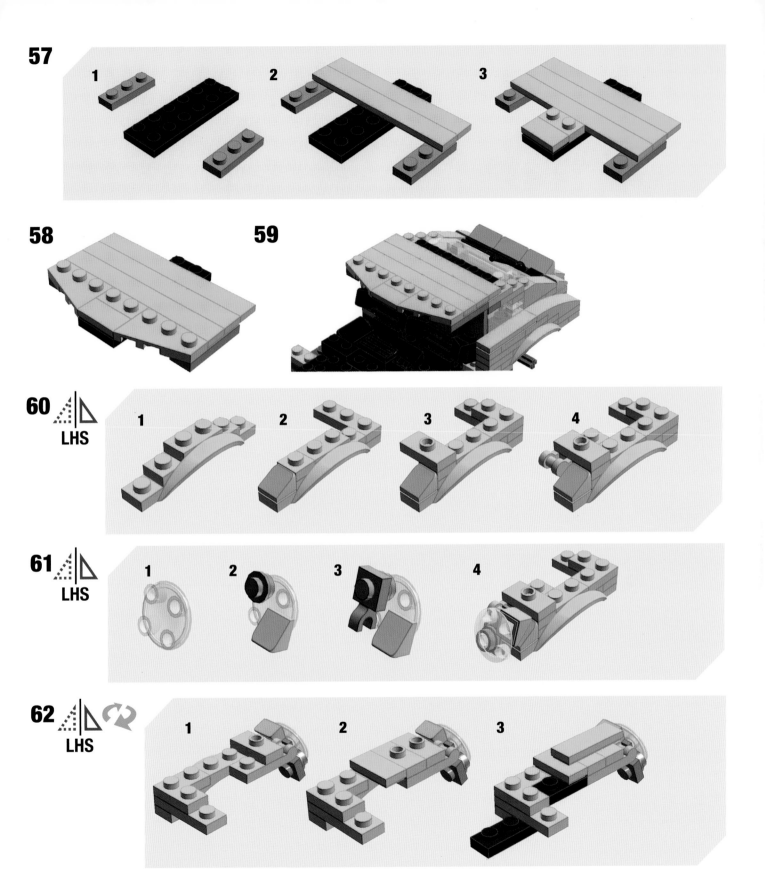

**58**

**59**

**60** LHS

**61** LHS

**62** LHS

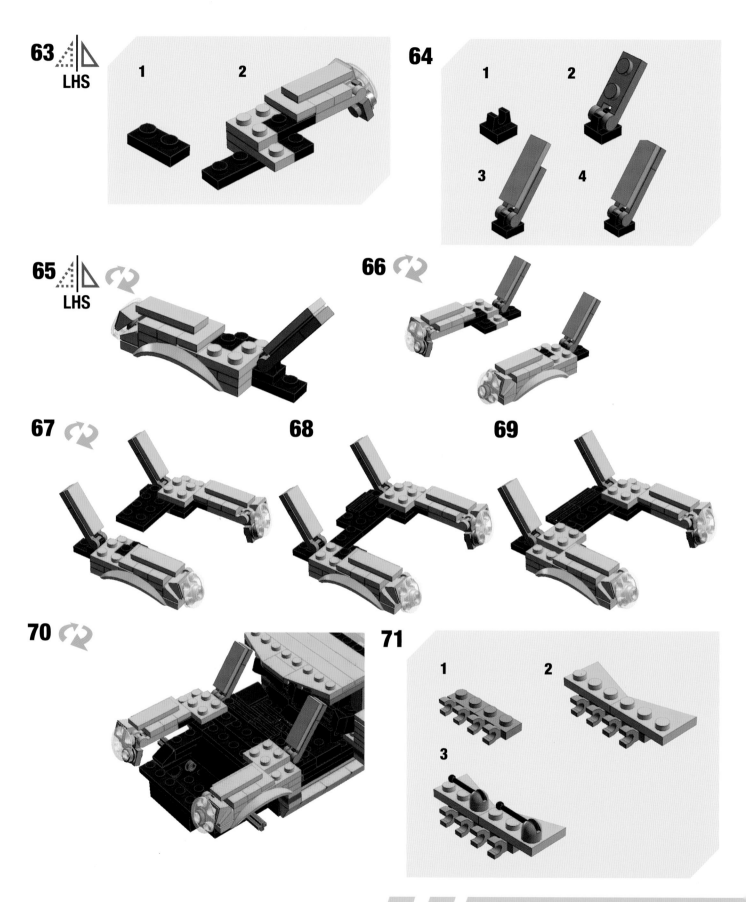

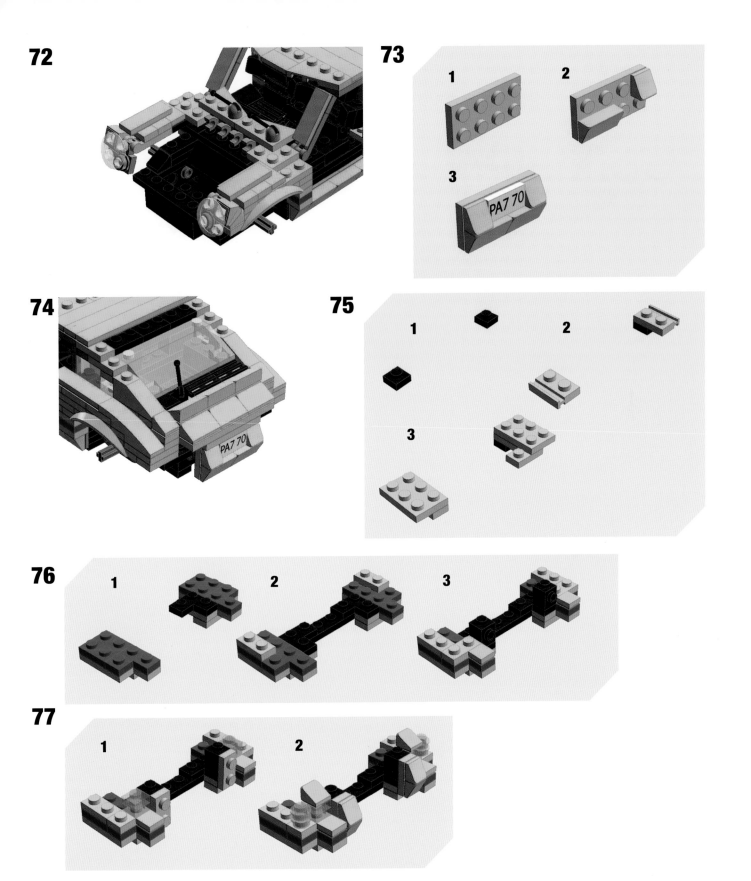

**72**

**73**
1

2

3

PA7 70

**74**

PA7 70

**75**
1

2

3

**76**
1

2

3

**77**
1

2

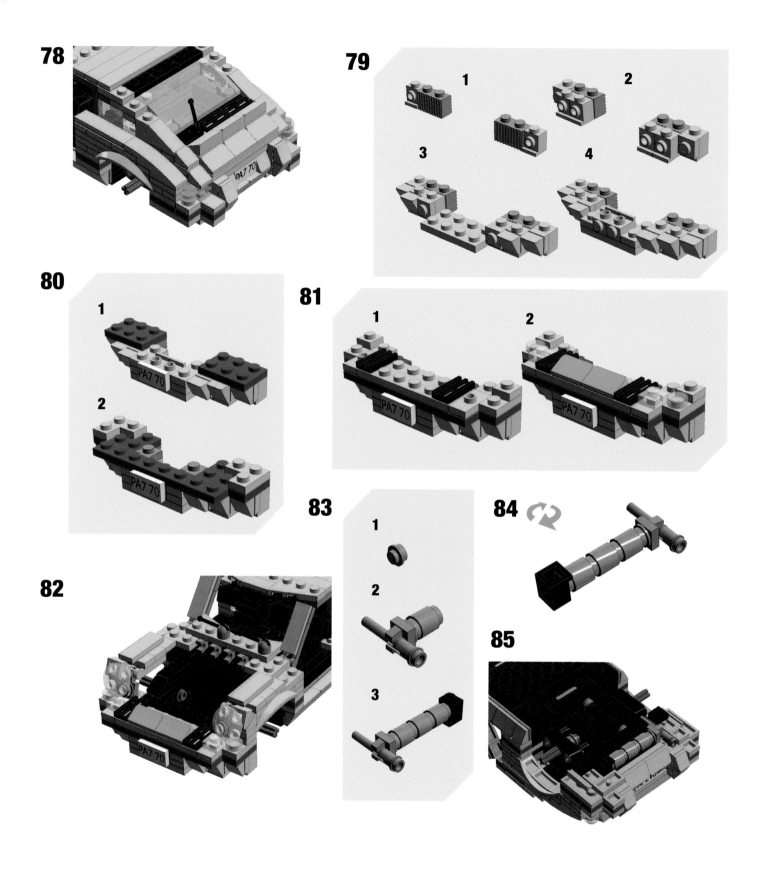

**78**

**79**

1

2

3

4

**80**

1

2

**81**

1

2

**83**

1

2

3

**84**

**82**

**85**

**86**

1  2

3  4  2×

**87** LHS

1

2

**88**

**89**

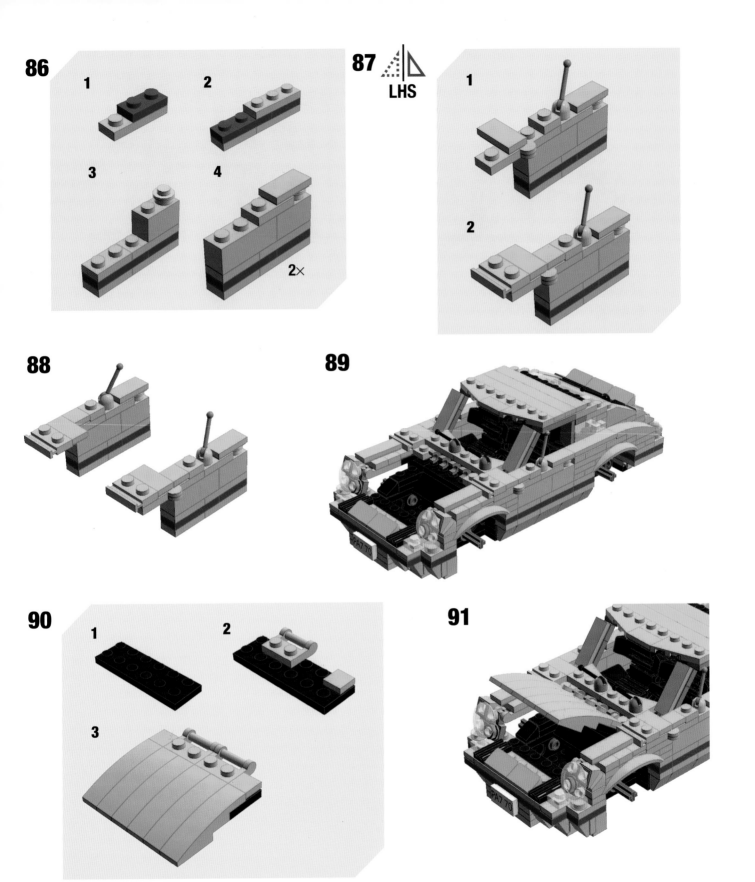

**90**

1  2

3

**91**

**92**

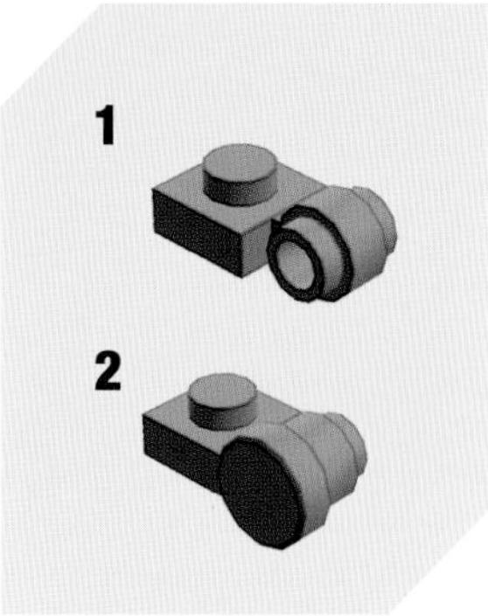

1

2

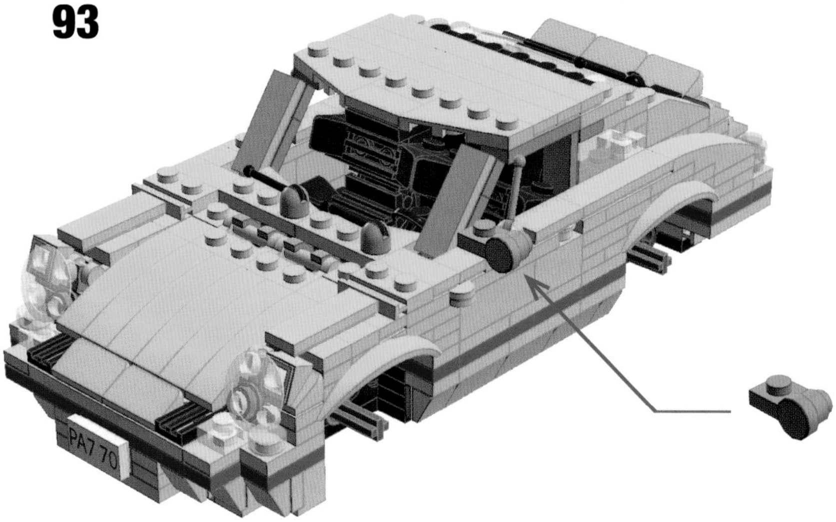

**94**

1

2

3

**93**

PA7 70

**95**

PA7 70

PA7 70

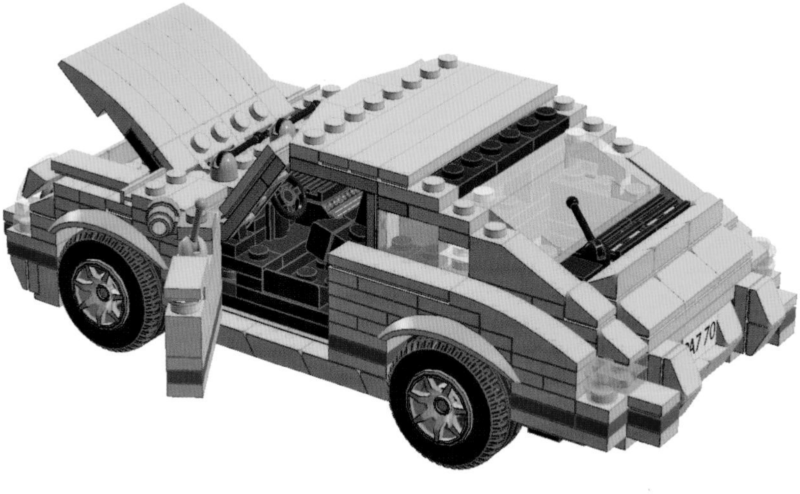

# ADVANCED

This is the fast end of the book—serious machines with serious performance. Along with their shape, performance cars are known for their powertrain performance—engines, gearboxes, and axles. The Plymouth Hemi 'Cuda sported plenty of performance for the money, a big engine wrapped up in budget clothes that made for a wild, wild ride. In complete contrast, the Bugatti Veyron provides the last word in vehicle complexity—16 cylinders, four turbochargers, 4-wheel drive, advanced electronics, and active aerodynamic spoilers.

These models are again presented in Miniland scale but include much more detailed chassis and engines, utilizing LEGO®'s Technic theme parts. As you assemble these models, you will even experience constructing major systems as they exist in the real cars. These are the functioning internal mechanical parts that are wrapped up in iconic bodywork.

Once the models from this book are completed, you should feel free to expand and develop the techniques further in the building of your own advanced brick cars.

# HEMI 'CUDA

The muscle car era was one of the automobile industry's golden eras. The formula was simple: small car, big engine.

This was all relative, of course. Even the US compacts were very large cars from the perspective of Europeans and the Japanese. The engine was not a relative measure—the V-8 fitted to the Plymouth shown was a mighty 7.0L at the time when American engines were measured in cubic inches—426 to be exact. And a feature of the engine formed part of the car's name Hemi—short for hemispherical combustion chambers, a method for achieving high compression ratio and large valve diameters.

'Cuda was just a shortened form of Barracuda, the official name of the car on which this model is based. Most Barracudas were a bit less wild than the Hemi version, with various engines of 3.2L to 7.2L capacity. For aficionados, though, the Hemi model is the real deal—perhaps even the greatest of all muscle cars. Coupes and a much more rare convertible were available, and the rarity of such cars is elevating the current market value—a 1971 Hemi 'Cuda convertible, one of eleven cars, sold for a staggering $3.5 million in 2014.

| | |
|---|---|
| **COUNTRY OF ORIGIN:** | USA |
| **PRODUCTION:** | 1971 |
| **NUMBER MADE:** | 16,159 (108 Hemis) |
| **LAYOUT/DRIVE:** | Front engine / Rear-wheel drive |
| **ENGINE:** | 426 cid (6,981 cc), 8 cylinders, V |
| **POWER / TORQUE:** | 424 bhp (317 kW) / 490 lb-ft (664.35 Nm) |
| **CONSTRUCTION / DOORS:** | Unibody / 2-door coupe |

To add to the drama, the Hemi 'Cuda was available in a number of wild colors, many of them citrus-toned, with matching groovy names. Year-on-year changes included various special paint schemes, including the black panels on the rear fenders of this car, which match the roof. For 1971, the car adopted twin headlamps, a one-year-only feature. The Hemi was also fitted with a shaker hood, an exposed air intake protruding from the hood—the intake "shakes" as the engine reacts to the mighty torque loads.

Alas, all golden eras must come to an end, and this one was brought down by insurance premiums, unleaded fuel, and vehicle emissions standards. For this reason, bona-fide muscle car legends remain the poster child for high-octane-fueled dreams.

**BODY COLOR**

15068-24 x2
2412-24 x2
2420-24 x6
2431-24 x5
2877-24 x2
3004-24 x2
3010-24 x2
3022-24 x5
3023-24 x15
3024-24 x16
3034-24 x2
3068-24 x2
3069-24 x6
3070-24 x4
3460-24 x1
3623-24 x4
3660-24 x2
3665-24 x2
3666-24 x4
3710-24 x6
4070-24 x2
4162-24 x1
50746-24 x12
6141-24 x2
6636-24 x2
61678-24 x4
63864-24 x2
85984-24 x10
87087-24 x2
93606-24 x2
62361-24 x2
73983-24 x2

2412-26 x2
2420-26 x13
2436-26 x4
2445-26 x1
2730-26 x2
2780-26 x14
2819-26 x1
2877-26 x2
3004-26 x2
3009-26 x1
30136-26 x2
3020-26 x5
3021-26 x6
3022-26 x5
3023-26 x29
3024-26 x18
3033-26 x1
3034-26 x2
3036-26 x2
3039-26 x2
3040-26 x2
3069-26 x2
32000-26 x2
32062-26 x7
32073-26 x1
3460-26 x13
32449-26 x1
3622-26 x2
3623-26 x18
3665-26 x10
3666-26 x4
3700-26 x1
3701-26 x3
3705-26 x2
3706-26 x1
3710-26 x11
3737-26 x1
3794-26 x11
3795-26 x6
3832-26 x2
4286-26 x2
44301-26 x2
44302-26 x2
4477-26 x2
4070-26 x14
4081-26 x2
4162-26 x1
6091-26 x4
6019-26 x2
60478-26 x4
6141-26 x10
85984-26 x4
62361-26 x2
45677-26 x1
3937-26 x3
3938-26 x1

50746-26 x2
55982-26 x4
58090-26 x4
73587-26 x1
87087-26 x2
99781-26 x2

2420-199 x2
2851-199 x4
2877-199 x2
32013-199 x6
32034-199 x4
3622-199 x2
3623-199 x2
3700-199 x2
4032-199 x1
6141-199 x4
61409-199 x2
2850-194 x4
2852-194 x4
2853-194 x2
2854-194 x1
3021-194 x1
3022-194 x1
3023-194 x10
3024-194 x4
3062B-194 x2
3069-194 x1
32123-194 x5
3460-194 x2
3623-194 x2
3665-194 x2
3700-194 x1
3832-194 x1
4070-194 x4
4162-194 x1
4274-194 x2
4477-194 x1
50746-194 x6
6141-194 x2
4589-194 x4
61903-194 x1
6541-194 x2
6562-194 x2
6589-194 x2
6590-194 x1
6632-194 x2
85984-194 x2
3938-194 x2
87087-194 x2
3023-40 x10
3024-40 x6
50746-40 x16
6141-40 x6
3023-41 x2
50746-41 x2
62701-315 x4
6562-5 x2
3024-182 x2
3069-1 x2
71137b-315 x2

**141**

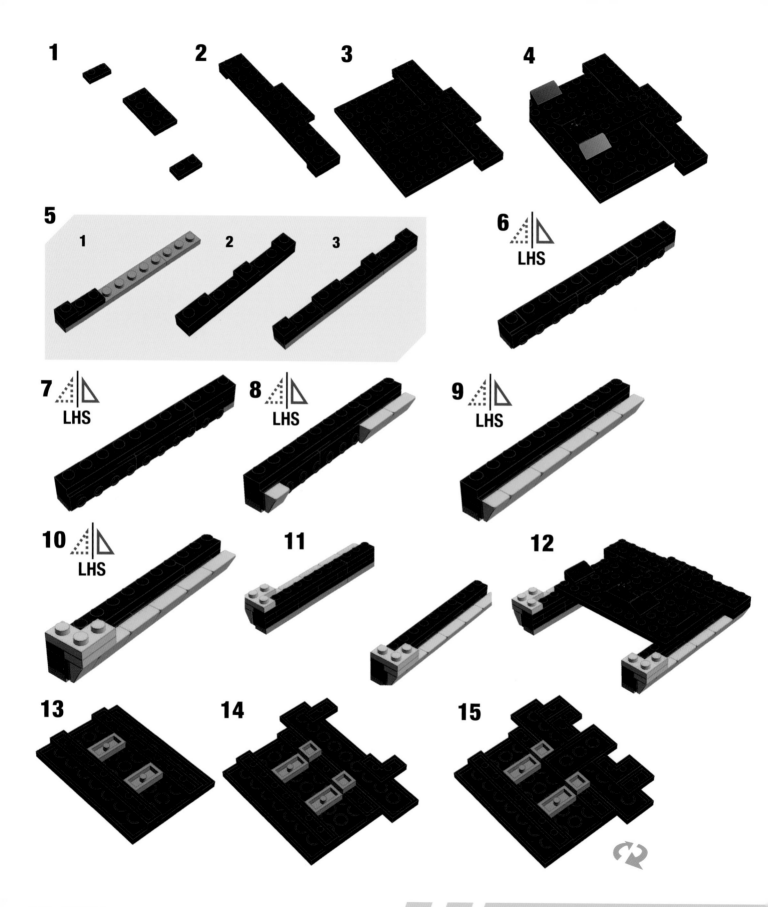

**1** **2** **3** **4**

**5**
1 2 3

**6** LHS

**7** LHS **8** LHS **9** LHS

**10** LHS **11** **12**

**13** **14** **15**

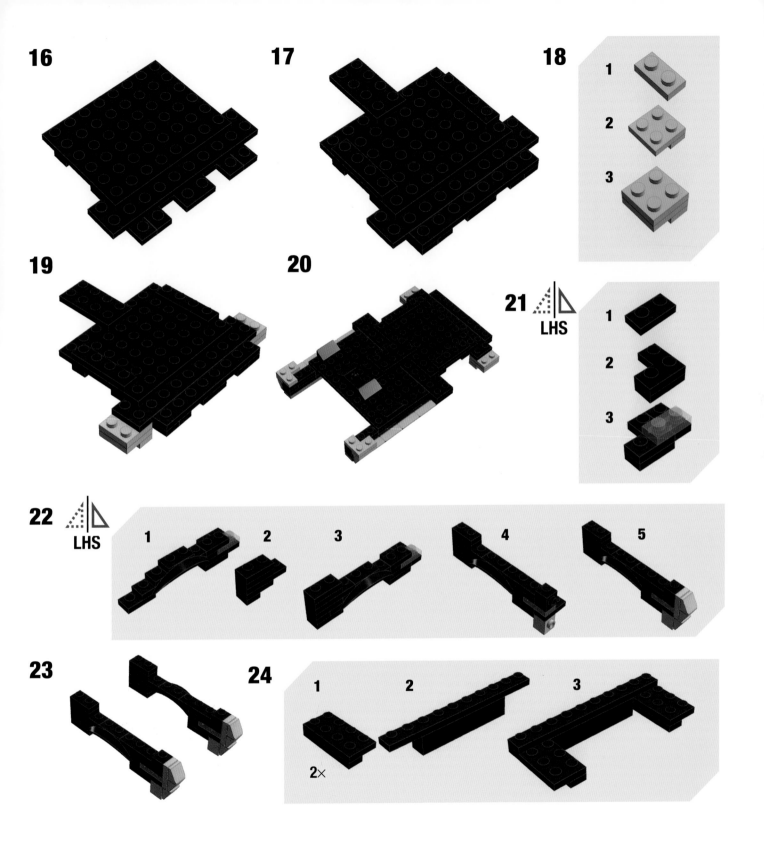

**16**

**17**

**18**
1
2
3

**19**

**20**

**21** LHS
1
2
3

**22** LHS
1  2  3  4  5

**23**

**24**
1  2  3
2×

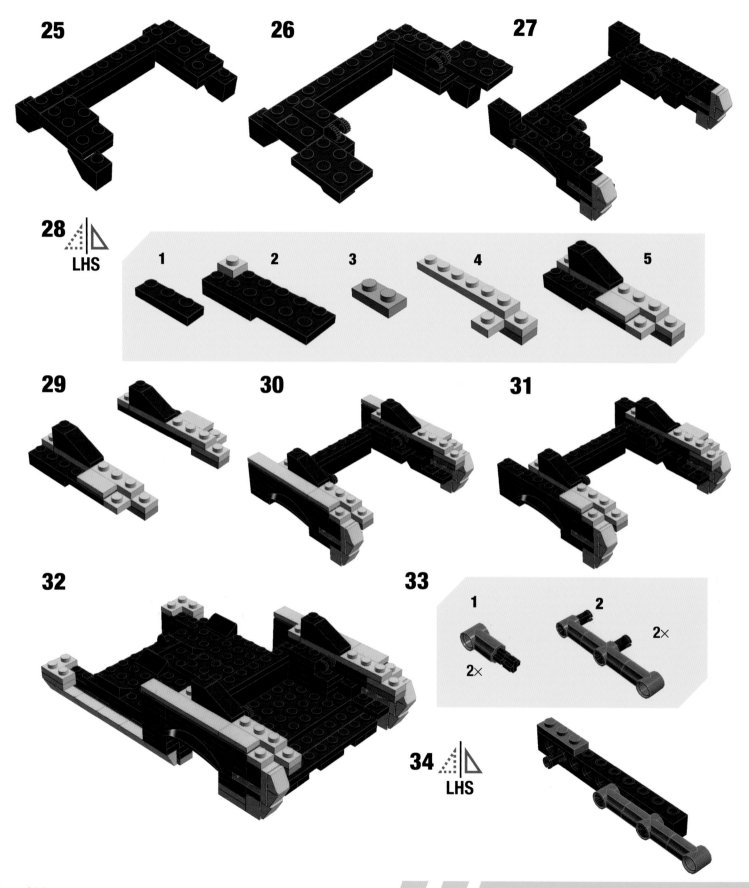

**25**

**26**

**27**

**28** LHS

1 2 3 4 5

**29**

**30**

**31**

**32**

**33**

1 2×

2 2×

**34** LHS

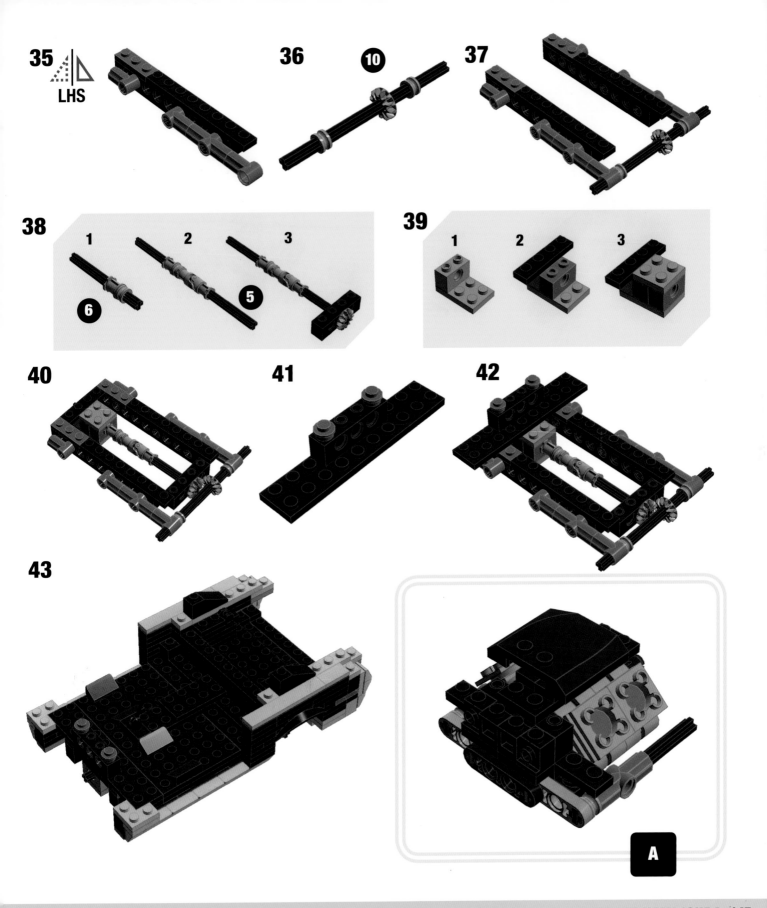

**35** LHS

**36**

**37**

**38**
1
6
2
3
5

**39**
1
2
3

**40**

**41**

**42**

**43**

**A**

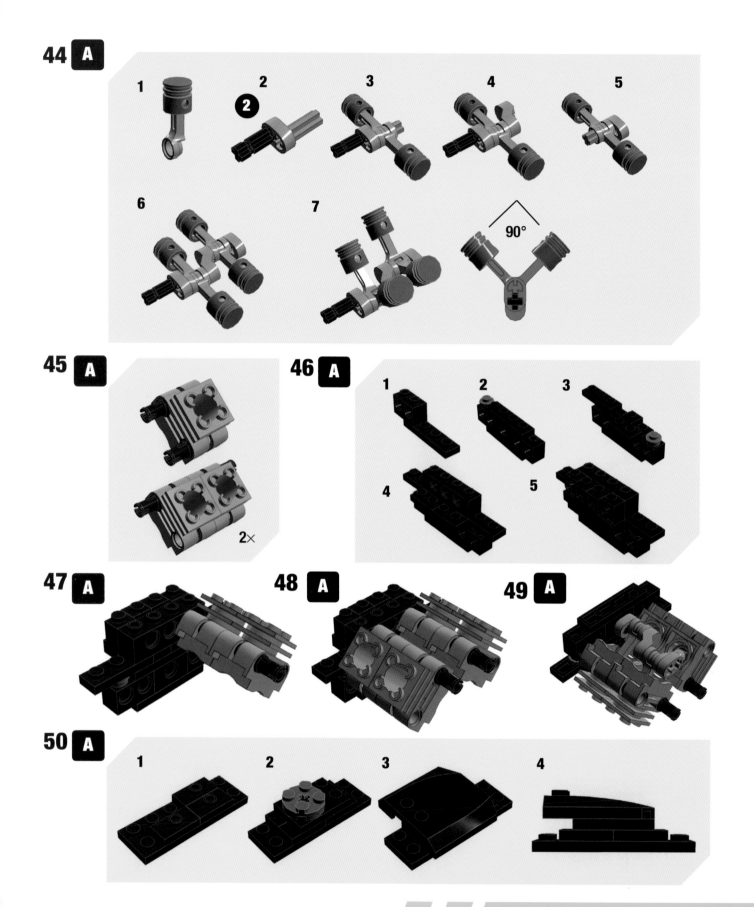

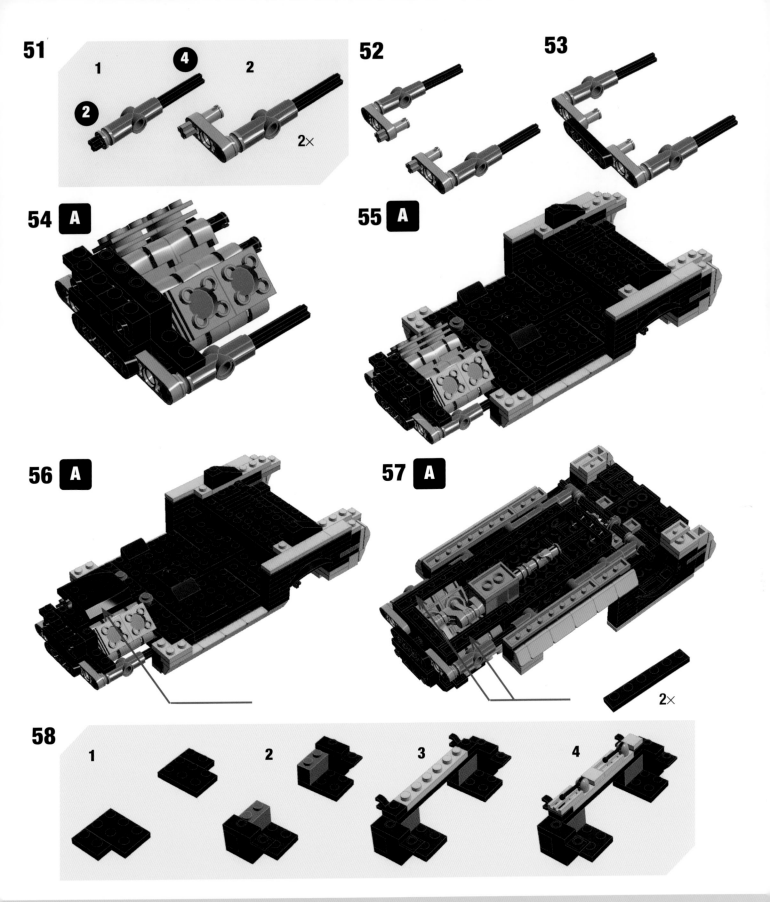

**51**

1    **4**    2

**2**

2×

**52**

**53**

**54** **A**

**55** **A**

**56** **A**

**57** **A**

2×

**58**

1    2    3    4

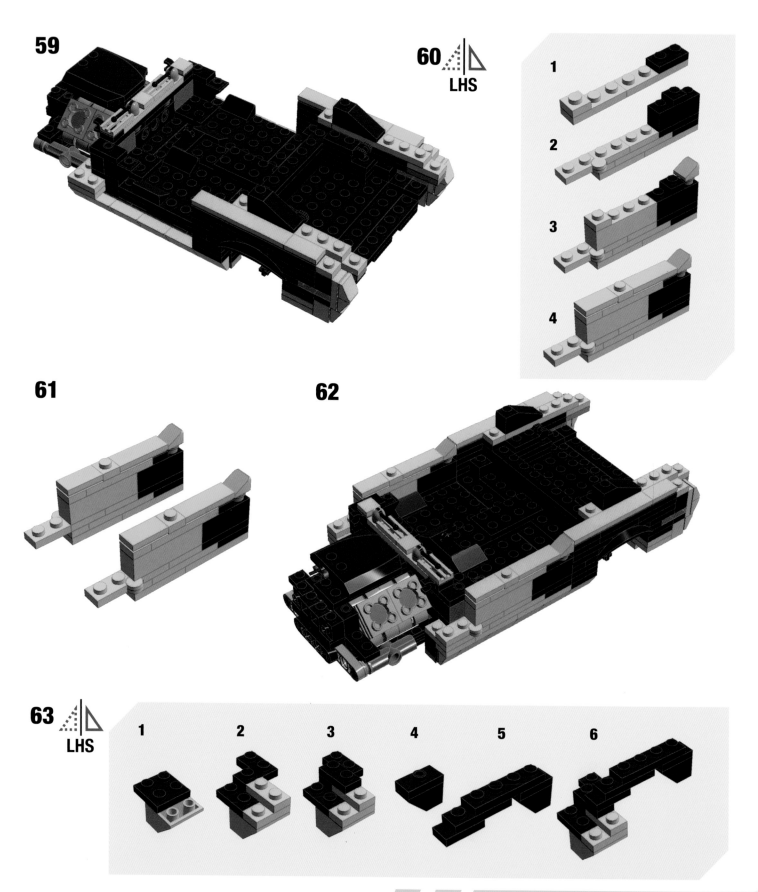

**59**

**60** LHS

1

2

3

4

**61**

**62**

**63** LHS

1 2 3 4 5 6

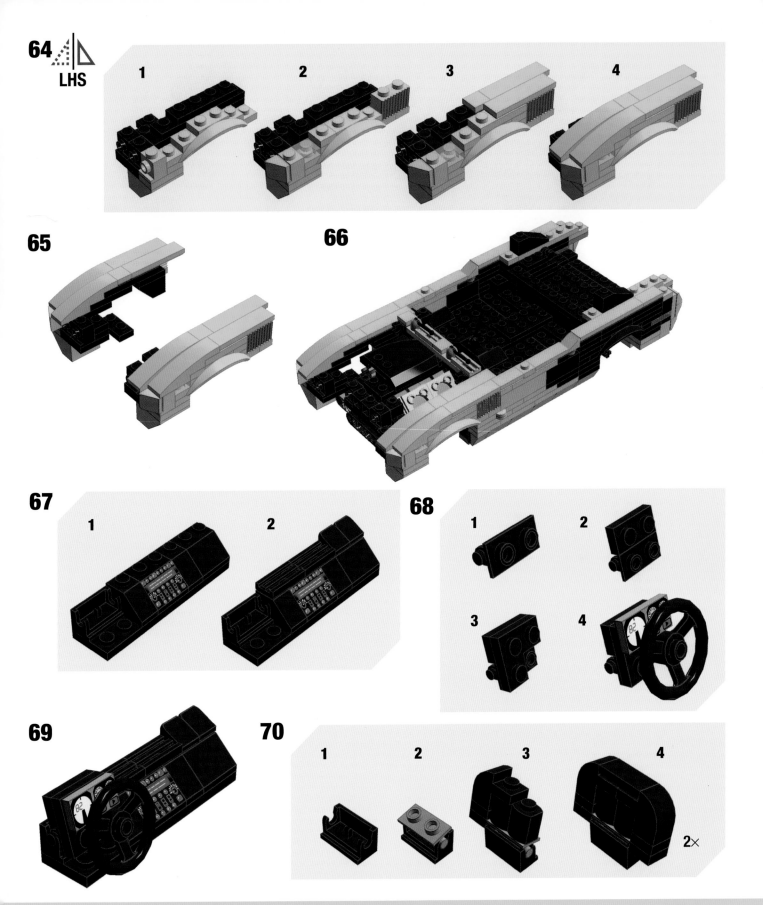

**71**

**72**

1

2×

2

**73**

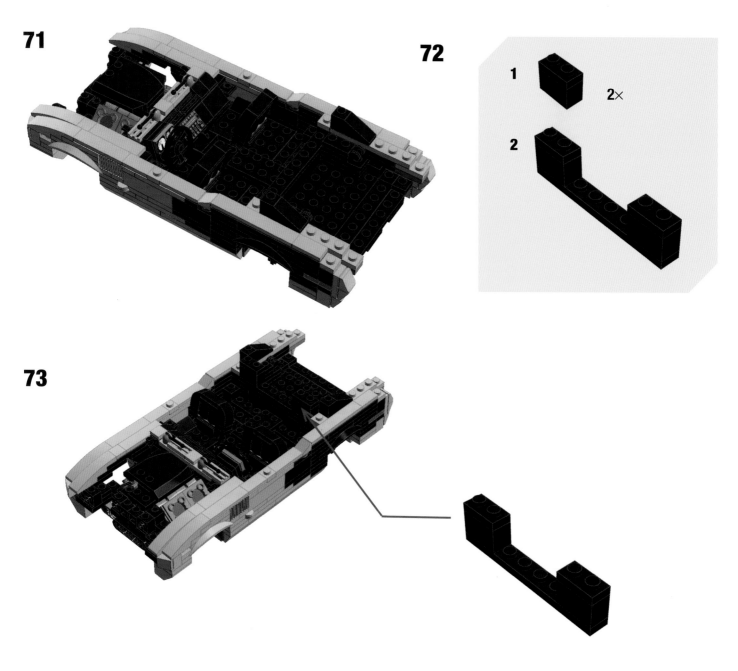

**74**

1

2

3

**75**

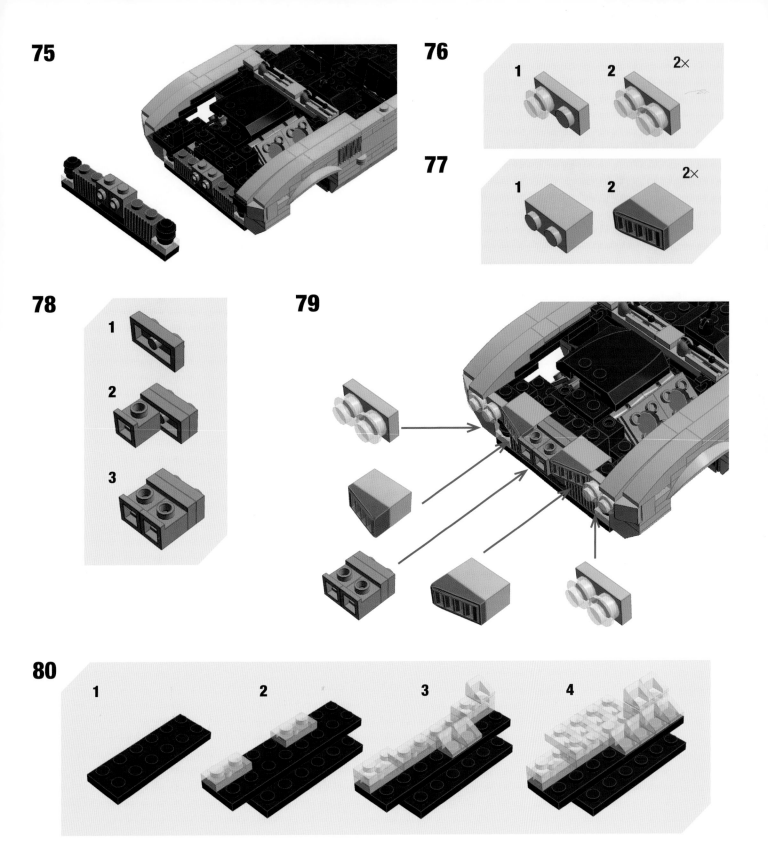

**76**

1  2  2×

**77**

1  2  2×

**78**

1
2
3

**79**

**80**

1  2  3  4

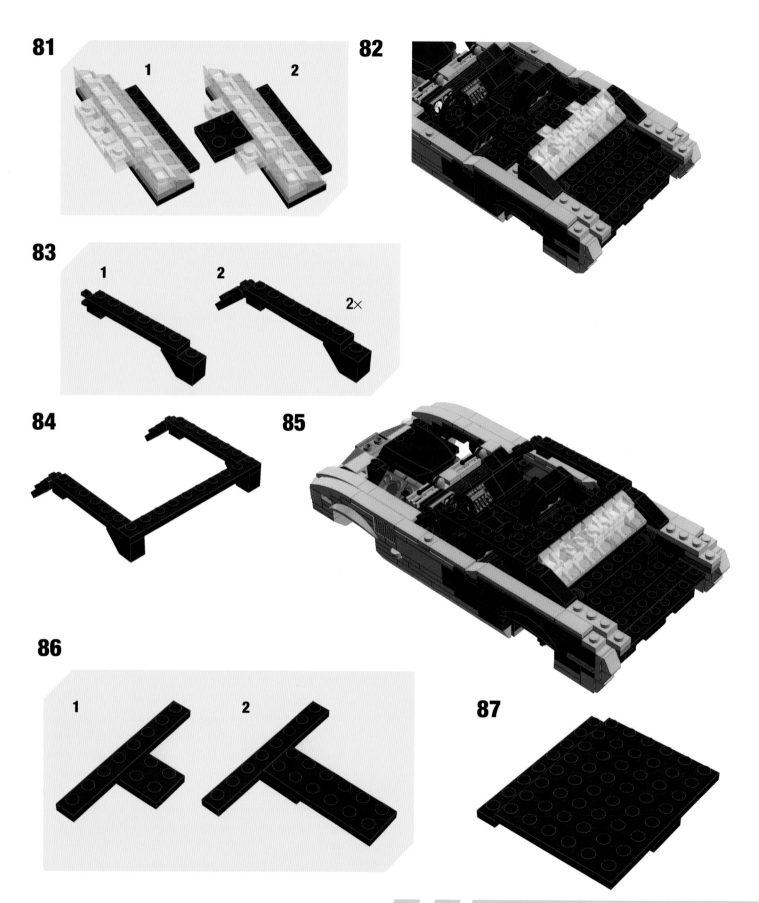

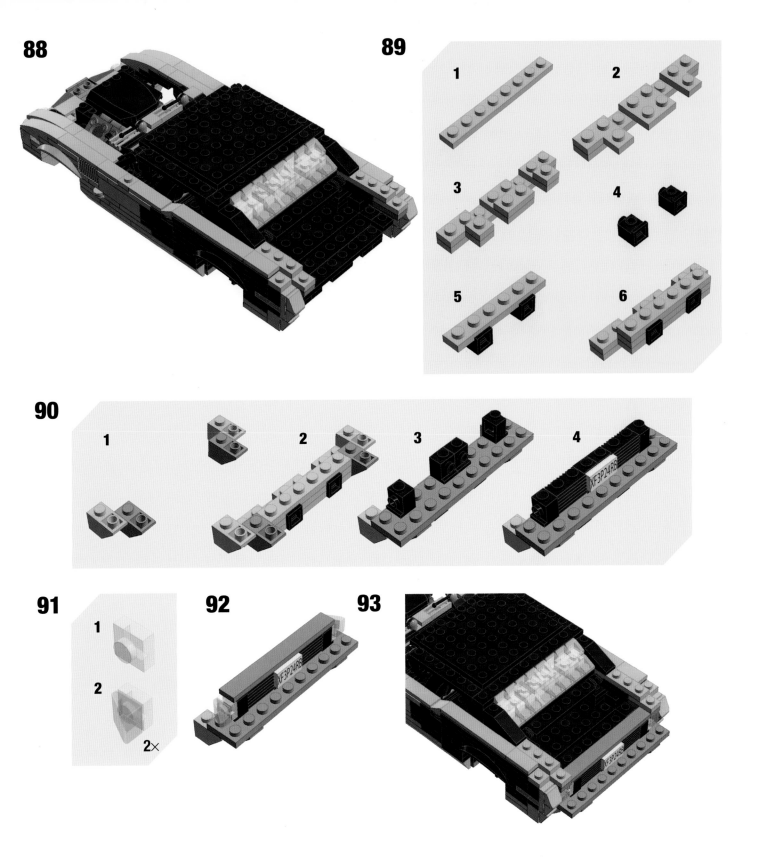

**88**

**89**
1
2
3
4
5
6

**90**
1
2
3
4

XF3P24RB

**91**
1
2
2×

**92**
XF3P24RB

**93**
XF3P24SC

**94**

1      2      3      4

**95**

**96**

1

2

3

4

**97**

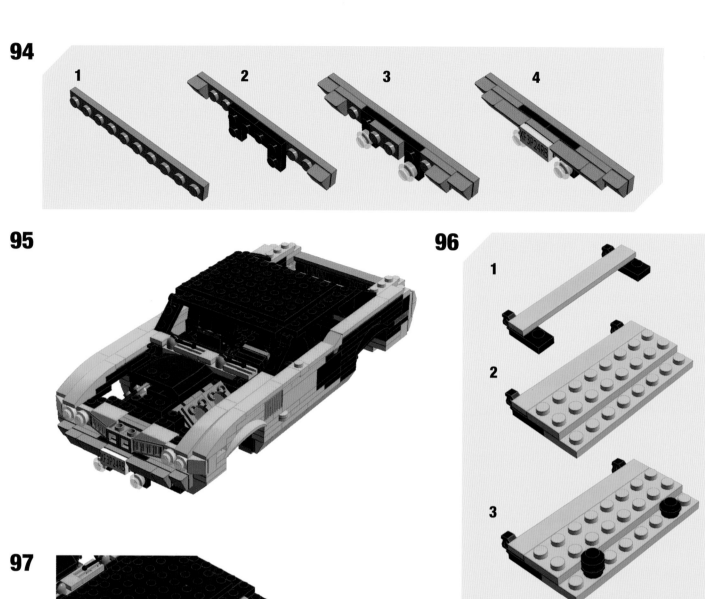
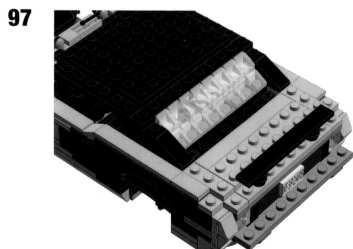
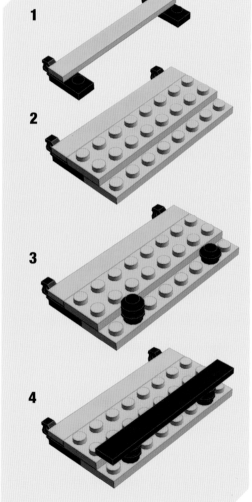

**98**

1      2             3

**99**

1                 2

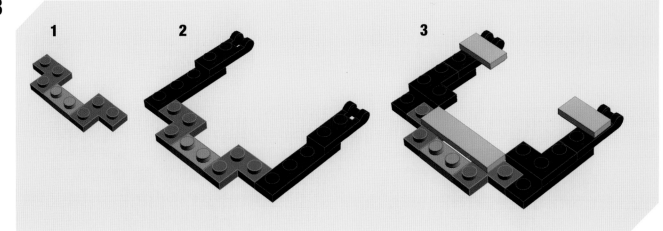

**100**

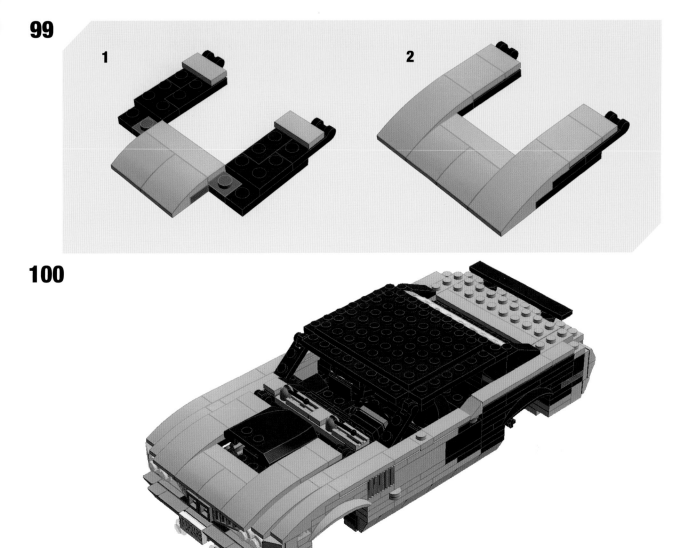

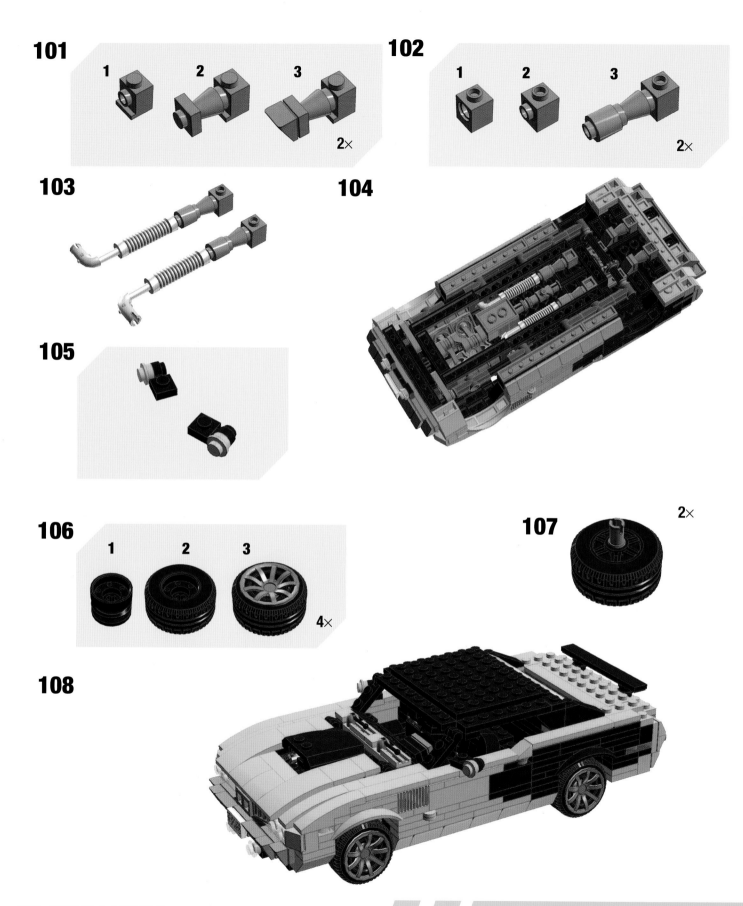

**101**

1  2  3

2×

**102**

1  2  3

2×

**103**

**104**

**105**

**106**

1  2  3

4×

**107**

2×

**108**

# GT Le MANS RACER

In the early 1960s, Henry Ford II courted Ferrari for the opportunity to purchase the company ahead of other automotive rivals. Ferrari had reportedly been keen on the deal, but Henry Ford II's offer was rebuffed by Enzo Ferrari due to disagreements over il Commendatore's desire to maintain directorial control over all of Ferrari's racing operations.

As grudge matches go, this was a doozy!

The Le Mans endurance race in France had become a Ferrari playground—it won six years straight from 1960 to 1965. Henry Ford II saw this as the place to strike at the heart of Ferrari and set about doing so with a Ford-powered and backed racing car—the GT40. Ford achieved its aim, winning from 1966 to 1969, and Ferrari was forced to sell the road-car business to FIAT while retaining control of the racing team.

In 2015, at the launch of the unexpected Ford GT supercar, the company announced that it would return to Le Mans the following year in celebration of the fiftieth anniversary of the 1966 1-2-3 win. Most commentators considered this to be a naïve ambition. Ford had obviously done its homework, selecting endurance-proven production components, including much of the 3.5L EcoBoost V-6 engine, along with robust prep work, and delivered on their promise. The four Ford Chip Ganassi factory team racers placed first, second, fourth, and ninth in the GTE Pro class.

The GT Le Mans racer is closely based on the limited-volume, road-going vehicle launched as a 2017 model year. A limited number of black and silver Le Mans 50 Year celebration road cars were made available following the 2016 race win.

| | |
|---|---|
| **COUNTRY OF ORIGIN:** | USA/Canada |
| **PRODUCTION:** | 2015–2016 |
| **NUMBER MADE:** | 4 chassis entered Le Mans 2016 |
| **LAYOUT / DRIVE:** | Mid engine / Rear-wheel drive |
| **ENGINE:** | 3.5L EcoBoost, 6 cylinders, V |
| **POWER / TORQUE:** | 600+ hp (450+ kW) / unspecified |
| **CONSTRUCTION / DOORS:** | Carbon-fiber unibody / 2-door coupe |

**Number of parts: 587**

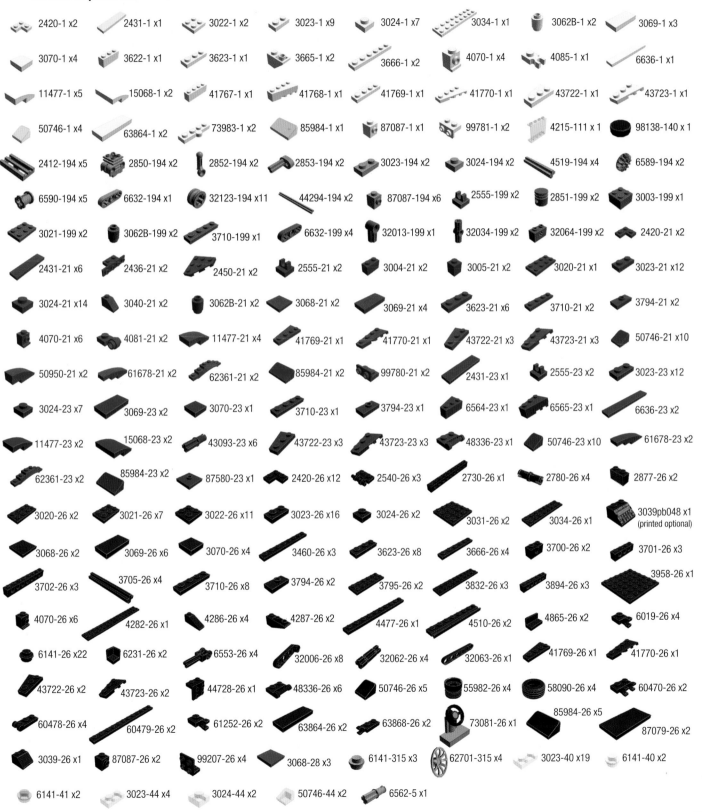

| | | | | | | | |
|---|---|---|---|---|---|---|---|
| 2420-1 x2 | 2431-1 x1 | 3022-1 x2 | 3023-1 x9 | 3024-1 x7 | 3034-1 x1 | 3062B-1 x2 | 3069-1 x3 |
| 3070-1 x4 | 3622-1 x1 | 3623-1 x1 | 3665-1 x2 | 3666-1 x2 | 4070-1 x4 | 4085-1 x1 | 6636-1 x1 |
| 11477-1 x5 | 15068-1 x2 | 41767-1 x1 | 41768-1 x1 | 41769-1 x1 | 41770-1 x1 | 43722-1 x1 | 43723-1 x1 |
| 50746-1 x4 | 63864-1 x2 | 73983-1 x2 | 85984-1 x1 | 87087-1 x1 | 99781-1 x2 | 4215-111 x 1 | 98138-140 x 1 |
| 2412-194 x5 | 2850-194 x2 | 2852-194 x2 | 2853-194 x2 | 3023-194 x2 | 3024-194 x2 | 4519-194 x4 | 6589-194 x2 |
| 6590-194 x5 | 6632-194 x1 | 32123-194 x11 | 44294-194 x2 | 87087-194 x6 | 2555-199 x2 | 2851-199 x2 | 3003-199 x1 |
| 3021-199 x2 | 3062B-199 x2 | 3710-199 x1 | 6632-199 x4 | 32013-199 x1 | 32034-199 x2 | 32064-199 x2 | 2420-21 x2 |
| 2431-21 x6 | 2436-21 x2 | 2450-21 x2 | 2555-21 x2 | 3004-21 x2 | 3005-21 x2 | 3020-21 x1 | 3023-21 x12 |
| 3024-21 x14 | 3040-21 x2 | 3062B-21 x2 | 3068-21 x2 | 3069-21 x4 | 3623-21 x6 | 3710-21 x2 | 3794-21 x2 |
| 4070-21 x6 | 4081-21 x2 | 11477-21 x4 | 41769-21 x1 | 41770-21 x1 | 43722-21 x3 | 43723-21 x3 | 50746-21 x10 |
| 50950-21 x2 | 61678-21 x2 | 62361-21 x2 | 85984-21 x2 | 99780-21 x2 | 2431-23 x1 | 2555-23 x2 | 3023-23 x12 |
| 3024-23 x7 | 3069-23 x2 | 3070-23 x1 | 3710-23 x1 | 3794-23 x1 | 6564-23 x1 | 6565-23 x1 | 6636-23 x2 |
| 11477-23 x2 | 15068-23 x2 | 43093-23 x6 | 43722-23 x3 | 43723-23 x3 | 48336-23 x1 | 50746-23 x10 | 61678-23 x2 |
| 62361-23 x2 | 85984-23 x2 | 87580-23 x1 | 2420-26 x12 | 2540-26 x3 | 2730-26 x1 | 2780-26 x4 | 2877-26 x2 |
| 3020-26 x2 | 3021-26 x7 | 3022-26 x11 | 3023-26 x16 | 3024-26 x2 | 3031-26 x2 | 3034-26 x1 | 3039pb048 x1 (printed optional) |
| 3068-26 x2 | 3069-26 x6 | 3070-26 x4 | 3460-26 x3 | 3623-26 x8 | 3666-26 x4 | 3700-26 x2 | 3701-26 x3 |
| 3702-26 x3 | 3705-26 x4 | 3710-26 x8 | 3794-26 x2 | 3795-26 x2 | 3832-26 x3 | 3894-26 x3 | 3958-26 x1 |
| 4070-26 x6 | 4282-26 x1 | 4286-26 x4 | 4287-26 x2 | 4477-26 x1 | 4510-26 x2 | 4865-26 x2 | 6019-26 x4 |
| 6141-26 x22 | 6231-26 x2 | 6553-26 x4 | 32006-26 x8 | 32062-26 x4 | 32063-26 x1 | 41769-26 x1 | 41770-26 x1 |
| 43722-26 x2 | 43723-26 x2 | 44728-26 x1 | 48336-26 x6 | 50746-26 x5 | 55982-26 x4 | 58090-26 x4 | 60470-26 x2 |
| 60478-26 x4 | 60479-26 x2 | 61252-26 x2 | 63864-26 x2 | 63868-26 x2 | 73081-26 x1 | 85984-26 x5 | 87079-26 x2 |
| 3039-26 x1 | 87087-26 x2 | 99207-26 x4 | 3068-28 x3 | 6141-315 x3 | 62701-315 x4 | 3023-40 x19 | 6141-40 x2 |
| 6141-41 x2 | 3023-44 x4 | 3024-44 x2 | 50746-44 x2 | 6562-5 x1 | | | |

**159**

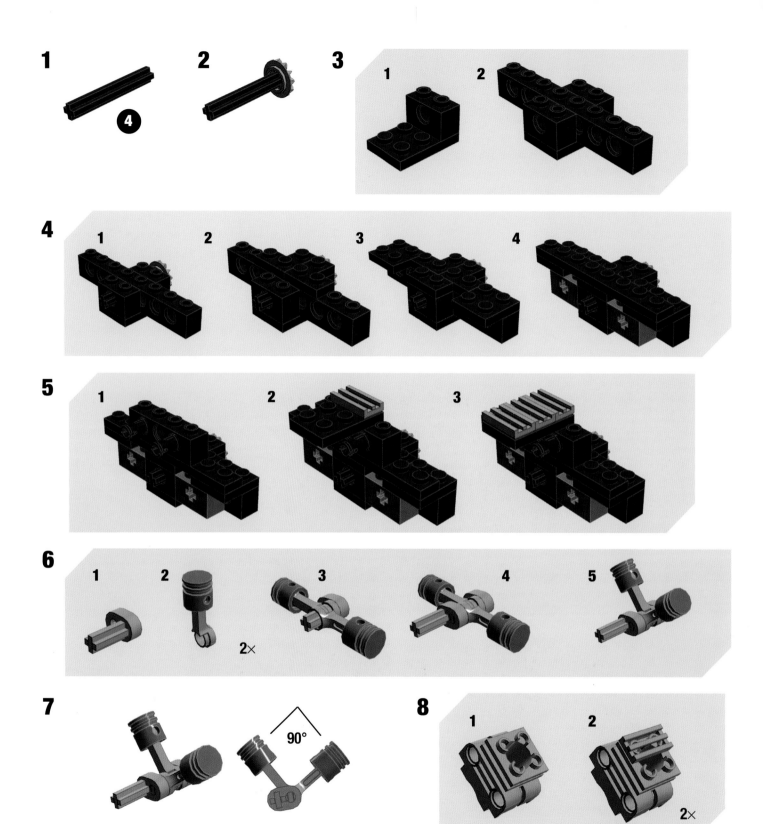

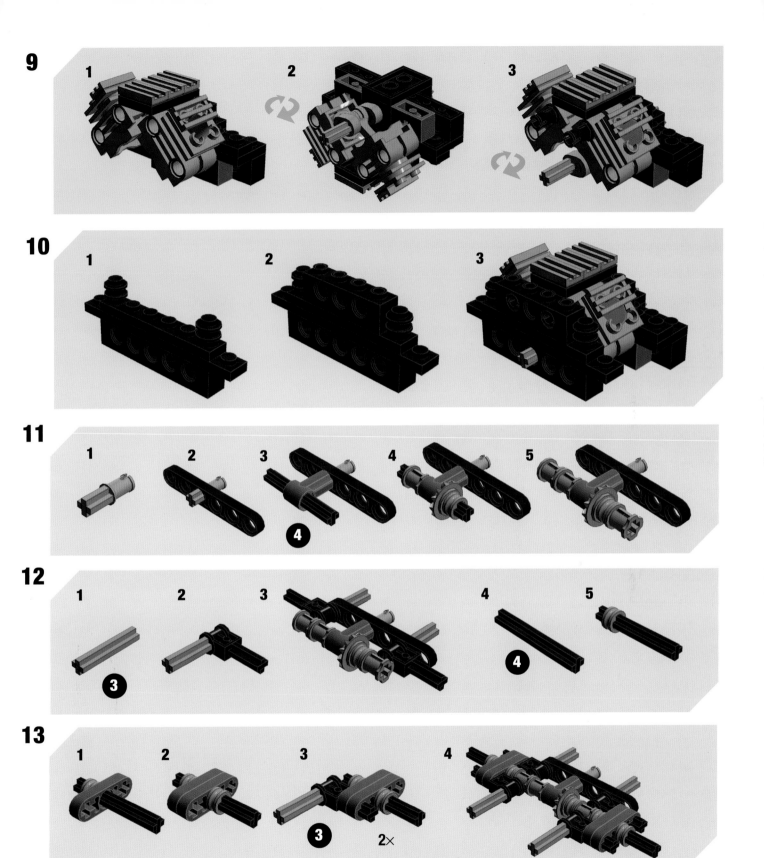

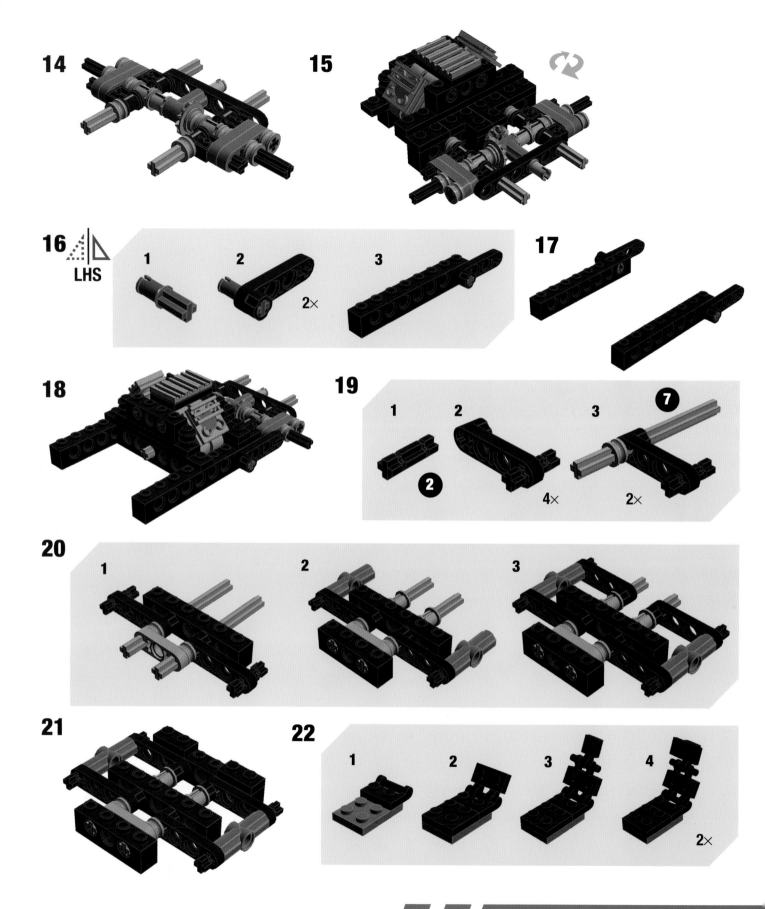

**14**

**15**

**16** LHS

1

2

3

2×

**17**

**18**

**19**

1

2

2

3

4×

7

2×

**20**

1

2

3

**21**

**22**

1

2

3

4

2×

**23**

**24**

**25**

1

2

**26**

1

2

**27**

**28**

**29**

**30**

1

2

2×

3

4

**31**

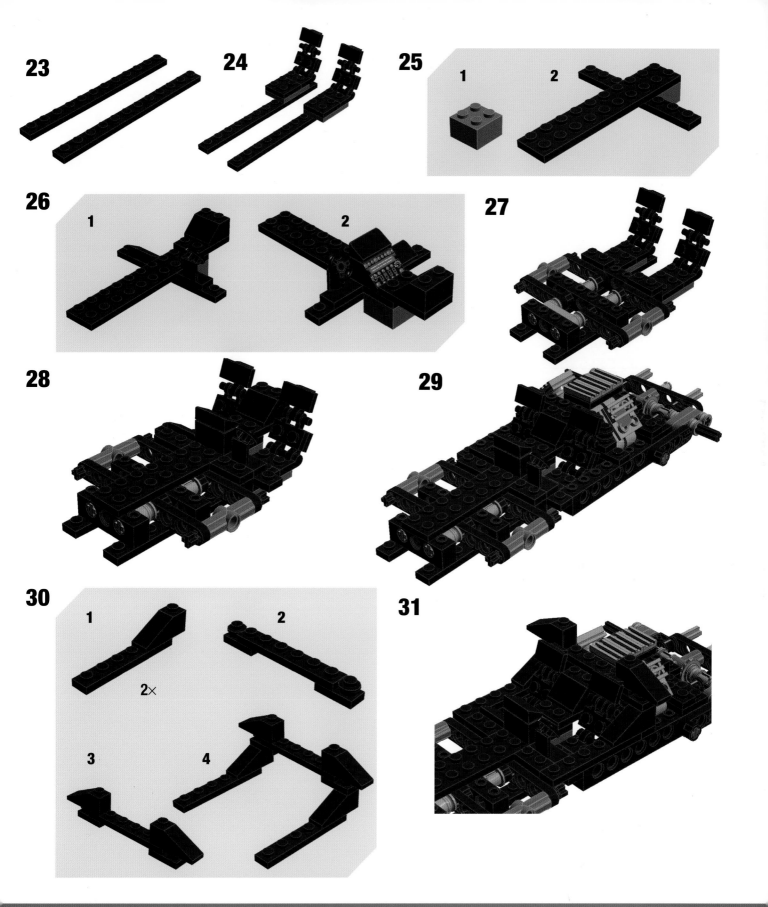

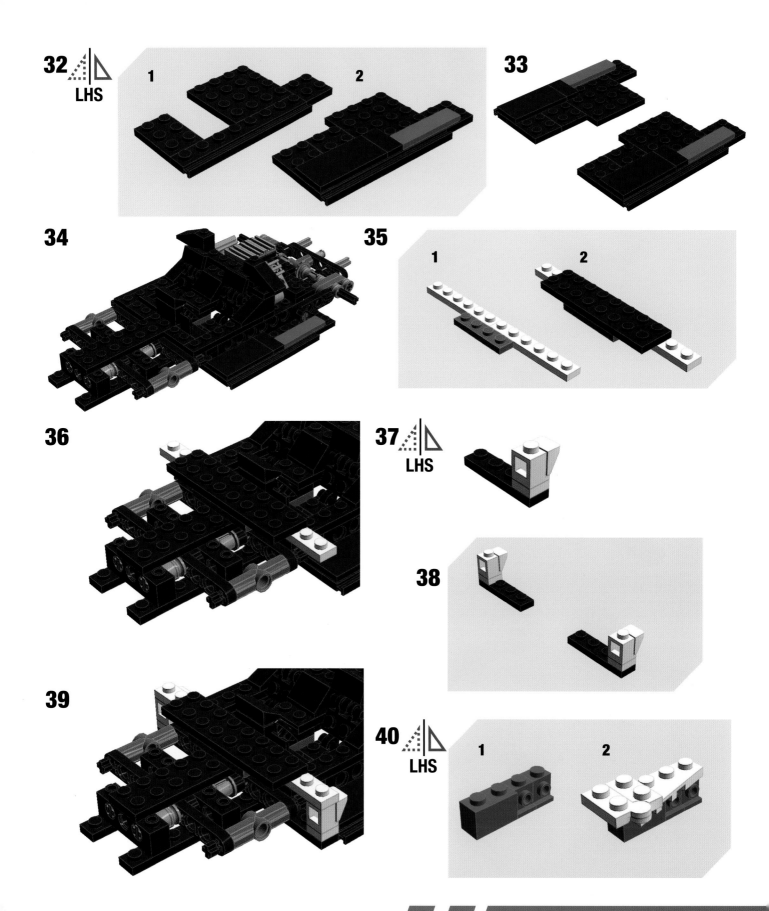

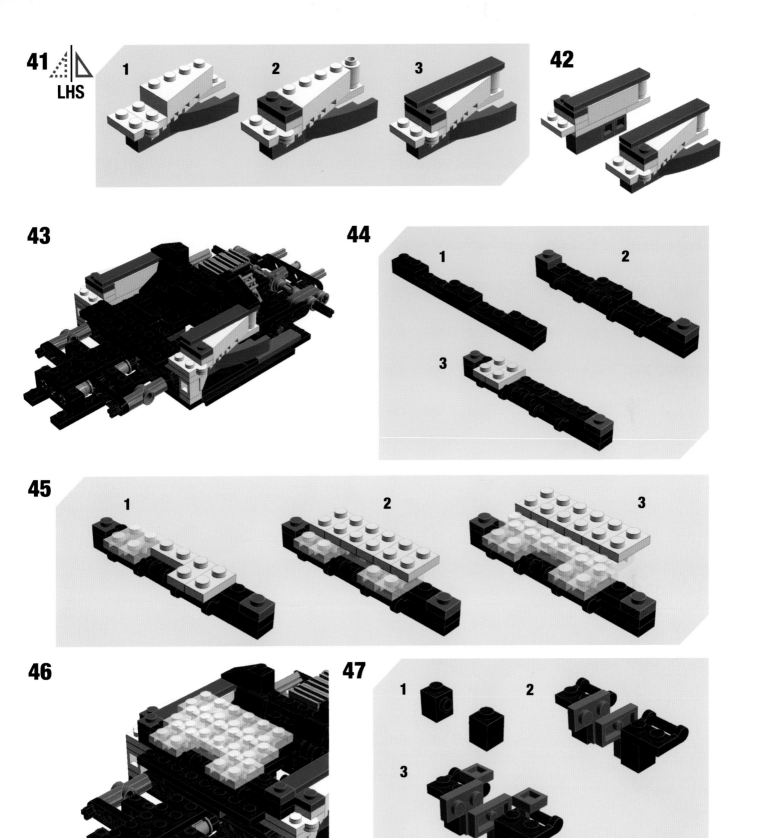

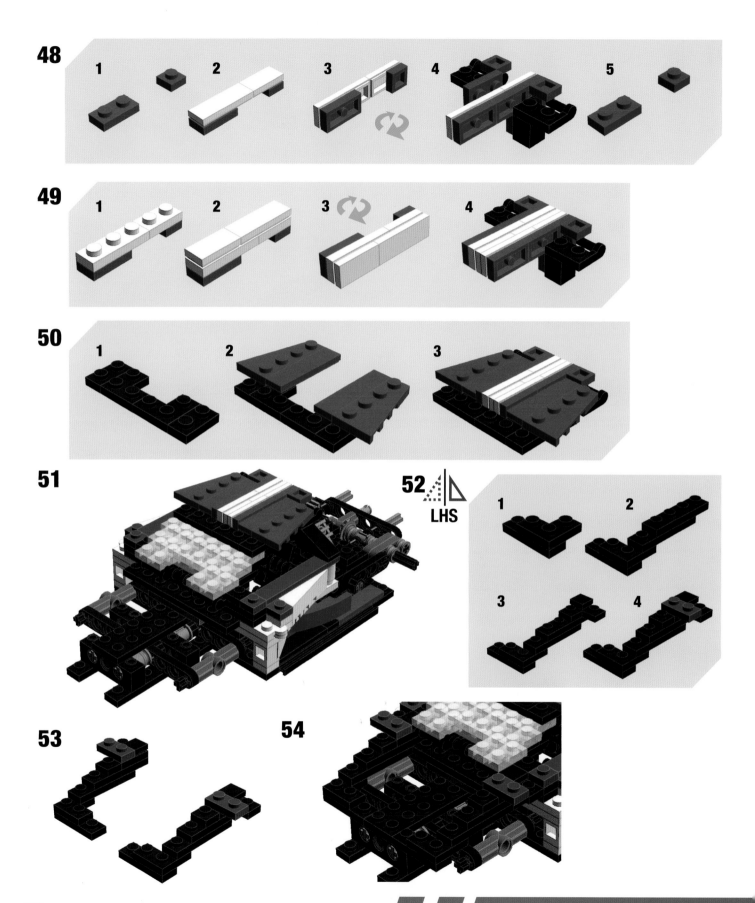

**55**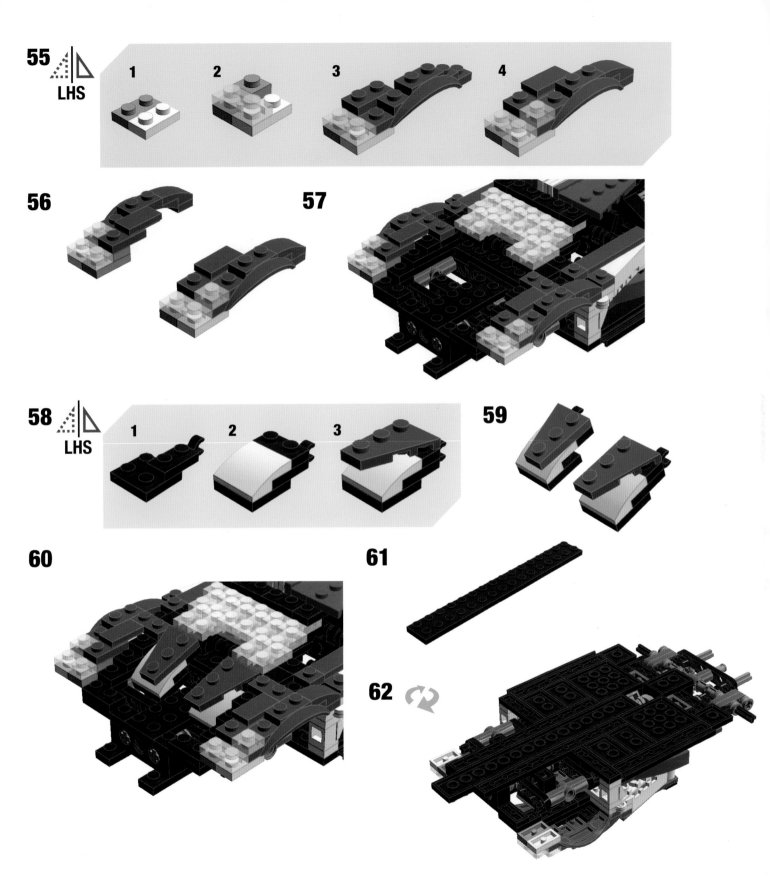

**LHS**

**1**  **2**  **3**  **4**

**56**

**57**

**58**

**LHS**

**1**  **2**  **3**

**59**

**60**

**61**

**62**

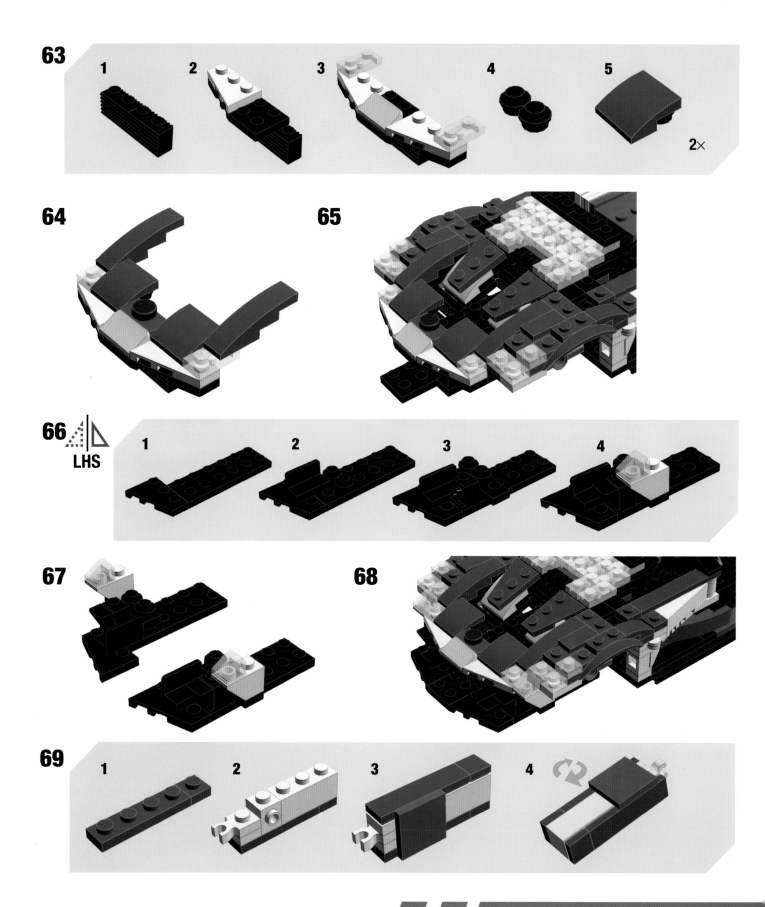

**70**

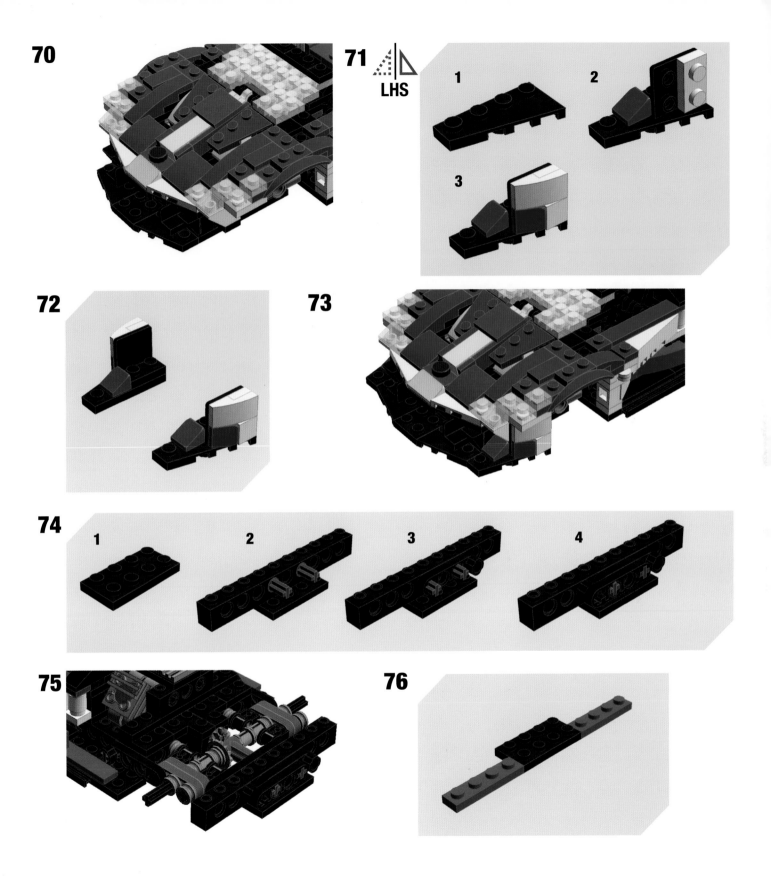

**71**

LHS

1

2

3

**72**

**73**

**74**

1

2

3

4

**75**

**76**

**77**

1

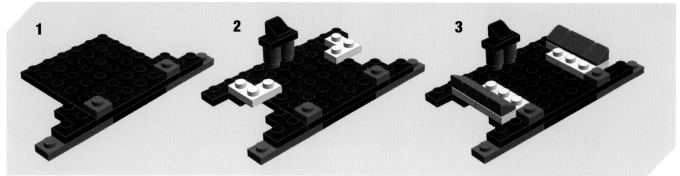

2

3

**78**

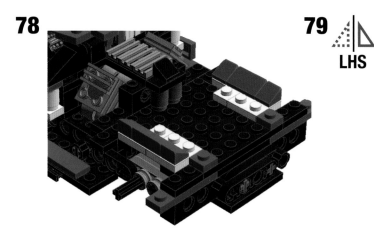

**79**
LHS

1

2

3

4

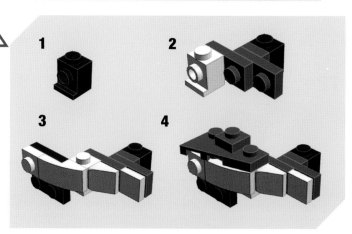

**80**
LHS

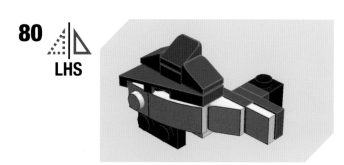

**81**

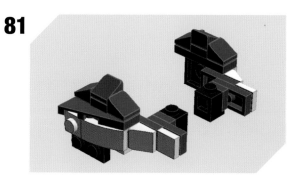

**82**

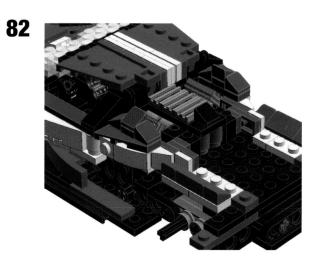

**83**

1

2

3

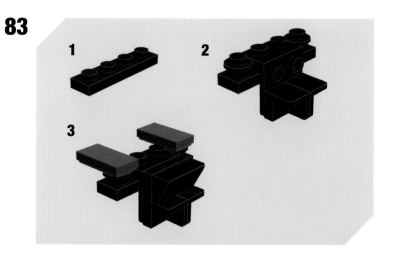

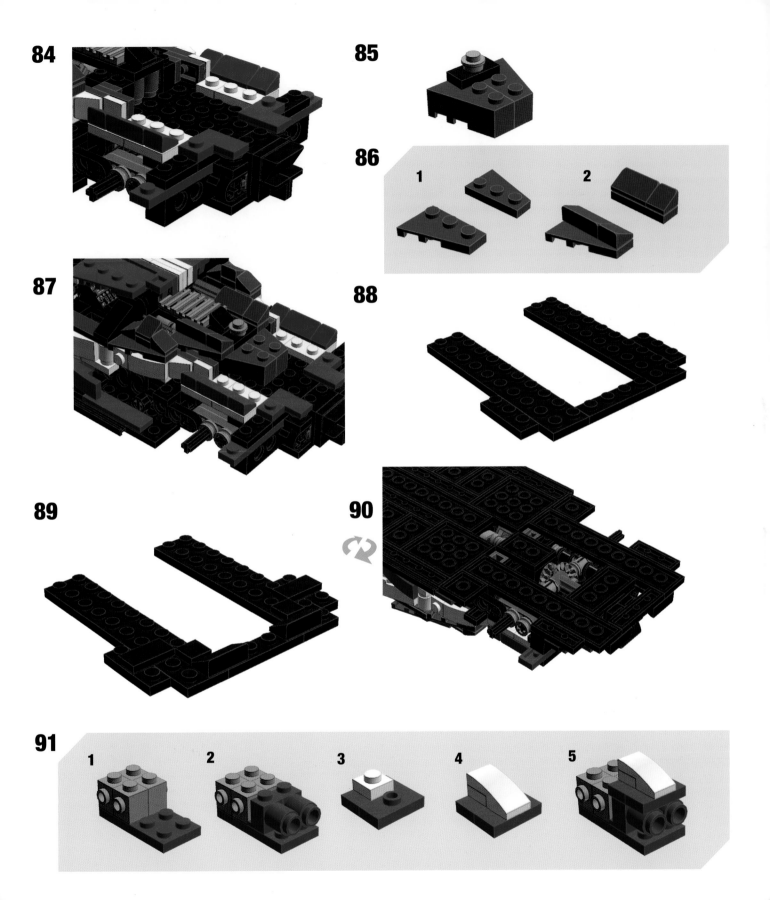

84

85

86
1    2

87

88

89

90

91
1    2    3    4    5

**92**

2×

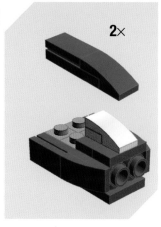

**93**

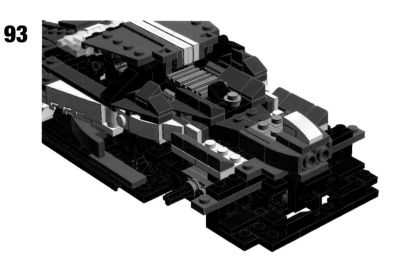

**94**
LHS

1     2     3     4     5

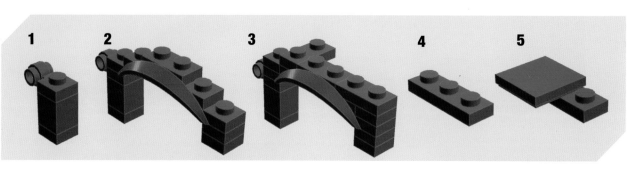

**95**
LHS

1     2     3     4

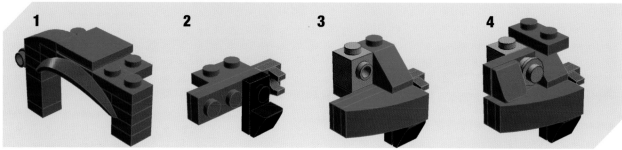

**96**
LHS

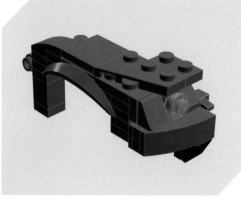

**97**

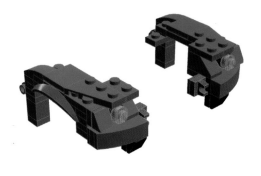

**98**

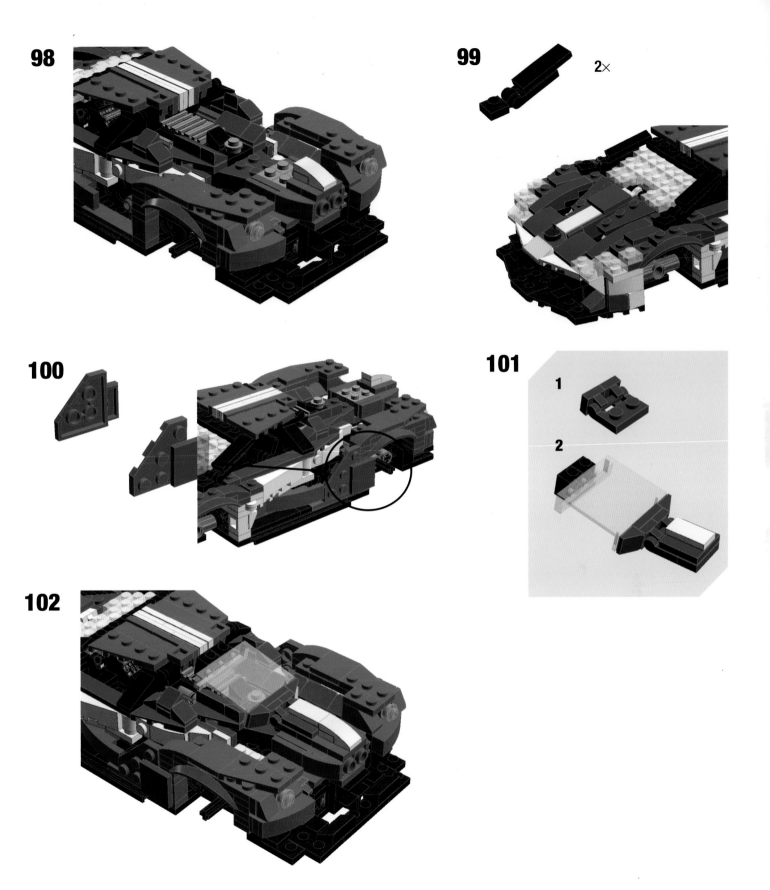

**99**

2×

**100**

**101**

1

2

**102**

**103**

1 2 3 4

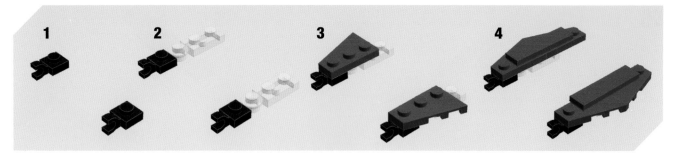

**104**

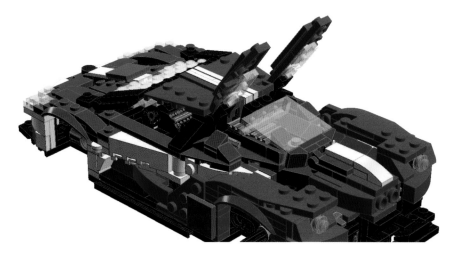

**105**

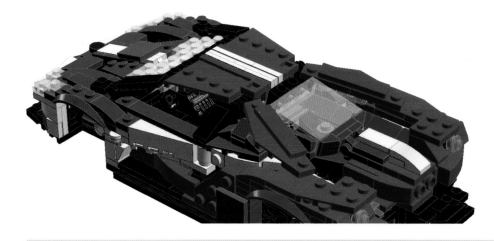

**106**

1 2 3 4

**107**

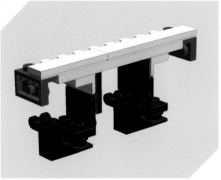

**108**

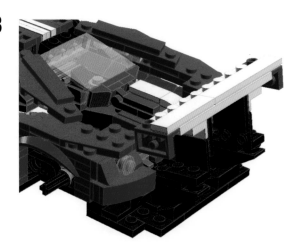

**109**

1
2
3
4×

**110**

2×

**111**

# BUGATTI
# VEYRON EB 16.4

Build the greatest car ever—this was the challenge laid down by Volkswagen Group Chief Ferdinand Piëch (grandson of Ferry Porsche and the creator of the mighty Porsche 917 Racer).

The Veyron was to be the most powerful (1,001 hp/736 kW), the fastest (253.81 mph/408.47 km/h), and the quickest (0 to 62 mph/100 km/h in 2.46 seconds) and set new benchmarks for almost all performance attributes.

The engine is a mighty 8.0L and 16 cylinders, boosted by four turbochargers. The twin-clutch transmission has 7 speeds and drives through all four wheels. The car is fitted with ten radiators to cool various systems.

To reach the 254 miles per hour (408 km/h) top speed, a special mode must be entered with the vehicle stationary. This driving mode uses the deployable rear wing from speeds between 137 and 213 miles per hour (220 and 343 km/h) to aid stability. Beyond this speed, the car lowers closer to the ground and retracts the spoilers to decrease drag—at the expense of downforce! Driving at 249 miles per hour (400 km/h) probably isn't a good idea on a public road. In fact, there are very few places where this can be done safely. Former BBC *Top Gear* presenter James May drove a Veyron at 259.49 miles per hour (417.61 km/h) at Volkswagen's Ehra-Lessien high-speed test track. The very steep banking on the track allows the car to run at very high speeds without scrubbing the tires through curves and losing speed—though this also pushes the driver down firmly into his or her seat!

All this car doesn't come cheap, and when sold new, the Bugatti Veyron cost about $1 million, though later exclusive versions were sold for more than twice this amount.

In 2016, Bugatti announced the replacement for the Veyron—a very similarly conceived V-16 hypercar called the Chiron.

**COUNTRY OF ORIGIN:** France

**PRODUCTION:** 2005–2015

**NUMBER MADE:** 450

**LAYOUT / DRIVE:** Mid engine / All-wheel drive

**ENGINE:** 7,992 cc, 16 cylinders, V

**POWER / TORQUE:** 1,001 hp (750 kW) / 1,100 lb-ft (1,500 Nm)

**CONSTRUCTION / DOORS:** Carbon-fiber monocoque / 2-door coupe

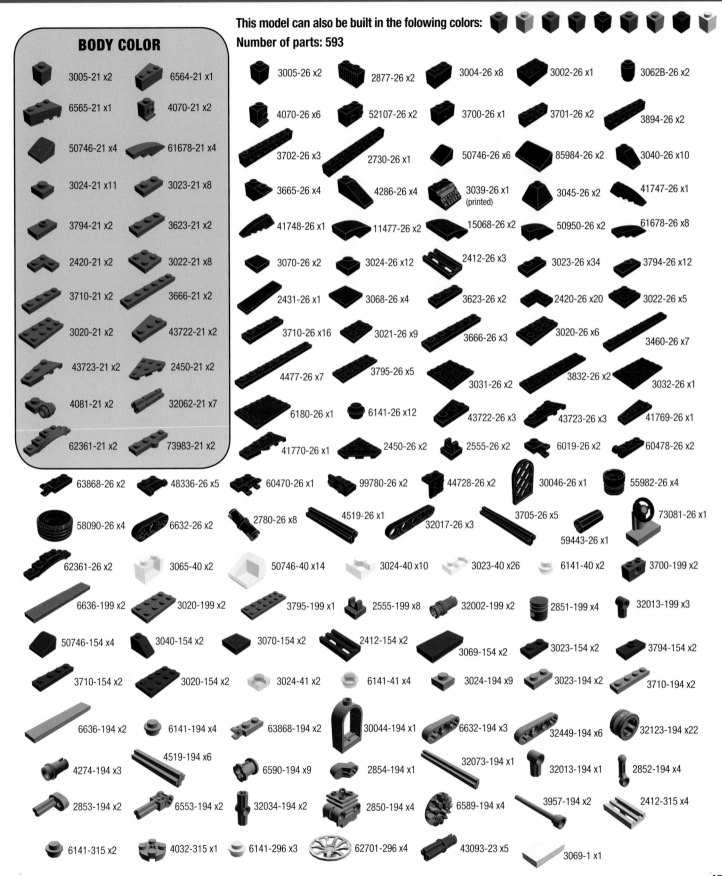

This model can also be built in the following colors:
Number of parts: 593

## BODY COLOR

3005-21 x2
6564-21 x1
6565-21 x1
4070-21 x2
50746-21 x4
61678-21 x4
3024-21 x11
3023-21 x8
3794-21 x2
3623-21 x2
2420-21 x2
3022-21 x8
3710-21 x2
3666-21 x2
3020-21 x2
43722-21 x2
43723-21 x2
2450-21 x2
4081-21 x2
32062-21 x7
62361-21 x2
73983-21 x2

3005-26 x2
2877-26 x2
3004-26 x8
3002-26 x1
3062B-26 x2
4070-26 x6
52107-26 x2
3700-26 x1
3701-26 x2
3894-26 x2
3702-26 x3
2730-26 x1
50746-26 x6
85984-26 x2
3040-26 x10
3665-26 x4
4286-26 x4
3039-26 x1 (printed)
3045-26 x2
41747-26 x1
41748-26 x1
11477-26 x2
15068-26 x2
50950-26 x2
61678-26 x8
3070-26 x2
3024-26 x12
2412-26 x3
3023-26 x34
3794-26 x12
2431-26 x1
3068-26 x4
3623-26 x2
2420-26 x20
3022-26 x5
3710-26 x16
3021-26 x9
3666-26 x3
3020-26 x6
3460-26 x7
4477-26 x7
3795-26 x5
3031-26 x2
3832-26 x2
3032-26 x1
6180-26 x1
6141-26 x12
43722-26 x3
43723-26 x3
41769-26 x1
41770-26 x1
2450-26 x2
2555-26 x2
6019-26 x2
60478-26 x2
63868-26 x2
48336-26 x5
60470-26 x1
99780-26 x2
44728-26 x2
30046-26 x1
55982-26 x4
58090-26 x4
6632-26 x2
2780-26 x8
4519-26 x1
32017-26 x3
3705-26 x5
73081-26 x1
59443-26 x1
62361-26 x2
3065-40 x2
50746-40 x14
3024-40 x10
3023-40 x26
6141-40 x2
3700-199 x2
6636-199 x2
3020-199 x2
3795-199 x1
2555-199 x8
32002-199 x2
2851-199 x4
32013-199 x3
50746-154 x4
3040-154 x2
3070-154 x2
2412-154 x2
3069-154 x2
3023-154 x2
3794-154 x2
3710-154 x2
3020-154 x2
3024-41 x2
6141-41 x4
3024-194 x9
3023-194 x2
3710-194 x2
6636-194 x2
6141-194 x4
63868-194 x2
30044-194 x1
6632-194 x3
32449-194 x6
32123-194 x22
4519-194 x6
4274-194 x3
6590-194 x9
2854-194 x1
32073-194 x1
32013-194 x1
2852-194 x4
2853-194 x2
6553-194 x2
32034-194 x2
2850-194 x4
6589-194 x4
3957-194 x2
2412-315 x4
6141-315 x2
4032-315 x1
6141-296 x3
62701-296 x4
43093-23 x5
3069-1 x1

**1**

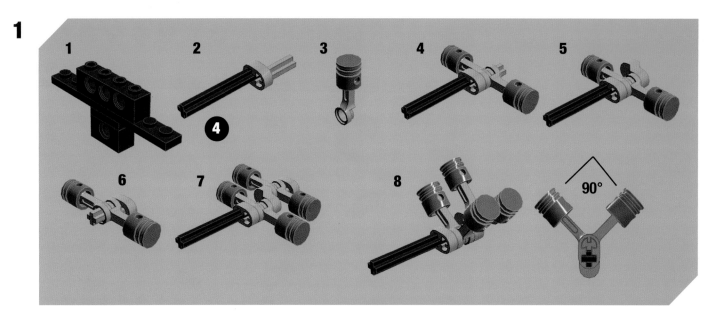

**2**

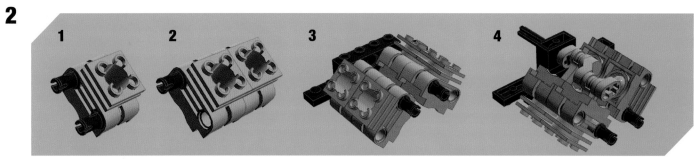

**3**

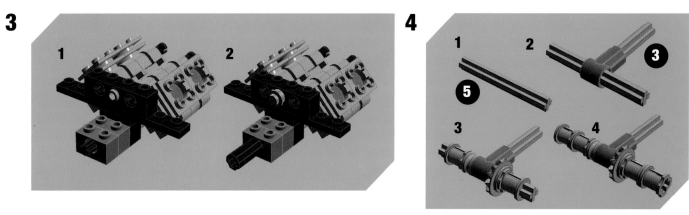

**4**

**5**

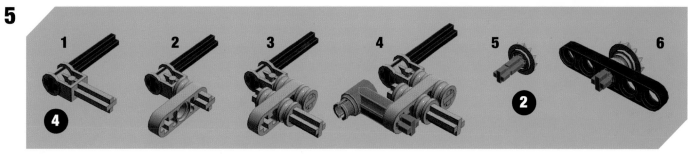

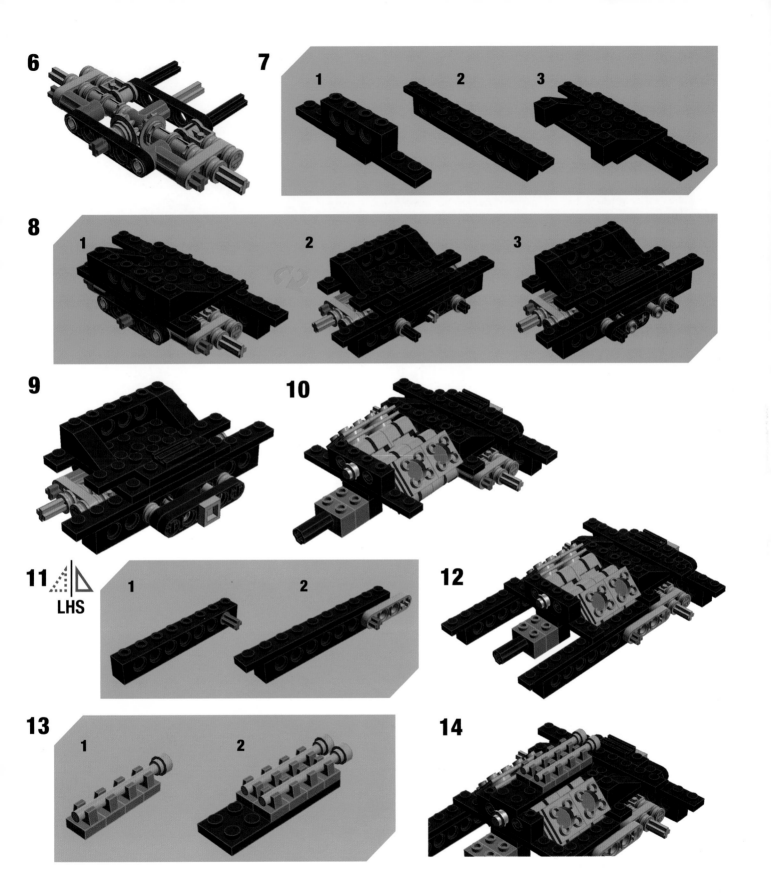

**6**

**7**
1     2     3

**8**
1     2     3

**9**

**10**

**11**
LHS
1     2

**12**

**13**
1     2

**14**

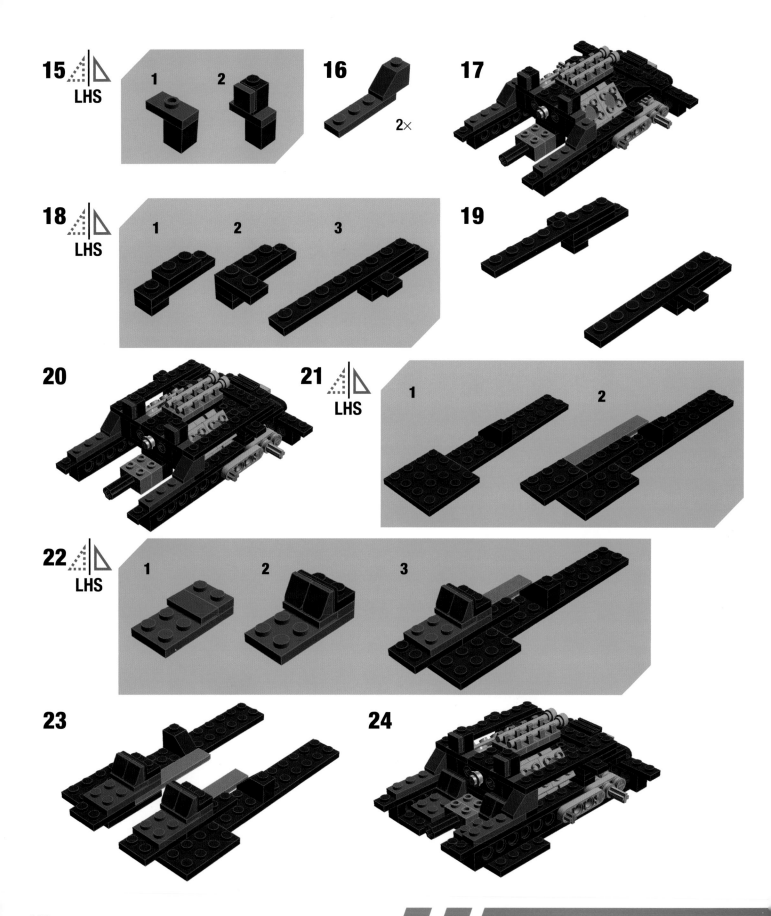

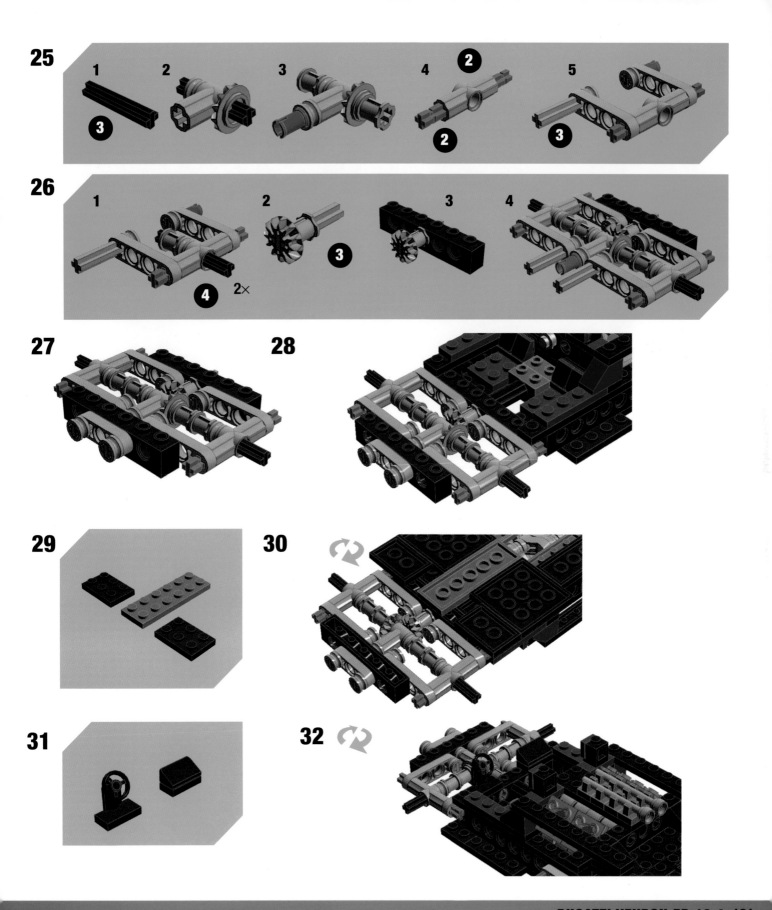

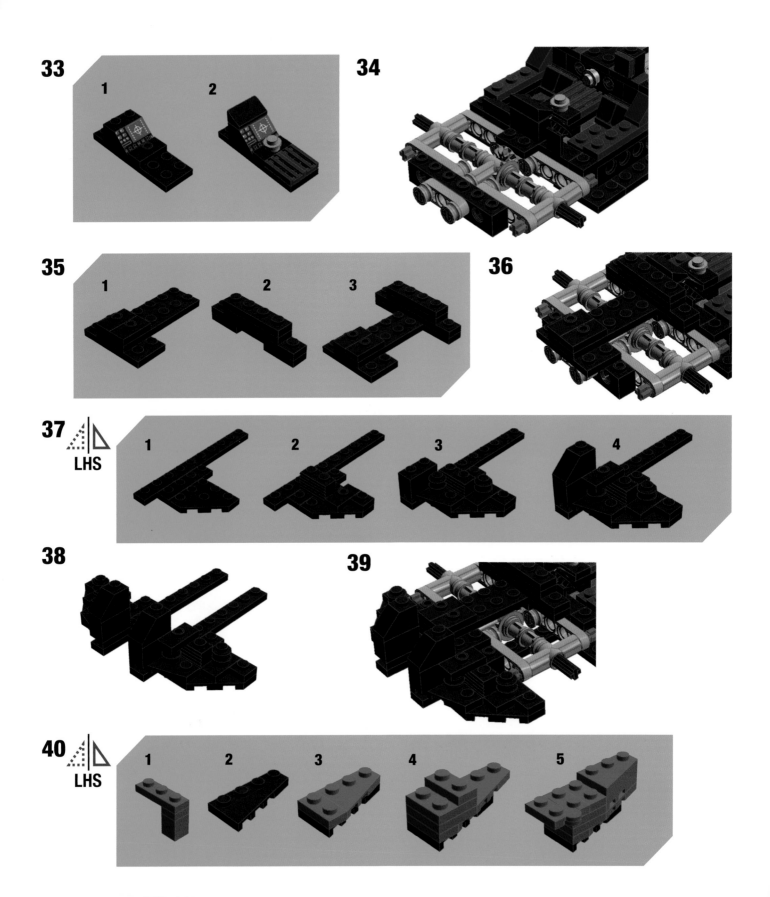

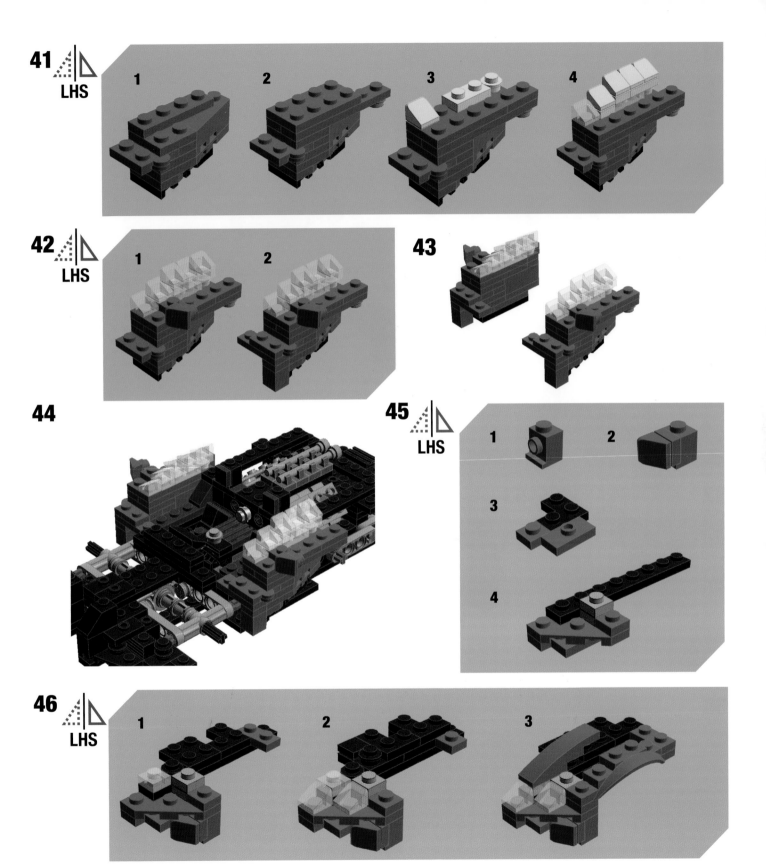

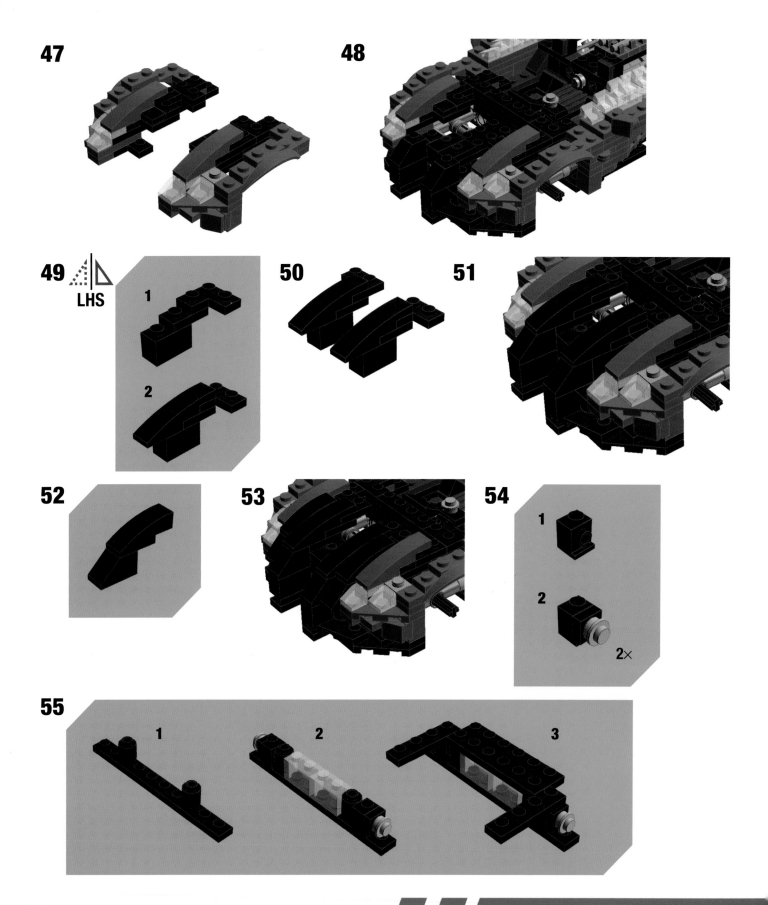

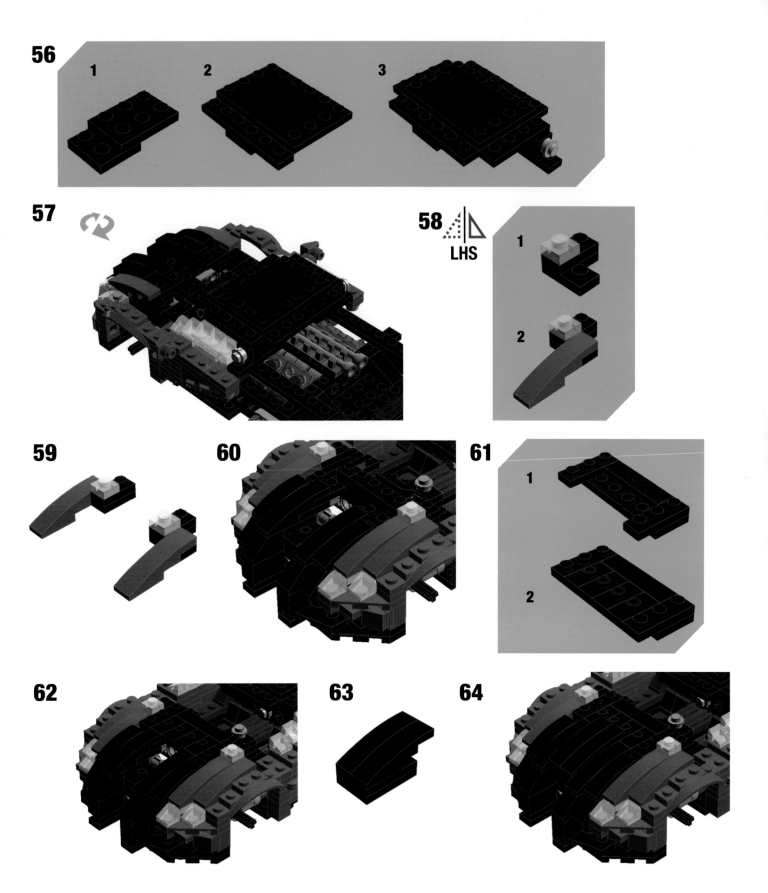

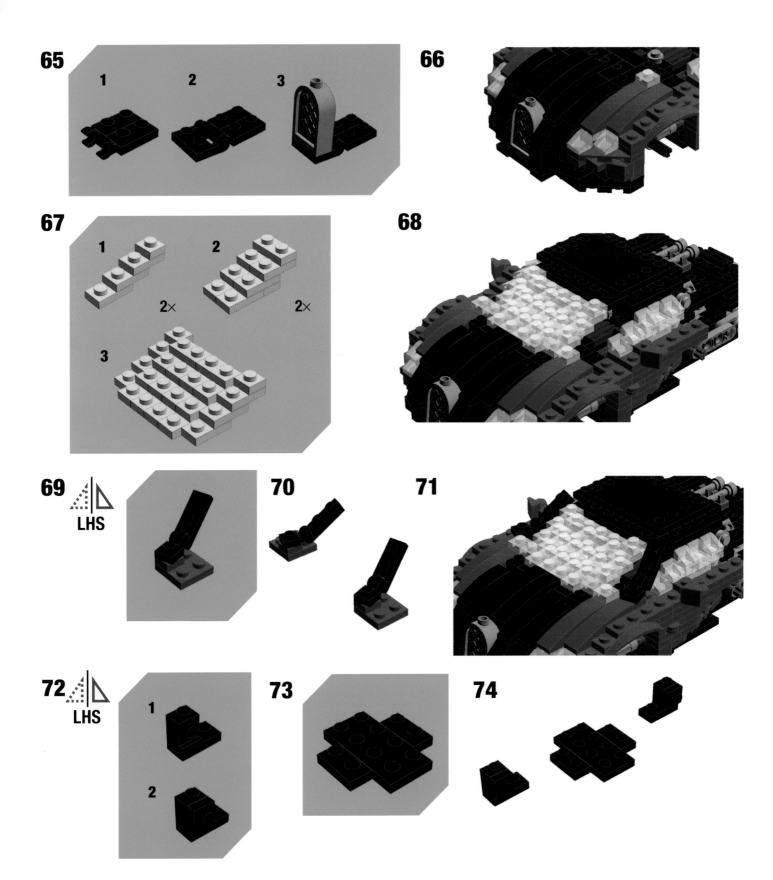

**65**

1    2    3

**66**

**67**

1    2

2×    2×

3

**68**

**69** LHS

**70**    **71**

**72** LHS

1

2

**73**    **74**

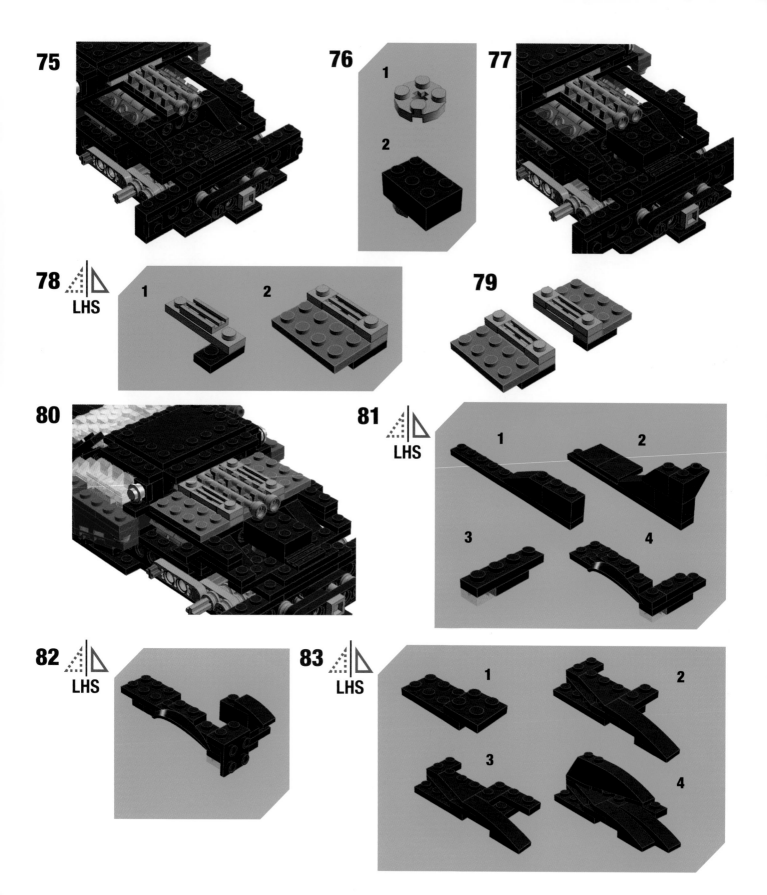

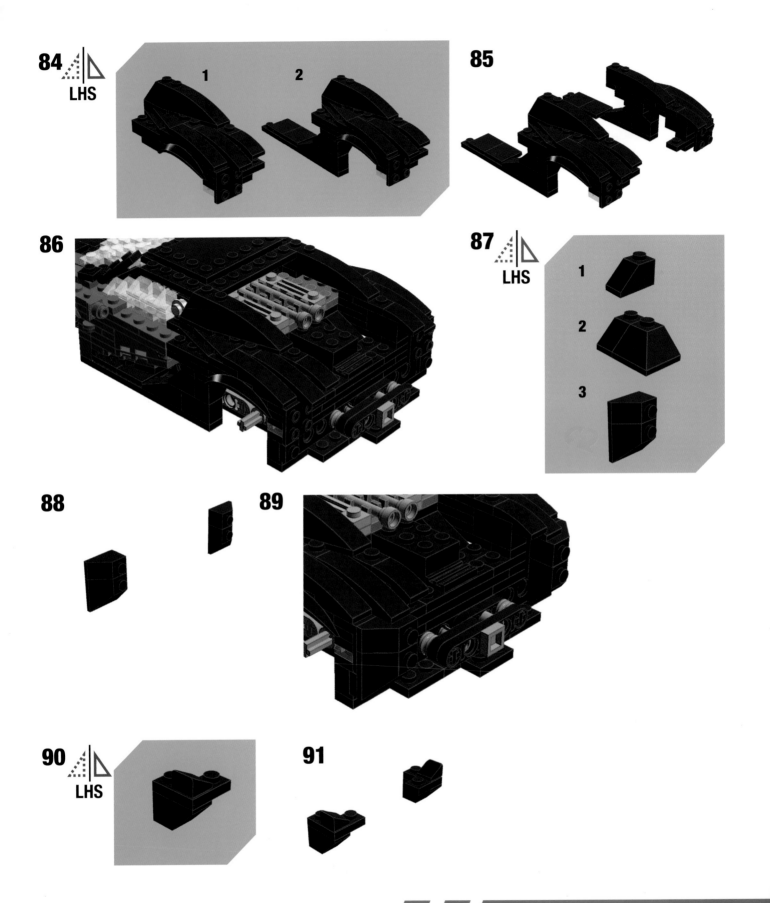

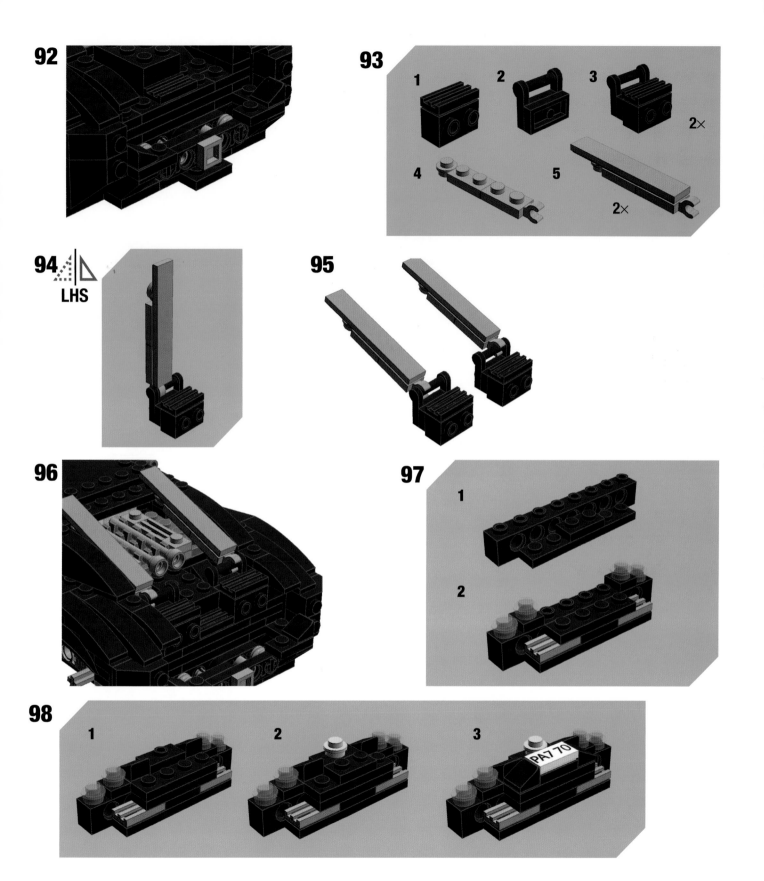

**92**

**93**
1
2
3
2×
4
5
2×

**94** LHS

**95**

**96**

**97**
1
2

**98**
1
2
3
PA770

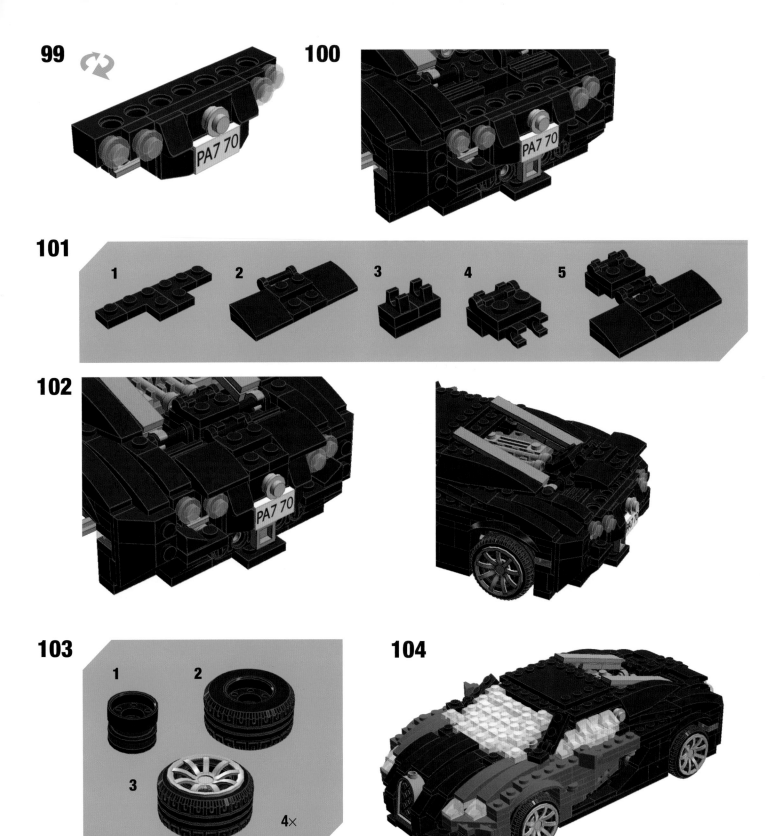

**99**

**100**

**101**

1

2

3

4

5

**102**

**103**

1

2

3

4×

**104**

# RESOURCES

## COMMUNITY

One of the great things about LEGO® is the worldwide community. There are LEGO Clubs in almost every country where LEGO is sold. Furthermore, if you are interested in a particular LEGO theme or creation type (like cars), there is likely a group on the internet that caters to this interest. The photo-sharing website Flickr is home to many specialist LEGO interest groups. The following websites may be useful starting points:

Official LEGO website: www.lego.com

Bricklink (part purchase): www.bricklink.com/v2/main.page

News and amazing creations of all types: www.brothers-brick.com

Extensive online community: www.eurobricks.com/forum

LEGO cars and other vehicles: www.thelegocarblog.com

## I DON'T HAVE ANY TECHNIC®— HOW CAN I BUILD THE COMPLEX MODELS?

To this good question, I have two answers:

1.  If your LEGO collection lacks any of the pieces required to build the model, you can buy them online. You can buy parts directly from the LEGO Company via the LEGO Shop@Home service—a place to purchase full LEGO sets, but also spare parts. This website is available across most of Europe, Asia, and the Americas. You can also purchase bricks via a service called Bricklink (see link above). Bricklink is a web service for thousands of individual stores around the world. Most will be able to supply common parts while others will also be able to supply specialist and rare parts. The LEGO Company has no affiliation with Bricklink, so there are more risks associated with pricing, purchase, and shipping.

2.  Many of the Intermediate and Advanced builds include Technic system suspension and engines. Understanding that both part availability and complexity/dexterity issues may discourage the building of these cars, it may please you to know that prior to designing these intricate assemblies, I nonetheless still needed my cars to have wheels attached, and so simpler techniques were employed. For most of the cars in this book, a variation of the following assembly should suffice:

## PART SUBSTITUTIONS

You may also find that you need parts that are unavailable from LEGO® or a third-party vendor. If this is the case, remember LEGO is a pretty adaptable building medium—there is always a way to build an assembly of parts other than the one shown here. Use your imagination and try with the parts you have access to. This is what expert MOC builders do every time they design their own models. It is the essence of their creativity.

## DETAILS AND CUSTOMIZATION

As you progress through the models, you will observe that they employ different part and assembly solutions for systems that might be common between vehicles. In particular, LEGO has wheels and tires that are available in close approximate geometric measurements. Though these wheels have a specific millimetric measure, it is much simpler to refer to them by their approximate LEGO part dimension.

In this book, most of the smaller models use wheels and tire combinations approximating 3-studs (24mm, or 1 inch), in various widths. Unfortunately, this does not quite mean that they will fit inside a 3-stud gap—so creative solutions are required to provide close-fitting wheel arches that nonetheless allow the wheel to spin freely. For the larger Miniland-scale cars, wheel and tire combinations approximating 4-studs (32mm, or 1¼ inches) are used; they closely fit a 4-stud gap. When building any of these models, please use the wheels and tires you have available. Not only that, there are a variety of creative ways of designing fancy wheel trims or hubcaps, and I encourage you to select designs that suit your style, as would a customizer in real life.

32mm: 55982 & 58090          24mm: 18976 & 18977

Most of the models in this book have been created to an exact specification of vehicle. The Porsche 911 is a case in point. There have been a great variety of 911s over fifty years. Each model is different. Even within a single year of production, there is considerable variation in details—wheels, spoilers, light units, seat designs, rear-view mirror placement, and antennae. If you want to follow the instructions precisely, enjoy. If you want to build the model with your own eye for customization, be my guest!

# ABOUT THE AUTHOR

**PETER BLACKERT** is perhaps uniquely positioned to write this book, being both a well-known and productive LEGO® modeller, and a design engineer for the Ford Motor Company. Peter has published hundreds of LEGO vehicle designs, including cars, trucks, motorcycles, and buses. In real life Peter spends his time in Ford's Asia-Pacific Engineering Centres in Geelong and Melbourne, Australia. His focus is on Powertrain and Chassis Systems Engineering—skills that are transferred to the detailed engineering suspension and engine design content included in many of his LEGO vehicles. Peter studied engineering at the University of Sydney and the Australian National University.

Peter has written this book to provide a challenge to a breadth of builders of all ages, and as a guide to advanced automotive engineering in compact scale.